Law, Society and Corruption

This book presents new socio-legal perspectives and insights on the social life of corruption and anticorruption in authoritarian regimes.

This book takes up the case of Uzbekistan—an authoritarian regime in Central Asia and one of the most corrupt countries in the world according to Transparency International's Corruption Perceptions Index—and examines the corruption that developed in a tightly closed authoritarian regime permeated by a large-scale shadow economy, a weak rule of law, and a collectivist legal culture. Building on socio-legal frameworks of legal compliance, living law and legal pluralism, the central argument of the book is that the roles, meanings, and logics of corruption are fluid, and depend on a myriad of structural variables, and contextual and situational factors.

This book will be of value to researchers, academics, and students in the fields of sociology of law, legal anthropology, and Central Asian studies, especially those with an interest in the intersection of law, society, and corruption in authoritarian regime contexts.

Rustamjon Urinboyev is Associate Professor in the Department of Sociology of Law at Lund University, Sweden, Professor in the Department of International Law and Human Rights at Tashkent State University of Law, Uzbekistan, and Adjunct Professor in the Department of Social Sciences, Tashkent State University of Economics, Uzbekistan.

Måns Svensson is Full Professor of Sociology of Law at the School of Education, Humanities and Social Sciences at Halmstad University, Sweden, and President of Jönköping University, Sweden.

Law, Society and Corruption

Lessons from the Central Asian Context

Rustamjon Urinboyev and Måns Svensson

Routledge
Taylor & Francis Group
LONDON AND NEW YORK

First published 2025
by Routledge
4 Park Square, Milton Park, Abingdon, Oxon OX14 4RN

and by Routledge
605 Third Avenue, New York, NY 10158

Routledge is an imprint of the Taylor & Francis Group, an informa business

British Library Cataloguing-in-Publication Data
A catalogue record for this book is available from the British Library

ISBN: 9781138592797 (hbk)
ISBN: 9781032822990 (pbk)
ISBN: 9780429952968 (ebk)

DOI: 10.4324/9780429952968

Typeset in Sabon
by Deanta Global Publishing Services, Chennai, India

Contents

Acknowledgements *vi*
Table of laws *viii*
Abbreviations *xii*

1 Understanding corruption in authoritarian regimes 1

2 Political environment and governance trajectories in Uzbekistan 39

3 Anticorruption laws, policies, and initiatives in Uzbekistan: An overview of the legal and institutional environment 55

4 Law, society, and corruption in Uzbekistan: A socio-legal analysis of macro-level developments 70

5 Corruption, informality, and coping strategies in meso-level arenas 87

6 The social life of corruption in micro-level arenas 104

7 The interplay between law, society, and (anti)corruption in authoritarian regimes 118

Index *127*

Acknowledgements

The completion of this book is the culmination of our 15 years of ethnographic study of law, society, and corruption in Uzbekistan, covering developments between 2009 and 2024. The initial idea for this book emerged in April 2009 when we travelled to Uzbekistan for our first ethnographic fieldwork. At that time, Uzbekistan was ruled by late-President Islam Karimov, under whom the country developed into a tightly closed and repressive authoritarian regime and was, therefore, nearly inaccessible to academic research. Given the repressive nature of Karimov's regime, we were aware of the possible methodological problems that might arise during our fieldwork. We, thus, decided to limit our research to participant observations and informal interviews. Our observations focused on the role of law in everyday life and—directly or indirectly—in various social arenas, observing, for instance, how state officials enforce laws and to what extent people adhere to laws when dealing with state officials. We also observed the commonplace and more or less taken-for-granted activities that signal the key features of social structures, norms, and interactions, which can stand for broader public policy developments.

Our fieldwork unconsciously brought into doubt many of our assumptions about the role of law and state–society relations in authoritarian regimes such as Uzbekistan. Despite the almost mythical coercive power of the political regime in Uzbekistan, especially the regime's ability to withstand internal and external challenges, we found that the state and its legal system had limited meaning in everyday life, and the coping strategies of ordinary citizens primarily relied on informal and extra-legal strategies. Even the behaviour of state officials was more influenced by the informal and extra-legal rules and practices than state law. We realised it was not state law, but the informal rules and norms ('living law') that had more meaning and influence in everyday life in Uzbekistan. On the last day of that first fieldwork trip to Uzbekistan (before departing for Sweden), we stayed at the Radisson Hotel in Tashkent. During a lengthy discussion and reflecting on our fieldwork experiences over a gin and tonic in the Radisson hotel's cosy bar, we talked about the omnipresence of the informal economy, the plurality of normative orders, the widespread presence of police and security forces in Uzbekistan, and the informal wealth redistribution in Uzbek society through extra-legal practices. In fact, ideas generated during our discussion at the hotel bar turned out to seed this book, ideas which germinated over the years. Given that this book was conceived as a bottom–up reflection of the interplay between law, society, and corruption, we have largely relied on our informants' stories, experiences, anecdotal evidence, and life trajectories in completing this project. We, therefore, dedicate this book to our resilient informants—heroes all—who agreed to share their everyday experiences of corruption and informality despite the risks and challenges this posed them.

We gratefully acknowledge the financial support we received from a number of funding agencies and institutions, all of which made this book possible: the Swedish Research Council ['The Multilevel Orders of Corruption' Project, dnr 2018-01425]; the Swedish Research Council ['Administrative Law Reform and Legal Integration in Hybrid Political Regimes' Project, dnr 2020-01734]; the European Commission H2020-MSCA-RISE-2019 'Central Asian Law' [grant number 870647]; the European Commission HORIZON-MSCA-SE-2021 'MOCCA: Multilevel Orders of Corruption in Central Asia' [grant number 101085855]; and Riksbankens Jubileumsfond [grant numbers MHI19-1428:1 and SAB22-0006]. We also express our gratitude to Lund University's Sociology of Law Department and Halmstad University's School of Education, Humanities, and Social Sciences for providing administrative and financial support. Last, but not least, we are indebted to Vanessa Fuller, English-language reviser in Language Services at the University of Helsinki, for editing and proofreading all of the chapters in this book.

Rustam Urinboyev and Måns Svensson
Lund, Sweden
February 2024

Table of laws

Primary laws

Administrative Liability Code (Law No. 2015--XII, adopted 1 April 1995, with accompanying amendments to date) 57
Article 15 62
Anticorruption Law (No. O‘RQ-419, adopted 3 January 2017) 3, 109
Article 21 78
Civil Code (Law No. 257-I, adopted 1 March 1997, with accompanying amendments to date) 57
Civil Code of the Republic of Uzbekistan (Law No. 163-I, adopted 21 December 1995)
Article 6 81
Code of Criminal Procedure (Law No. 2013-XII, adopted 1 April 1995, with accompanying amendments to date) 57
Criminal Code (Law No. 2014-XII, adopted 1 April 1995, with accompanying amendments to date) 57, 61, 109
Draft Law of the Republic of Uzbekistan ‘On Conflicts of Interest’ (No. QL-922, under Senate consideration) 57, 68, 75
Draft Law of the Republic of Uzbekistan ‘On the Declaration of the Incomes and Property of Civil Servants’ 57, 67–68, 73, 75
Draft Law of the Republic of Uzbekistan ‘On the Public E-Registry of Persons Convicted of Corruption Offences’ 57
Foreign Corrupt Practices Act (FCPA) 45
Labour Code of the Republic of Uzbekistan (No. O’RQ-798, adopted 30 April 2023) 62
Article 121 78
Law No. 257-I, adopted 1 March 1997, with accompanying amendments to date 57
Law No. 2013-XII, adopted 1 April 1995, with accompanying amendments to date 57
Law No. 2014-XII, adopted 1 April 1995, with accompany amendments to date 57

Law No. 2015-XII, adopted 1 April 1995, with accompanying amendments to date 57
Law of the Republic of Uzbekistan 'On Administrative Procedures' (No. O'RQ9457, adopted 10 January 2019) 64
Law of the Republic of Uzbekistan 'On the Anticorruption Assessment of Normative Legal Acts and Their Drafts' (No. O'RQo-860, adopted 9 August 2023) 57
Law of the Republic of Uzbekistan 'On Anticorruption Expertise and the Assessment of Normative Legal Acts and Their Drafts' (No. O'RQ-860, adopted 9 August 2023) 64–65
Law of the Republic of Uzbekistan 'On Combating Corruption' (No. O'RQ-419, adopted 3 January 2017) 56, 63–64, 68
Law of the Republic of Uzbekistan 'On Courts' (No. O'RQ-703, adopted 29 July 2021) 72
Law of the Republic of Uzbekistan 'On the Dissemination of Information and Ensuring Access to Legal Aid' (No. O'RQ-443, adopted 8 September 2017) 64
Law of the Republic of Uzbekistan 'On Guarantees of the Freedom of Entrepreneurial Activity' (No. O'RQ-328, adopted 3 May 2012) 75
Law of the Republic of Uzbekistan 'On Internal Affairs Bodies' (No. O'RQ-407, adopted 18 March 2017) 72
Law of Republic of Uzbekistan 'On Investments and Investment Activities' (No. O'RQ-598-son, adopted 27 January 2020) 75
Law of the Republic of Uzbekistan 'On Public Civil Service' (No. O'RQ-788, adopted 8 August 2022) 57
Article 13 72
Article 19 78
Law of the Republic of Uzbekistan 'On Public Control' (No. O'RQ-474, adopted 13 April 2018) 64
Law of the Republic of Uzbekistan 'On Public Procurement' (No. O'RQ-684, adopted 22 April 2021) 56, 64
Law of the Republic of Uzbekistan 'On the Prosecutor's Office' (No. 257-II, adopted 7 November 2001) 72
Law of the Republic of Uzbekistan 'On the Protection of Victims, Witnesses, and Other Participants in the Criminal Process' (No. O'RQ-515, adopted 16 July 2019) 64
Law of the Republic of Uzbekistan 'On the Regulation of Conflicts of Interest' to be adopted 1 January 2022) 79
Law of the Republic of Uzbekistan 'On the Representative for the Protection of the Rights and Legal Interests of Business Entities (Business Ombudsman) under the President of the Republic of Uzbekistan' (No. O'RQ-440, adopted 30 August 2017) 75

Bylaws (decrees, resolutions, and decisions)

Decree (No. PF-6013, adopted 29 June 2020) of the President of the Republic of Uzbekistan 'On Additional Measures to Improve the Anticorruption System in the Republic of Uzbekistan' 59
Decree No. PF-6257, adopted 6 July 2021 67
Decree of the President of the Republic of Uzbekistan 'About the strategy of actions for further development of the Republic of Uzbekistan' (PF-4947, adopted 7 February 2017) 47
Decree of the President on 'Additional measures for the further improvement of the system of anticorruption in Uzbekistan' (No. PF-5729 of 27.05.2019) 3
Decree of the President of the Republic of Uzbekistan 'On Additional Measures of Improvement to the Anticorruption System' (No. PF-6013, adopted 29 June 2020) 56
Decree of the President of the Republic of Uzbekistan "On Combating Corruption' (No. PF-6257, adopted 6 July 2021) 79
Paragraph 4 73
Decree of the President of the Republic of Uzbekistan 'On the Fundamental Improvement of the System of Raising Legal Awareness and Legal Culture in Society' (No. PF-5618, adopted 10 January 2019) 65
Decree of the President of the Republic of Uzbekistan 'On Measures to Create an Environment of Zero Tolerance for Corruption, to Drastically Reduce Corruption-Causing Factors in the Governance of State and Society, and to Increase the Participation of the Public in These Processes' (No. PF-6257, adopted 6 July 2021) 57
Decree of the President on the Republic of Uzbekistan 'On Measures to Further Improve the System of Fighting Against Corruption in the Republic of Uzbekistan' (No. PF-5729, adopted 27 May 2019) 56
Decree of the President of the Republic of Uzbekistan 'On Measures to Introduce a System for Rating the Effectiveness of Anticorruption Efforts' (No. PQ-81, adopted 12 January 2022) 57
Decree of the President of the Republic of Uzbekistan 'On Measures to Radically Enhance the Role of Civil Society Institutions in the Process of the Democratic Renewal of the Country' (No. PF-5430, adopted 5 May 2018) 65
President's decree 'On the approval of the concept of administrative reform in the Republic of Uzbekistan (No PF-5185, adopted on 8 September 2017) 46, 51
Resolution of the Cabinet of Ministers of the Republic of Uzbekistan 'On Additional Measures to Ensure Compliance with the Rules of Conduct by Public Civil Servants (Annex 1 "On the Code of Ethics for Public Civil Servants")' (No. 595, adopted 15 October 2022) 57, 78

Resolution of the Cabinet of Ministers of the Republic of Uzbekistan 'On the Approval of the Regulation on the Procedure for Rewarding Persons Who Reported a Corruption Offence or Assisted in the Fight against Corruption' (No. 829, adopted 31 December 2020) 56
Resolution 'On Measures to Implement the Provisions of the Law of the Republic of Uzbekistan "On Combating Corruption"' 58

Abbreviations

ACN	Anti-Corruption Network for Eastern Europe and Central Asia
CEO	chief executive officer
CPI	Corruption Perceptions Index
EU	European Union
FCPA	Foreign Corrupt Practices Act
GDP	gross domestic product
GPO	General Prosecutor's Office
IMF	International Monetary Fund
NGO	non-governmental organisation
OECD	Organization for Economic Co-operation and Development
TI	Transparency International
UNCAC	United Nations Convention against Corruption
UNDP	United Nations Development Programme

Chapter 1

Understanding corruption in authoritarian regimes

Introduction

On 14 May 2019, we were on an aeroplane flying to Uzbekistan to conduct ethnographic fieldwork. The Turkish Airlines flight from Istanbul to Tashkent (the capital city of Uzbekistan) took just under six hours. Taking in the panoramic view of Tashkent from our seats on the aeroplane, we were full of excitement: this was our first fieldwork trip to Uzbekistan after the death of Islam Karimov on 2 September 2016. Given recent political developments and the opening up of Uzbekistan to the outside world, we were eager to collect empirical data on corruption and the informal practices that developed in a tightly closed authoritarian regime. Under President Islam Karimov, who ruled the country with an iron fist from 1989 until his death in 2016, Uzbekistan was consistently listed as one of the most repressive, corrupt, and closed authoritarian regimes in the world (ICG 2007, Freedom House 2013). With the death of Islam Karimov and the instalment of Shavkat Mirziyoyev as President of Uzbekistan, the crucial question for both domestic and foreign actors, institutions, and analysts became whether, how, and to what extent these events would impact modes of governance and state–society relations in the country.

For us—two sociologists of law who have been conducting fieldwork on law, society, and (anti)corruption in Uzbekistan since 2009—these developments prompted multiple intriguing questions. For instance, we wondered whether and how the new leadership would address the challenges associated with the kleptocracy, weak rule of law, dysfunctional legal institutions, and systemic corruption that became part-and-parcel of governance in Uzbekistan. Uzbekistan has regularly ranked as one of the most corrupt countries in the world according to Transparency International's (TI) Corruption Perceptions Index (TI 2016a, 2022). Academically, studies have shown that informal practices and transactions have become so omnipresent and influential in Uzbekistan that it is no longer possible to distinguish between formal and informal economies (Kandiyoti 2007, Markowitz 2008, Rasanayagam 2011, Trevisani 2022). As Rasanayagam (2011, p. 682) noted,

DOI: 10.4324/9780429952968-1

'what we might think of as informal economic activity is just one expression of a more general informalisation of state, society, and lifeworlds following the collapse of the Soviet Union'. Indeed, we confirmed such accounts during the course of our extensive fieldwork in Uzbekistan from 2009–2016, during which we also observed the ever-growing role of informal norms, practices, and networks in both state and non-state arenas (Urinboyev and Svensson 2013a, 2013b, 2017, Adams *et al.* 2018). In the words of one of our informants operating on the foreign currency exchange black market, the governance system that evolved in the post-Soviet period was simply a *bardak sistema* ('mess or disordered system'), where it was nearly impossible to act fully legally and people were compelled to straddle between legality and illegality in everyday situations. Under the *bardak sistema*, only a few found a 'golden middle' (*zolotaya seredina*) and became successful, whereas many others either lost their jobs or businesses and often landed in prison given their inability to navigate the bureaucratic hurdles.

When we returned to Uzbekistan in May 2019, we noticed that the governance mode and political climate were shifting in post-Karimov Uzbekistan. In contrast to early pessimistic predictions, newly installed President Mirziyoyev openly acknowledged the failure of the Karimov-era governance practices and presented himself to the local population and the outside world as a reformer, expressing an eagerness to open up the tightly closed country, modernise the system of governance, curb systemic corruption, and attract foreign investors to a largely underexploited Uzbek market. Under the Karimov government, it was nearly impossible for citizens to express their critical views and challenge arbitrary decisions and actions of state institutions and officials. Unlike his predecessor, Mirziyoyev launched an ambitious reform programme under the notion that 'the state should serve its citizens, not vice versa'. He established an online 'virtual reception portal', where ordinary citizens can voice their grievances, lodge complaints against corrupt and dishonest state officials, and make policy recommendations to the President's Office. These e-governance initiatives were further extended, with all ministries and state agencies also launching their own online reception portals. In addition to the online platform, the President's reception houses, known as *halq qabulhonalari* ('people's reception houses'), were established and opened in all regions of Uzbekistan. Furthermore, the return to a convertible currency was one of the most significant changes. The official exchange rate (4200 Uzbek soum to US$1) was adjusted to the black-market rate (8100 soum) overnight on 5 September 2017. As a result, people no longer had any incentive to exchange their money on the black market, leading to a drastic drop in black-market transactions. Our initial impression was that formal and informal practices in Uzbekistan—at least on the surface level of everyday interactions—began to align.

The pace of changes was also visible in the state's anticorruption rhetoric. Unlike during the Karimov era when it was nearly impossible to express any opinion criticising public policy developments in the country, corruption suddenly became a fashionable topic of discussion in the Uzbek political landscape. In fact, *Ijtimoiy Fikr* (Public Opinion), a state-sponsored polling organisation which usually offered an extremely positive view of the political, economic, and social life in Uzbekistan, presented the results of its latest survey in 2018, where 57% of respondents believed that corruption was a widespread phenomenon in the country. In addition, the report, presented by an expert group from the Republican Interdepartmental Commission on Combating Corruption, mentioned that, in the first half of 2017, 1130 criminal cases were opened against 1566 officials suspected of engaging in corruption (Podrobno.uz 2017). Wherever we looked—at institutions such as banks, hospitals, universities, bazaars, and *mahalla* ('neighbourhood communities')—we saw the government's anticorruption rhetoric visible in flyers and banners warning of the legal penalties associated with offering or asking for bribes. At the legislative and policy-making levels, Uzbek authorities produced numerous legislative initiatives, policies, and strategies to combat corruption. Uzbekistan adopted a long-awaited 'Anticorruption Law' on 4 January 2017 (No. O'RQ-419 of 03.01.2017). This law was further supplemented by a Decree of the President on 'Additional measures for the further improvement of the system of anticorruption in Uzbekistan' (No. PF-5729 of 27.05.2019), which led to the launch of a national monitoring system aimed at improving the ranking of Uzbekistan on global indicators, such as TI's Corruption Perceptions Index and the World Bank's Doing Business Index. The culmination of these changes was the establishment of a new Anticorruption Agency in 2020, tasked with coordinating anticorruption efforts in the country.

Accordingly, these processes produced widespread euphoria and expectations among Uzbek citizens, state officials, foreign actors, and analysts whereby opening up the previously tightly closed country would lead to political and economic transformations in the country. A palpable example of these post-Karimov developments emerged through the numerous international conferences on good governance, the rule of law, and anticorruption organised by central-level institutions and ministries in Tashkent. Thus, as a part of our fieldwork, we were also invited to attend a conference on anticorruption and the rule of law reforms in Uzbekistan, an international event organised by one of the central government institutions in Uzbekistan. This conference proved useful not simply because of its focus on anticorruption and rule-of-law issues, but also because of its (unforeseen) value in generating empirical data on multifaceted meanings, logics, and the functional roles of informal and extra-legal practices. Given its intersectoral nature, the conference brought together scholars, practitioners, experts, and analysts from various countries. One noteworthy feature of the conference was a lavish gala dinner provided by the conference organisers at one of the fanciest restaurants in Tashkent, which also included live music and performances by popular Uzbek musicians. Because this conference included nearly 100 participants, we assumed that the related expenses were funded either by the Uzbek government or by international organisations or development agencies operating in Uzbekistan.

On 27 January 2020, eight months after this conference, we travelled to the Fergana Valley of Uzbekistan, to a village we call 'Beshkapa', where we conducted our ethnographic fieldwork. During our fieldwork, we regularly visited the village's social hotspots, such as the *guzar* ('community meeting space') and *choyxona* ('teahouse'), where village residents meet each other on a daily basis and conduct the bulk of village-level information exchanges. Because we visited these social spaces frequently, we met and interacted with more than 100 villagers during our fieldwork. On one such visit, we met Azim, a local entrepreneur (*rassiychi*) who exports the village's agricultural products (i.e., cherries, cucumbers, grapes, apples, etc.) to bazaars and markets in various Russian cities. Given the transnational dimension of his business, he had to deal with the legal system and various state institutions in terms of preparing paperwork, paying customs duties, and securing legal protections when he encountered problems in Russian bazaars. When we introduced ourselves as researchers studying law, society, and corruption in Uzbekistan, Azim quickly mentioned the conference in Tashkent we had attended in 2019. Much to our surprise, he possessed detailed information about the logistics of the conference, including the name of the hotel where participants stayed, the meals provided during the catered lunch, and the restaurant where we had that gala dinner. We were intrigued by how and why a local entrepreneur residing in a remote village in rural Fergana possessed such detailed information about the logistics of a conference organised by a key institution from the central Uzbek government. When we asked him why he knew so much about a conference, which had nothing to do with his profession, he replied with a cunning smile that he had paid for all of the conference lunches and dinners, including the lavish gala dinner.

This fortuitous encounter with Azim, an 'invisible funder' of the conference lunches and dinners, reminded us of the Karimov-era informal agreements between the state and business sectors, where businesses financed various projects, programmes, events, and other informal requests from state institutions. In return, state institutions, particularly law enforcement bodies, provided various informal benefits and privileges to businesses or ignored them when they operated outside the law. Based on our previous understanding of the everyday business realities in Uzbekistan, we assumed that Azim could expect a favour, support, or *kryshovanie* ('protection') from the respective state institution when conducting his transnational business (e.g., when he gets into trouble or faces a legal challenge). This encounter with Azim also provided us with a clue regarding the existence of informal rules and extra-legal practices in Uzbekistan which allow things to work under the conditions of authoritarian governance. Often, the central government assigns numerous tasks and responsibilities to various state institutions without allocating adequate funding and resources from the state budget. Yet, lower-level institutions are still expected to fulfil all of the orders and tasks coming from the centre, a catch-22 situation leading to informal agreements and alliances between state institutions and businesses. Thus, the state itself induces its institutions to invent and utilise various informal and extra-legal practices in order to comply with centrally adopted policies, laws, and decisions.

We observed many similar situations in meso- and micro-level social arenas, illustrating that the use of informal and extra-legal practices has become a *modus operandi* in everyday life in Uzbekistan. One case involving road asphalting in the Beshkapa village and the informal practices revolving around it serve as another poignant example. Given budgetary limitations across Uzbekistan, local governments (*hokimiyats*) have limited financial capacity and cannot asphalt the roads of villages and *mahallas* when the need arises for various reasons. Rather than following a needs-based approach, the asphalting of village and *mahalla* roads is implemented within the framework of 'Prosperous Village' (*Obod Qishloq*) and 'Prosperous *Mahalla*' (*Obod Mahalla*),[1] two state programmes approved by the president, which contain the list of select villages and *mahallas* whose roads are slated for asphalting in 2022–2026. Another way to asphalt the roads of *mahallas* is the 'My Road' (*Mening yo'lim*) initiative within the framework of the Open Budget programme,[2] a citizen-led participatory budgeting system through which citizens campaign and vote for infrastructure projects benefiting their village and *mahalla*. Villages and *mahallas* whose residents are the most active and collect more votes win the battle and receive funding from the state for road asphalting. Interestingly, however, asphalting the roads of one of the *mahallas* in the Beshkapa village was completed neither through the aforementioned state programmes nor through the Open Budget programme. Instead, the asphalting project was funded based on the political influence of one household in the *mahalla* which had a relative who worked in the General Prosecutor's Office (GPO) of Uzbekistan. Akmal (pseudonym) occupied a key position at the GPO, a position for which the duties amongst other tasks included the exercise of control and supervision over the implementation of legislation in the construction sector. This meant that the Committee for Roads, which held primary responsibility for road asphalting in the country, was also under his supervision. Obviously, it was in the interest of the head of the committee to maintain good relations with Akmal. Consequently, these hierarchical power relations brought asphalt to the roads of the *mahalla* where Akmal's relatives lived, an outcome that would not have occurred if Akmal had not used his legal and political influence. From a legal standpoint, this situation

1 https://www.president.uz/oz/lists/view/5078
2 https://openbudget.uz/home

may be interpreted as an informality or extra-legal practice coming closer to the international legal definitions of corruption. However, when interpreted from the *mahalla* members' perspectives, this practice represented neither an 'abuse' nor a 'private gain' as the diversion of state resources (asphalt) to the *mahalla* benefitted the wider community, a public good to which all *mahalla* members (i.e., taxpayers) were legally entitled.

Our fieldwork observations further reinforced our initial assumptions that mainstream (anti)corruption frameworks have limited applicability and utility in authoritarian contexts. Such contexts are characterised by dysfunctional institutions, a weak juncture between the state and society, strong traditions of informal law, a weak rule of law, and, often, multiple social forces promoting alternative norms for social behaviour and social order. More specifically, we wondered whether it is appropriate to apply the 'principal–agent model' or the 'collective action approach to corruption' framework to situations where the state (central government) itself induces its institutions and civil servants to resort to informal and extra-legal practices and transactions (empirical example concerning conference logistics) or to micro-level mundane processes where ordinary citizens are compelled to use informal channels to gain access to the public good (asphalt) to which they are legally entitled (i.e., using nonlegal methods to enforce their rights prescribed by law). Accordingly, these points indicate that corruption 'is not always a matter of black and white' (De Graaf 2007, p. 43); as such, corruption should not be understood merely in terms of the legal culture, institutional configurations, ways of thinking, and circumstances typical for Western societies. The prevalent ethnocentrism (Western-centrism) to understanding (anti) corruption may neglect intricacies, everyday dynamics, and the alternative orders and rationalities which inform the meaning of corruption and informal practices in non-Western settings (Al-Ramahi 2008, Kubbe and Varraich 2019). Likewise, informality may complement the state and allow people to deal with legal uncertainty and bureaucratic hurdles when formal rules and procedures do not apply (Polese *et al.* 2018). Hence, one possible inference from the above observations is that there might be valid reasons for reevaluating the nature of informal, nonlegal practices, and transactions (that is, 'corruption', from a legal standpoint) not simply as instances of individual greed and personal venality, but also as reflections of society's informal rules, local needs and circumstances, everyday power relations, and as cultural and affective repertoires that coexist and work parallel to formal institutions.

The above considerations have informed our position in this book, which is intended to produce new empirical and theoretical insights on understanding and counteracting corruption in authoritarian regimes. Our aim lies in going beyond the widely held assumptions that explain the persistence and ubiquity of corruption in authoritarian regimes with reference to a weak rule of law, kleptocratic elites, dysfunctional institutions, and arbitrary law enforcement. We argue that the legal landscape of authoritarian regimes should not be viewed from a 'black-and-white' perspective, a simplistic approach which largely ignores the dynamic life and logic of corruption on different levels and social arenas. Indeed, a growing body of literature demonstrates that even in contexts characterised as authoritarian regimes, citizens have agency and can evade, use, enforce, reinterpret, and shape the operation of law and state institutions (Solomon and Gadowska 2018, Zaloznaya 2020, Marat and McCarthy 2021).

In exploring and understanding (anti)corruption in the context of authoritarian regimes, we build on and attempt to extend existing paradigms (i.e., the principal–agent model and the collective action approach) by drawing from theories and perspectives in the field of socio-legal studies, namely (1) socio-legal perspectives on legal compliance; (2) the concept of 'living law'; (3) a legal pluralism perspective; and (4) the concept of legal consciousness/culture. The integration of these theoretical concepts into an overarching framework allows us to understand society's basic social fabric, which may encompass both formal and informal forms of normative ordering. We argue that understanding a society's basic social fabric, normative orders, and the mechanism and factors that make people obey or break the law (legal compliance) serve as a lens via which to understand the emergence, explanation, persistence, and ubiquity of corruption. To do so, these processes are explored in a post-socialist context, specifically using the case of Uzbekistan, which offers an intriguing example of (anti)corruption and informal practices developed within a tightly closed authoritarian regime, as well as an internationally significant (yet under-researched) case given its position as one of the most corrupt countries in the world according to TI's Corruption Perceptions Index (TI 2022). Before presenting the proposed theoretical framework, we provide a review of the academic and policy debates in the field of (anti)corruption in the next section.

Academic and policy debates in the field of (anti) corruption: A state-of-the-art review

There have been extensive discussions in academic and policy circles about why corruption remains a persistent and pervasive phenomenon in many parts of the world. The initial view that 'corruption greases the wheels of economic growth' in the newly independent states of Africa and Asia (Leff 1964, Leys 1965, Huntington 1968, Scott 1972) has lost its validity in light of the current ever-growing global coalition against corruption, spearheaded by TI and the World Bank (Sampson 2005). According to these international bodies, this entire debate is now closed: corruption, as they confidently assert, is 'the abuse of public office/entrusted power for private gain' (World Bank 2002, TI 2007) and thus 'sands the wheels of economic growth' (cf. Méon and Sekkat 2005). This relies on the understanding that corruption, primarily affecting weak states in Eastern Europe, Africa, Asia, and Latin

America, is the primary cause of poverty and inequality (World Bank 2013). Corruption distorts public expenditures, increases the costs of running businesses, deters foreign investors, and leads to social instability, a weak rule of law, and bad governance (Mauro 1997, Johnson 2005, Mungiu-Pippidi and Hartmann 2019).

In view of these developments, a new global anticorruption movement has emerged over the last three decades (Sampson 2005). Accordingly, this global movement, consisting of diverse actors, such as policymakers, academic researchers, international organisations, anticorruption agencies, civil society organisations, investigative journalists, law enforcement authorities, advocacy groups, and individual activists, has devised countless strategies and approaches to diagnose and combat corruption. The World Bank created 'six strategies to fight corruption' in addition to its '10 ways to fight corruption' (Lopez-Claros 2014, Hunja 2015), TI recommended '5 key ingredients' to eradicate corruption (TI 2016b), while the World Economic Forum suggested '5 ways to beat global corruption' as well as '3 key steps to end corruption' (Glencorse 2014, Vlassis 2015). At the same time, the volume of academic literature on (anti)corruption has rapidly increased in the fields of economics and political science, the two disciplines that have contributed most extensively to the corruption literature and significantly shaped the globally circulating set of anticorruption models, frameworks, policies, and laws (Rose-Ackerman 1999, Acemoglu and Verdier 2000, Langbein and Knack 2010, Rothstein 2011, Della Porta and Tarrow 2012). Most of this mainstream literature, either implicitly or explicitly, regards corruption as a sign of social instability, a weak rule of law, and bad governance, frequently using 'disease' and 'cancer' metaphors to describe corruption.

At present, the most established framework regarding how to understand and counteract corruption is the principal–agent model (Klitgaard 1988, Groenendijk 1997, Andvig *et al.* 2001, Adserà *et al.* 2003, Besley 2006, Mungiu 2006). Resting on economistic assumptions and legal centralistic perspectives, the principal–agent model views corruption as a situation in which an agent (e.g., civil servant) violates the trust of their (honest/benevolent) principal (public or a cabinet minister) by taking a bribe in return for a favourable decision or to steal from the state's coffers. This model assumes that two interlinked factors increase a state official's penchant for engaging in corrupt practices: first, the existence of wide discretionary power when making decisions over access to resources or acquiring a licence, such as the allocation of land, the award of a licence, or major construction contract; and, second, the risk of being caught remains low when engaging in corrupt practices. These factors imply that agents who engage in corrupt practices are rational actors and make a cost–benefit analysis when deviating from their formal duties related to a public role in favour of private gain. Put in Klitgaard's (1998, p. 4) terms, 'Corruption is a crime of calculation, not passion.'. The principal–agent model is thus based on the understanding that corruption can be deterred if the costs exceed the benefits or if the risk of being caught is rather high. Thus, when viewed through the lens of the principal–agent model, anticorruption reform appears quite straightforward: principals can combat corruption by increasing the costs, surveillance, and severity of the penalty for corrupt practices to such an extent that agents are discouraged from engaging in corruption.

Accordingly, the principal–agent model influenced the design of many anticorruption policies, laws, development aid projects, and programmes worldwide (Persson *et al.* 2013, Schwertheim 2017a). It is, therefore, unsurprising that many anticorruption efforts and programmes are often based on the assumption that the best way to combat corruption is to develop institutional and legal configurations and socioeconomic settings which would negatively affect agents' motivations to engage in corrupt practices (Rothstein 2018). In this regard, mainstream anticorruption approaches emphasise the need to improve institutional and regulatory frameworks by frequently focusing on (1) formal law enforcement and improving the rule of law; (2) the behaviour of agents in particular public office settings and measures to limit their discretionary power; (3) the system of formal rules and institutions; (4) the role of political institutions, elections, and competition amongst political elites; (5) enhancing government's accountability by supporting democratisation and increased public oversight; and (6) independent media and the formation of strong civil society institutions (Galtung 1998, Acemoglu and Verdier 2000, Johnson 2005, Shah 2007, Heidenheimer and Johnston 2011, Kaufmann *et al.* 2011, Della Porta and Tarrow 2012).

Although the principal–agent model provides straightforward tools for assessing and combating corruption, it may have limited utility in social settings characterised by systemic corruption, a weak rule of law, and an authoritarian regime. A growing body of literature argues that the definition of an (honest/benevolent) principal and (corrupt) agent may differ depending upon the political context and forms and types of corruption (Persson *et al.* 2013, Rothstein 2018, Mungiu-Pippidi and Fazekas 2020). Under the classical approach, which is concerned with situations of bureaucratic corruption, rulers represent the principal and the bureaucracy represents the agent (Becker and Stigler 1974). When applying the principal–agent model, policymakers, practitioners, and analysts assume that corruption stems from the unlawful actions of the agent, and the principal takes on the role of controlling corruption (Galtung 1998, Andvig *et al.* 2001, Mungiu 2006). But, when it comes to political corruption, it is actually the ruling elite—not the bureaucrats—who gain the most from corrupt practices. In heavily corrupt and authoritarian social contexts, it is the rule rather than the exception that political elites and decision-makers engage in corrupt practices. Therefore, in such social settings, it is an exceptionally difficult task to identify who may act as an honest principal. If the ruling elite is heavily corrupt and reluctant to implement genuine anticorruption reforms, the principal–agent model would hardly produce the expected outcomes since no actors exist to willingly counteract corruption (Andvig *et al.* 2001, Persson *et al.* 2013). This dilemma led some to view rulers as agents and ordinary citizens (the public) as honest principals (Adserà *et al.* 2003, Besley 2006). Yet, this approach is also problematic given its insensitivity to the nature of the political regime. In heavily corrupt settings, it is unlikely that the public can act as a principal and exert significant pressure given that corrupt political elites may use various legitimation techniques and coercive measures to contain dissent. As a result, the public (principals) have little or no power to monitor or hold public officials (agents) accountable (Schwertheim 2017a). These contextual differences, therefore, cast doubt on the universal applicability and relevance of the principal–agent model.

Reflecting on these complexities, several new frameworks were developed to better diagnose and counteract corruption in social settings characterised by rampant corruption and a weak rule of law. One of these key frameworks is the 'collective action approach' (Persson *et al.* 2013), which views corruption as a 'collective action problem' rather than a 'principal–agent problem'. Drawing from their fieldwork in Kenya and Uganda, two African countries plagued by systemic corruption, Persson *et al.* (2013) argue that one of the main reasons anticorruption reforms in non-Western societies fail is that they view and conceptualise corruption as a principal–agent problem. Using Elinor Ostrom's (1998) collection action theory as an analytical tool, Persson *et al.* (2013) suggest that, in exceptionally corrupt social settings, corruption resembles a collective action problem rather than a principal–agent problem. Under this conceptualisation, corruption is viewed as an expected behaviour resulting from the prevailing social norms in which an agent's choices and decisions regarding how to act are influenced by their perception and expectation of other agents' behaviours. This approach stresses the collective over the individual nature of corruption, focusing on the norms, behaviours, and levels of trust in society as the primary challenges facing anticorruption efforts. In other words, corruption can be viewed as the standard operating procedure in society: agents may be well aware that corruption is pernicious, but because they believe everyone is doing it, they have no reason to refrain from corrupt practices (Rothstein 2018). As a result, any anticorruption effort built on the principal–agent model is likely to fail or may even lead to detrimental effects, since it does not reckon with the prevailing sociolegal context of heavily corrupt countries. The collective action approach, therefore, calls for a distinct design to anticorruption strategies, promoting inclusive community engagement geared towards building trust and integrity (Marquette and Peiffer 2015, Schwertheim 2017b).

Given its strong emphasis on society's informal rules and practices, the collective action approach led to the proliferation of scholarly literature focusing on the interconnections between corruption and norms (Banerjee 2016, Camargo and Passas 2017, Kubbe and Engelbert 2017, Urinboyev and Svensson 2017, Ellis 2019, Köbis *et al.* 2020). The bulk of these studies explore issues such as (1) why people engage in corrupt behaviour even though they themselves consider it wrong; (2) the role and influence of social norms or unwritten/informal rules on individuals' actions and decisions; (3) how social norms, pressures, and influence penetrate state institutions; and (4) whether social norms provide incentives to individuals to be corrupt, thereby facilitating corruption. Another strand of the literature explores how differences in political regimes, cultural traditions, social norms, gender, and internalised values shape an individual's moral preferences and consideration of their behaviour in daily social life and official/institutional settings (Esarey and Chirillo 2013, Kubbe 2017, Esarey and Schwindt-Bayer 2018, Kubbe and Engelbert 2018, Barnes and Beaulieu 2019). Some researchers argue that democracies tend to develop strong anticorruption norms due to their integration into Western international networks and organisations and normative and economic pressures, whereas authoritarian regimes tend to have a high corruption rate given their reluctance to embrace democratic and anticorruption norms and values (Heidenheimer and Johnston 2011, Kostadinova 2012, Kubbe 2017, Kubbe and Engelbert 2018). One possible inference from the 'corruption and norms' literature is that corruption becomes the social norm in settings riddled with systemic corruption, implying that anticorruption campaigns in exceptionally corrupt societies should primarily focus on changing prevailing social norms and cultural repertoires rather than simply punishing deviant behaviour (*cf.* World Bank 2015).

However, critical perspectives—often resulting from anthropological studies of corruption—have argued that corruption should not be viewed as culturally determined since there is no empirical support demonstrating that corruption is more prevalent in societies where it is culturally accepted (De Sardan 1999, Pardo 2004, Haller and Shore 2005, Hasty 2005, Smart and Hsu 2007, Torsello and Venard 2016). Debunking accounts that view corruption through the lens of social norms or as a 'collective action problem', anthropologists view corruption as a social phenomenon without moral evaluation, refraining from condemning activities (as corrupt or noncorrupt) socially accepted by the population. Simultaneously, anthropologists do not justify corruption as a morally and culturally accepted practice. Rather, they argue that society's moral codes and norms should not be used as a cause or an explanation for why corruption is prevalent (i.e., 'the standard operating procedure') in a particular social setting. In doing so, anthropologists argue for the necessity of using a contextual and multiple moralities approach by paying attention to different—and at times conflicting—moral and normative standpoints. In fact, in countries ranked as extremely corrupt in TI's Corruption Perceptions Index, most people have strong norms against corruption, as observed in the example of post-Soviet countries such as Kyrgyzstan, Russia, Ukraine, and Uzbekistan, where ordinary people condemn corruption as morally wrong but feel compelled to engage in corrupt practices given a weak state capacity to address it (Polese

2008, Ledeneva 2013, McMann 2015, Urinboyev *et al.* 2018). Consequently, the neutral, value-free approach to corruption, as anthropologists suggest, may allow us to gain a more accurate understanding of corruption, with alternative views leading to new investigations and establishing better and more context-sensitive anticorruption policies (Torsello and Venard 2016).

Another factor adding to this complexity is that the universal definitions of corruption tend to be Western-centric and rely upon the separation of the state (or its agents) from the rest of society, where salaried public officials, politicians, bureaucrats, and judges are expected to draw a sharp distinction between their personal interests and the public resources they administer (Nuijten 2003, Haller and Shore 2005). Any deviation from formal rules and duties of a public role in favour of private gain is interpreted as an act of corruption. Quantitative analyses of these processes lead to a set of correlations between specific factors and corruption, forming the basis of prescriptions against corruption. These measurement tools rely on the assumption that the public–private dichotomy is fixed and, thus, can be applied universally to measure corruption across countries. However, challenging (Western-centric) mainstream definitions and approaches, anthropological accounts of corruption have provided abundant evidence to support the claim that the public–private dichotomy is context-dependent and the meaning of terms such as 'abuse', 'public', 'private', and 'benefit/gain' varies according to local legal and cultural standards (Gupta 1995, Haller and Shore 2005, Nuijten and Anders 2007, Rothstein and Torsello 2013). Rather than using the universal definition of corruption, anthropologists adopt an 'emic' approach and investigate how local people think about and perceive the world in which they live (Torsello and Venard 2016). In doing so, anthropologists probe the ways in which certain informal and illegal practices and transactions (which are perceived as instances of corruption from a legal or economistic standpoint) may also reflect people's desires to fulfil their family and kinship obligations (Urinboyev and Svensson 2017), socialise and maintain membership in their community and networks (Rivkin-Fish 2005), avoid gossip and social sanctions (Lazar 2005), gain or preserve social status and reputation (Pardo 1996), and secure more moral and affective support from the surrounding community and kinship networks (Lomnitz 1995). Given that traditions, moral codes, and social norms vary across cultures, it is possible that each culture could have quite different ideas regarding what constitutes corruption (Pani 2016). Likewise, what is termed corruption from an outsider's perspective is often linked to a code of values and behaviours widely known and accepted from an insider's perspective (Gupta 1995, Werner 2000).

Rationale and aims

As shown above, (anti)corruption has become a buzzword in both academic and policy debates over the last three decades. Notwithstanding the unrelenting global efforts to understand and combat corruption, one thing seems clear: there is no such thing as a remedy to this 'cancer'. Corruption today remains part and parcel of everyday life in many parts of the world. Indeed, global anticorruption initiatives and efforts from the last three decades can be regarded as huge policy failures: one of the largest implementation gaps in history between formal and informal institutions of governance (Heywood 2018, Rothstein 2018, Mungiu-Pippidi and Heywood 2020). There are at least three main factors contributing to these failures, which we elaborate below.

First, most anticorruption frameworks and international definitions of corruption (e.g., presented by TI and the World Bank) are viewed as universally applicable regardless of the culture in which they are applied. This understanding is especially prevalent in economics and political science, the two disciplines that have significantly shaped policy and academic discourses regarding (anti)corruption. Rather than critically reflecting on various policy failures, global (Western-centric) anticorruption bodies and strategies continue to rely on a 'one-size-fits-all' approach. However, these approaches fail to consider the contextual factors and mechanisms explaining the persistence of corruption, given that people in various cultures have quite different ideas regarding what constitutes corruption (Lloyd Bierstaker 2009) and react differently to the institutional and regulatory norms imposed (Heywood 2018). This implies that, in some cultures and societies, corrupt practices may be deemed not only morally acceptable, but also functionally and socially cohesive, which may not be the case in other cultures. Part of the reason for the broad failure of anticorruption policies is that they do not account for cultural differences and fail to consider the contextual factors and mechanisms explaining the persistence of corruption. From this perspective, informal or illegal practices and transactions (corruption from a legal standpoint) not only mirror kleptocracy, individual greed, or survival strategies, but may also reflect society's informal norms and non-monetary currencies such as respect, prestige, social status, solidarity, trust, and kinship norms which constitute the basic social fabric of a society. Accordingly, informal, illegal practices and transactions that would be labelled corruption from a supranational (Western-centric) and/or nation-state legal perspective may be considered legitimate practices according to society's informal norms and moral codes. These informal norms and moral codes render any efforts towards combating corruption a complex endeavour and potentially counterproductive from a societal perspective. However, when they are perceived as corrupt and battled, the risk is that the basic social fabric and cohesion are weakened and distorted, possibly leading to social instability. Likewise, any anticorruption strategies should be designed based on a deep knowledge of these 'informal legal orders' that determine the rights and wrongs of everyday social behaviour.

Second, research on (anti)corruption remains rather fragmented and has thus far not been synthesised into an overarching and integrated framework

(Prasad *et al.* 2019). Interdisciplinary communication remains lacking, and researchers show insufficient interest or outright reluctance to engage with corruption research undertaken in academic disciplines beyond their own fields (Jancsics 2014). Much of the corruption literature stems from economics, political science, law, criminology, and organisational and business studies, and partly from social and legal anthropology. Each discipline has its own preoccupation and disciplinary concerns in the study of (anti)corruption: (1) economists are interested in understanding the causes of corruption and its impact on economic life; (2) political scientists often examine top–down processes and macro-level topics, such as the role of political institutions, the regulation or freedom of speech in relation to corruption, corruption's influence on political factions and parties, corruption's functional role in political systems, and corruption's nexus with democracy, civil society, and development; (3) legal scholars and criminologists view corruption through the lens of crime and investigate diverse topics such as bribery, kickbacks, white-collar crime, and state crime through the lens of the system of formal rules and procedures; (4) organisational and business ethics approaches to corruption primarily focus on bribe-giving practices, examining organisational rules and procedures, codes of conduct, anticorruption ethics and compliance systems, and organisations and businesses' reactions to regulatory frameworks; and (5) anthropologists study corruption as a social phenomenon without engaging in moral evaluations, taking into account the view of the observed/informants, and thereby avoiding condemning activities that are socially cohesive and accepted by a population. As shown above, academic research on (anti)corruption is vast, but approaches and models developed by various disciplines remain largely isolated from each other. Thus, we cannot rely merely on economic explanations and legal centralistic approaches (i.e., the principal–agent model) as a basis for understanding and counteracting the problem of corruption. It is also problematic to conceptualise corruption as a collective action problem resulting from the prevailing social norms given that this approach runs the risk of regurgitating the 'culture of corruption' (De Sardan 1999) thesis, potentially leading to ethical and political concerns, particularly in non-Western societies. At the same time, anthropological approaches to corruption, despite their ability to produce a value-free and contextual understanding of the multifaceted meanings of corruption, have a penchant for romanticising the functional role of informal and illegal transactions. Whilst specific informal/illegal 'corrupt' practices may benefit certain individuals, social groups, and communities, they may also carry harmful social consequences for others, thereby leading to power asymmetries and social inequalities. Thus, given the multifaceted meaning, logic, and morality of informal/illegal practices and transactions in different societies, neither economic-based attempts, legal centralistic perspectives, nor anthropological and cultural explanations can sufficiently explain why some countries are corrupt and why others succeed in establishing effective anticorruption mechanisms. This reality indicates the need for an interdisciplinary study of corruption, combining perspectives from various disciplines. Such an approach may provide a more nuanced understanding of corruption capable of informing anticorruption laws and policies.

Third, as argued earlier, most anticorruption frameworks and international definitions of corruption (e.g., presented by TI and the World Bank) are Western-centric; nevertheless, they are viewed as universally applicable regardless of the culture in which they are applied. As a result, the majority of the corruption research and anticorruption interventions continue to apply the principal–agent model as a basis for understanding and combating corruption. However, as a growing body of literature argues (Persson *et al.* 2013, Rothstein 2011, Marquette and Peiffer 2015), there are limitations to understanding corruption only as a 'principal–agent problem'. This stems from the fact that such honest principals may not exist in reality, or principals may themselves participate in corrupt behaviour, particularly in the context of authoritarian regimes where elites in the higher echelons of power engage in kleptocratic practices. Given the differences in state–society relations, governance, and legal cultures, mainstream (anti)corruption frameworks and assumptions reflecting the Western liberal–democratic context may have limited utility in authoritarian regime contexts. These concerns become particularly relevant when we consider the increasing number of authoritarian regimes over the last three decades, a global trend frequently referred to as the 'third wave of autocratization' (Lührmann and Lindberg 2019) or 'authoritarianism goes global' (Diamond *et al.* 2016). These points lead us to argue that we should fine-tune existing frameworks or devise a new framework when analysing (anti)corruption in nondemocratic regimes.

In light of the obvious failure of global anticorruption initiatives, there has been a growing call within academic circles to rethink existing approaches and definitions of corruption, arguing for the necessity to better understand what corruption is, why it occurs, how it can be measured, and what we can do to stop it (Graycar and Prenzler 2013, Holmes 2015, Schwickerath *et al.* 2016, Heywood 2018, Rothstein 2018, Mungiu-Pippidi and Heywood 2020, Pozsgai-Alvarez 2020). Critically reflecting on 'one-size-fits-all' approaches and definitions, Mungiu-Pippidi and Fazekas (2020) proposed that a future (anti)corruption research agenda should aim to develop new corruption indicators which (1) rest on a theoretically sound understanding of the process of corruption, (2) rely on objective data describing actor behaviour, (3) are defined at the micro-level such as on individual transactions, and (4) allow for consistent comparisons across countries, organisations, and time.

In this book, whilst emphasising the usefulness of the existing (anti)corruption frameworks, we respond to Mungiu-Pippidi and Fazekas' (2020) call to move beyond 'one-size-fits-all' approaches. More specifically, we aim to produce new theoretical insights and empirical material for understanding (anti)corruption in the context of authoritarian regimes. Theoretically, we intend to do so by drawing upon theories and perspectives in the field of socio-legal studies, namely (1) socio-legal perspectives on legal compliance, (2) the concept of 'living law', (3) a legal pluralism perspective, and (4) the concept of legal consciousness/culture. Doing so will help us understand society's basic social fabric and the mechanisms and factors that make people obey or break the law. We suggest that the integration of these theoretical concepts into an overarching framework allows us to understand (anti) corruption both from interdisciplinary and multilevel perspectives, focusing on mutually transforming interactions between global, transnational anticorruption laws, initiatives, discourses and institutions, national-/central-level institutions, initiatives, policies, and laws, as well as across local, meso-, and micro-level actors, social norms, and practices. Empirically, we rely on various case studies from Uzbekistan, an authoritarian regime in Central Asia riddled with systemic corruption. This allows us to examine (anti)corruption and informal practices developed in a tightly closed authoritarian society, as well as draw broader implications on the multifaceted meanings of corruption in non-Western social settings permeated by informality, a weak rule of law, inefficient institutions, and an authoritarian legal culture. We present a more detailed overview of our proposed framework, which we call a 'hybrid compliance framework', in the sections that follow.

Socio-legal perspectives on legal compliance

In constructing our proposed hybrid compliance framework for studying, understanding, and counteracting corruption in authoritarian regimes, we draw from several theories and perspectives in the field of socio-legal studies—namely, socio-legal perspectives on legal compliance, the concept of 'living law', the legal pluralism perspective, and the concept of legal consciousness. In this section, we present a brief overview of three specific socio-legal perspectives on legal compliance and then explain why these need additional theoretical concepts to fit with the socio-legal context of authoritarian regimes.

A specific focus on legal compliance and the ambition to understand why people obey or break state law remains the default approach in socio-legal studies. Generally, within socio-legal studies, we can identify three main perspectives on legal compliance: (1) the instrumental perspective, (2) the normative perspective, and (3) the expressive perspective.

First, the instrumental perspective on legal compliance is closely associated with the deterrence literature—that is, economistic-based assumptions. Such assumptions argue that, when deciding whether to comply with or break a law, people usually estimate the tangible, immediate incentives and penalties associated with following that law—that is, the personal gains and losses resulting from different kinds of behaviour (Krislov *et al.* 1972, Gibbs 1975, Tittle 1980, Levitt and Miles 2008, Paternoster 2010). Essentially, people decide to comply with various laws not because they believe in the legitimacy of a law or because they follow their own personal ethics and morality, but because they make instrumental decisions about compliance, calculating the likelihood that they will face a punishment if they do not comply. For example, increasing the severity and certainty of punishment for bribery is frequently viewed as an effective way of combating corruption. This serves as a typical example of an instrumental perspective whereby legislators and policymakers seek to obtain compliance through legal sanctions, assuming that legal sanctions change the costs of a behaviour and render compliance cheaper than noncompliance. Given its focus on rewards and punishments as a tool to shape and control people's behaviours, the instrumental perspective is often referred to as the study of social control (Krislov *et al.* 1972, Wood 1974). Social control refers specifically to moulding people's behaviours by manipulating access to valued societal resources or by imposing or threatening to impose sanctions. This implies that legal authorities attempt to modify behaviour by rewarding compliance with the rules and punishing or threatening to punish violations of rules. The principal–agent model, which views corruption as a crime of calculation, is largely influenced by the instrumental perspective/deterrence literature.

Second, the normative perspective relies on the understanding that people are more likely to obey a law when they view laws more generally as just and moral and/or view the authorities enforcing laws as legitimate moral authorities (Tyler 2006, Bilz and Nadler 2009). Specifically, when a law reflects society's prevailing norms and moral codes regarding appropriate social behaviour, people voluntarily assume the obligation to follow legal rules. Likewise, a law's legitimacy heavily depends on how well or badly the legal rules and outcomes align with the public's moral intuitions (Robinson and Darley 1995, Nadler 2004, Mullen and Nadler 2008). Because of these normative influences, psychologists often refer to the normative perspective as 'internalised obligations'—that is, obligations for which people have taken personal responsibility. There are two types of internalised obligations: (1) a normative commitment through legitimacy and (2) a normative commitment through personal morality. The first type of internalised obligation suggests that citizens comply with a law because of their belief that the legal authorities they are dealing with have a legitimate right to dictate behaviour; this represents an acceptance by people of the need to bring their behaviour into line with the dictates of an external authority (Friedman 1975). The second type of internalised obligation is derived from a person's desire to behave in a way that accords with their sense of justice and personal morality. Like beliefs that accord legitimacy to authorities, personal morality is an internalised sense of obligation characterised by voluntary compliance. It differs from legitimacy in content, however. Personal morality is not a feeling of an obligation to an external political or legal authority; instead, it is an internalised obligation to follow one's personal sense of what is morally right or wrong.

In both types, people's reactions to a law are determined by their beliefs and attitudes about what is ethically and morally appropriate rather than by their assessment of the costs and benefits of breaking that law. This represents the key feature distinguishing the normative perspective from the instrumental perspective. The normative perspective thus suggests that we should focus on people's internalised norms of justice, legitimacy, and obligation and thereby explore what citizens think about and understand as their values.

Finally, the most recent contribution to theoretical debates in legal compliance is the expressive perspective. This perspective is based on the postulate that legal compliance cannot be explained entirely by a law's behavioural effects (deterrence and incapacitation) and legitimacy (moral authority), but also requires consideration of a law's expressive power, which creates an incentive for compliance (McAdams 2000a, 2000b, 2015). According to McAdams (2015), a law has two types of expressive powers (causal mechanisms) influencing behaviours and producing compliance: (1) a coordinating function and (2) an information function. A law's coordinating function is visible in its capacity to guide and coordinate people's actions by offering a means of avoiding a collision. The possible risk of collision makes people comply with a law, rendering that law self-enforcing. Because a law is full of requirements, we may easily overlook its suggestive influence, which coordinates people's actions by making a particular outcome salient, channelling their behaviour in that direction. In this way, legal expression provides a coordinating 'focal point' for behaviour. A law also carries information power, which is visible in its ability to convey or 'signal' information to people regarding how to behave properly and safely in different social situations and arenas. The fact that political and legal authorities allow people to do something yet prohibit doing other things is itself information. People's desires for self-preservation create an incentive to comply with a law. Updating information also affects people's beliefs and behaviours, also rendering a law self-enforcing. Based on these considerations, McAdams (2015) argues that a law carries expressive powers independent of the legal sanctions and the legitimacy considerations.

We note, however, that each of the three legal compliance perspectives discussed above carry limitations when explaining why people comply with or break a law (i.e., engage in or refrain from corrupt/illegal practices). An excessive reliance on the instrumental perspective is problematic for several reasons. If deterrence-based strategies alone were sufficient, political and legal authorities would easily secure legal compliance by focusing on social control strategies and manipulating the rewards and punishments associated with obeying or disobeying a law. The instrumental perspective and the principal–agent model are based on a similar logic in that they both view rewards and punishments as effective means to secure compliance. Although the idea of shaping people's behaviours through the instrumental perspective may appear easy and straightforward, these strategies consume large amounts of public resources and are unsustainable in the long term. In addition, granting excessive power to political and legal authorities may lead to unintended consequences, given the fact that authorities may use that power to advance their own interests or the interests of a particular group or individual over the interests of the public. It is rather naïve to assume that authorities have integrity, are benevolently motivated, and use their power and legitimacy to promote the interests of the public. The way in which power is exercised and its possible effects heavily depend upon the motives and competence of those exercising it. These concerns are especially relevant in authoritarian regimes, where political and legal authorities often use legal sanctions, coercion, and surveillance to suppress dissent and free speech and to legitimise their predatory practices.

Moreover, the normative perspective hardly works in authoritarian regimes, where the state and its legal system lack legitimacy and clash with the morality of the people. Personal morality resembles a double-edged sword in its interplay with the legal system: it can lead to compliance with laws, but it can also lead to noncompliance when a specific law, a political decision, or the actions of a state official enforcing a law are incompatible with a person's morality and ethics. It is unsurprising then that political and legal authorities strive for greater legitimacy in the eyes of the people, given that legitimacy provides them with discretionary power they can use to govern. The erosion of the legitimacy of political and legal authorities may lead to dramatic consequences in society and instigate people's widespread noncompliance with a government's laws and policies. Therefore, as Tyler (2006) maintains, legitimacy represents a reservoir of loyalty via which authorities can capitalise, giving them the required discretionary power to govern effectively. These concerns are particularly relevant in the context of authoritarian regimes, which lack legitimacy due to their excessive reliance on coercive strategies, a weak rule of law, ubiquitous corruption, and dysfunctional institutions.

Ensuring legal compliance through the expressive perspective is also problematic in the context of authoritarian regimes. In nondemocratic regimes, given that political and legal authorities are viewed as an instrument of oppression and an expression of the will of kleptocratic elites (and, thereby, lack broader legitimacy), it is unlikely that laws can fulfil their coordination and information functions. Rather than creating an incentive for compliance, state law creates fear and, at the same time, resentment which may trigger a silent form of resistance amongst the people. People may react to and resist state laws by disobeying and/or resorting to informal practices. As a result, state law must compete with other informal, non-state forms of normative ordering, potentially serving as an alternative (to state law) 'focal point' for behaviour.

As illustrated above, these three perspectives on legal compliance provide useful insights when we attempt to understand why corruption remains a persistent and pervasive phenomenon despite numerous legal interventions and policy measures. However, whilst placing legal compliance at the centre of our attention, we also argue that (anti)corruption cannot be satisfactorily understood without exploring the role of society's informal legal orders. These arguments become particularly relevant in the context of authoritarian regimes, where political and legal authorities face enormous resistance from other social forces when implementing their policies. A state's laws and regulations must compete with the norms of other social forces that promote different versions of how people should behave (Migdal *et al.* 1994, Migdal 2001). This implies that we must also examine the issue of legal compliance (i.e., why people obey or break a state law) through the lens of normative pluralism—that is, multiple forms of normative ordering operating in a society (e.g., social norms, customs, etiquette, traditions, religion, personal morality, etc.) which may influence social behaviour more effectively than state law. Thus, legal compliance should be examined not only by simply focusing on why people obey or break a state law but by also considering why people are more inclined to follow non-state, informal forms of normative ordering. With these considerations in mind, in the next section, we provide a brief review of existing research on law and legal compliance in authoritarian regimes.

Law and legal compliance in authoritarian regimes

In this section, we briefly review extant research on the role of law and legal compliance in authoritarian regimes. Here, we aim to explain why three socio-legal perspectives on legal compliance should be contextualised when dealing with local categories and needs and multifaceted meanings of power relations and exchange in authoritarian regimes. In this respect, this review of extant scholarly literature indicates that research on the functioning of law in authoritarian regimes can be conditionally divided into three broad streams, as we elaborate below:

(1) Law as an expression of the will of an authoritarian regime. This research strand encompasses studies that view law as a means of political domination and coercion by an authoritarian regime. Such research highlights a regime's full control over the enactment of central laws and regulations in various areas considered pivotal to maintaining control over the state and society (Bogdanova 2018, Kovács and Scheppele 2018, Şerban 2018, Favarel-Garrigues 2021, Marat and Sutton 2021).
(2) The legal field as a space of competition between the executive branch and other actors and institutions. This research strand includes works arguing for the necessity of going beyond conventional approaches which view law and legal institutions in authoritarian regimes as solely an expression of the political will of the executive branch (Solomon 2004, 2008, Kurkchiyan and Kubal 2018, Hendley 2020, Lu 2021). Such

studies illustrate that ample evidence exists indicating that, in authoritarian states, there are spaces where law is not a tool freely manipulable by the executive branch but is also wielded by other societal actors, such as courts, legal practitioners, the business sector, and society at large.

(3) Parallel legal orders, both formal and informal, operating in an authoritarian regime context. This research strand includes studies that examine the role of law in authoritarian regimes from a legal pluralistic perspective by including in their analysis informal norms and practices, such as social norms, customs, traditions, and moral codes. Extensive literature exists which focuses on the role of informal norms in shaping the legal landscape of authoritarian regimes (Urinboyev *et al.* 2018, Gans-Morse 2020, Wilson 2020, Dzmitryieva 2021, Isabaeva 2021, Ismailbekova 2021, McCarthy *et al.* 2021). Specifically, such studies have highlighted that informal norms are not simply unspoken/unwritten means to regulate societal relationships, but also have a strong impact on the content and implementation of official law. In particular, the close interplay between official law and unofficial norms becomes visible in three specific areas: the economic sector, society at large, and institutional actors such as courts. These works, therefore, demonstrate the existence of strong empirical support for the claim that the operation of law in authoritarian regime contexts is influenced by a complex web of normative forces, in which both state law and informal norms play a pivotal role.

This brief survey of the literature on the functioning of law in authoritarian regimes suggests that the legal landscape of authoritarian regimes should not be viewed from a 'black-and-white' perspective. Rather, there is a need for a comprehensive account of how state law and non-state forms of normative ordering engage in mutually transforming interactions, thereby shaping the legal landscape of authoritarian regimes. A growing body of literature, especially socio-legal accounts focusing on post-communist contexts, has begun challenging the dominant understanding of law in authoritarian regimes by producing empirically grounded accounts of how law is negotiated and shaped in everyday interactions between a state and society, organisations, and individuals, and between law enforcement officials and other government entities (Solomon and Gadowska 2018, Zaloznaya 2020, Marat and McCarthy 2021). Such studies demonstrate that, even in authoritarian regime contexts, citizens have agency and can evade, use, enforce, reinterpret, and shape law in everyday situations.

Constructing a hybrid compliance model for understanding (anti)corruption in authoritarian regimes

As argued in the previous sections, making people obey a law represents a complex task. This task is especially challenging in authoritarian regime contexts where the state and its legal system lack legitimacy given the extensive use of surveillance and coercion, leading to a disjuncture between the state and society. We can, however, observe the existence of multiple forms of normative ordering in a society whereby people follow or operate outside state law. Although the existing three perspectives on legal compliance offer various explanations for why people break or comply with a law, one pattern emerges as consistent across them: people tend to view state law as the only source of normative order in society but do not account for the role of society's informal norms. Hence, law often faces the challenge of competing or co-existing with informal legal orders such as social norms, customs, or religious norms, which also operate as a focal point of reference, coordinating and influencing people's daily behaviours. Accordingly, the theoretical premise of our proposed hybrid compliance model relies on the understanding that there is not a single, integrated set of rules in any society encoded in law or sanctified by religion or enshrined as rules for daily social behaviour. Quite simply, there is no uncontested and universally applicable normative code that guides people's lives—the very nature of the normative order is determined by the outcomes of struggles and the interplay between multiple norms and orders. As such, supranational law and nation-state laws are not opposing but rather lie in tension or coexist with other formal and informal norm structures (e.g., social or religious) promoting different types of sanctioned behaviours. Likewise, the state and its laws are rarely the main source of social order/control in a society and face enormous resistance from other (formal and informal) forms of normative ordering.

Eugen Ehrlich was one of the first scholars to fully recognise the plurality of normative orders, and his living law theory remains a useful tool for studying the normative pluralism inherent in different working normative orders. In *Fundamental Principles of the Sociology of Law*, Ehrlich (1912) distinguishes between law created by the state (juristic law and statutes) and informal norms produced by non-state social associations (living law). Ehrlich claims that a 'living law' is not directly linked to the state or its legal system, but to the inner order of various social associations. By 'the inner order of social associations', Ehrlich means society's reflexive web of expectations that grant power and meaning to norms. Thus, for Ehrlich, it is not state law, but the 'living law' of various social associations that dominates everyday life itself even if it is not codified or formally recognised/endorsed by the state (Banakar 2008, Urinboyev 2013). In this way, Ehrlich designates the entirety of law dominating everyday life and social relations as the living law, whereas he refers to a law created/codified by a state as state law or juristic law. He advises us that if we seek to better understand the coexistence of and clashes between different normative orders, we should attentively observe everyday life, the relations of domination, and actual habits of people, and enquire into people's thoughts regarding the opinions of those relevant to them in their surrounding environment and related to proper social behaviours. Thus, equipped with the concept of 'living law', we argue that we cannot satisfactorily explore the nature, forms, and causes of corruption without considering the informal norms, practices, and moral codes operating within various social associations in society (the 'living law').

Ehrlich's idea that state law is not the only regulator of social, economic, and political life is also reflected in the scholarly literature on legal pluralism (Moore 1973, Griffiths 1986, 2003, Merry 1988, Tamanaha 2001, von Benda-Beckmann 2002). Legal pluralism emphasises the coexistence of and clash between multiple sets of rules or 'legal orders' moulding people's social behaviours: the law of the nation-state, indigenous customary rules, religious decrees, moral codes, and the practical norms of social life. From this perspective, law may consist of any rules (written or unwritten) that influence social behaviours and are acted upon by certain groups as binding obligations. In other words, law should be defined by its function and social recognition, not by its form. Thus, state law is merely one amongst many other legal orders within a society. As such, a society is a place of legal pluralism where a wide range of norms, including both official laws and informal norms, coexist and/or clash. Classic legal anthropology studies and the more recent legal pluralism scholarship have described the emergence of 'semi-autonomous social fields' or 'non-state forms of normative ordering' (i.e., informal legal orders) with their own forms of regulation and informal norms, many of which contradict state law (Moore 1973, Tamanaha 2001, Roberts 2005, Pirie 2006). Thus, from a legal pluralism perspective, informal/illegal transactions that would be labelled corruption from a state law and/or supranational perspective may very well be considered morally acceptable and socially cohesive practices according to local morality, social norms, and traditions.

The above discussions suggest that society consists of multiple formal and informal norms that shape people's legal consciousness/culture, daily behaviours, and reactions to different social situations and circumstances. In their seminal work on legal consciousness, Ewick and Silbey (1998) argue that every individual inevitably participates in the social construction of (official) legality through their own personal behaviour. Several categorisations of an individual's position vis-à-vis official law have been proposed, such as 'before the law', 'with the law', and 'against the law' (Ewick and Silbey 1998) as well as 'under the law' (Fritsvold 2009) and 'around the law' (Augustine 2019). However, recent work has argued for the necessity of broadening our state law-centric understanding of legal consciousness/culture by incorporating insights from the legal pluralism scholarship. Building upon Ehrlich's (1912) theory of living law, Hertogh (2018) puts forward the proposition that informal, non-state forms of normative ordering can also be viewed as sources of legal order capable of shaping people's legal consciousness/culture (perceptions, experiences, behaviours, and practices). Based on Hertogh's (2018) conceptualisation, it can thus be argued that there is no one dominant normative order shaping people's legal consciousness. Instead, the very nature of legal consciousness is determined by the outcomes of struggles and the interplay between different normative orders.

Equipped with the aforementioned perspectives, we argue that the study of legal compliance and its interconnections with (anti)corruption should reckon with society's legally plural social fabric, potentially encompassing normative phenomena of quite different kinds. These informal forms of normative ordering shape people's attitudes towards law and social behaviours (i.e., legal compliance) as much as, or possibly more than, state law. Such points are particularly relevant in the context of authoritarian regimes where the state and its legal system lack legitimacy and social acceptance. Thus, the analysis of (anti)corruption should move beyond economic-based approaches or legal centralistic approaches and, thereby, deal with the multiple forms of normative ordering, everyday power relations, conflicts, contradictions, social sanctions, and norms that constitute the basic social fabric (the 'living law') of a society.

These propositions inform our proposed hybrid compliance framework for understanding (anti)corruption in authoritarian regimes. Thus, one of the distinctive features of our proposed framework lies in the investigation of corruption beyond the established paradigms (i.e., the principal–agent model and the collective action approach) and its focus on multiple sources of legal compliance (both formal and informal norms) as a lens via which to understand the emergence, explanation, persistence, and ubiquity of corruption. Our central argument in this book is that the measures and tools adopted to understand and combat corruption should extend beyond a merely economistic view and (Western-centric) legal centralistic approaches. In addition, we argue that, to convince people to act within the realms of state law, a structure replacing not only economic opportunity but also reducing the gap between state law and a society's informal norms and rules (the 'living law') must be in place.

Method, approach, and fieldwork

This book is based on extensive ethnographic field research we conducted between 2009 and 2023 (a total of 20 months) in Tashkent city and the Fergana region of Uzbekistan. The first author—given his Uzbek ethnicity, command of the local language, village origin, and cultural competence—has extensive contacts and social networks enabling him to participate in the daily life of Fergana, becoming *svoi* ('one of us, those who belong to our circle'). - The second author, from Sweden (non-native), provided an external perspective to our fieldwork by interrogating the meaning, function, and logic of taken-for-granted activities and prevailing social norms in Uzbekistan. Our ethnographic toolkit (Reyes 2020), in this sense, includes both 'internal' and 'external' perspectives, affording a holistic view of the field sites in question. Owing to our cooperation with Uzbek universities and our extensive networks, we secured a research permit for fieldwork in Uzbekistan, granting us direct access to the study of (anti)corruption and informal practices in the country. Because we collected empirical material in two different locations in Uzbekistan, we present it separately for each locale. This allows us to provide a detailed and clear description of our fieldwork, including the data collection strategies and the selection of informants and fieldwork sites.

During our fieldwork in Tashkent (the capital city of Uzbekistan), we relied on various qualitative methods of data collection, involving the use of observations and informal interviews, key informant interviews, semi-structured interviews, and case studies of corruption. Combining these multiple techniques allowed us to collect first-hand, original empirical data on central-level institutions, anticorruption laws, policies, and initiatives, as well as how they are perceived, experienced, and renegotiated in various social arenas and in everyday situations. For example, we conducted observations and informal interviews in state institutions where state officials and citizens come into contact with one another on a daily basis (i.e., healthcare institutions, schools, universities, tax offices, and traffic safety enforcement). We also conducted key informant interviews with lawyers, local corruption researchers, anticorruption experts, public prosecutors, members of Parliament, policymakers, and practitioners who design and enforce anticorruption laws and policies. The interviews focused on understanding: (1) the internal logic of national anticorruption institutions and regulations and (2) the reception, interpretation, and impact of global, transnational anticorruption institutions, initiatives, indicators, and discourses at the domestic level. When conducting fieldwork in state institutions, we relied on ethnographic approaches and collected personal anecdotes, biographical trajectories, and bureaucratic itineraries, providing a 'thick description' (Geertz 1973) of the context.

In the Fergana region, the primary methods of data collection during our fieldwork consisted of observations and informal interviews. We conducted observations and interviews in rural areas, namely in the village's social spaces and at events during which most residents come together and exchange information on a daily basis. Specifically, we regularly visited such social hotspots as the *guzar* ('community meeting space') and *choyxona* ('teahouse'), as well as life-cycle events, rituals, and socialising events including weddings, births, circumcision ceremonies, funerals, and monthly get-togethers (*gap*) of village residents. These hotspots are public and open to all village residents and guests. Our informants in the village consisted of a diverse group of individuals with a variety of social positions, ranging from people of influence to ordinary residents. We classified the following social groups as 'people of influence', individuals who negotiated and shaped local politics: (1) *mahalla* leaders who administrated daily affairs and arranged mutual aid practices and life-cycle events; (2) religious leaders who provided religious and moral guidance to the local community; (3) wealthy, successful entrepreneurs (*rassiychilar*) and families in the village who exported village-cultivated fruits and vegetables to Russia; (4) local-level state officials (both medium-level and low-level officials) and their family members who lived in the different *mahallas* of the village; and (5) female leaders of the village and *mahallas* who led and arranged rituals; established the standards for gift exchanges during weddings, births, and circumcision ceremonies; and adjudicated domestic violence and family conflicts. By contrast, we classified those informants not falling into one of the above categories as 'ordinary residents/people' in this study. Notably and importantly, this group nevertheless indirectly shaped local politics by spreading gossip, rumours, and stories.

These strategies allowed us to gain a nuanced understanding of the multi-faceted meanings, logics, and morality of corruption, informal transactions, and practices within different state institutions, and social groups and actors in Uzbek society. We collected a rich stock of ethnographic material on the role of law and informal rules and norms in everyday life, and, either directly or indirectly, in both state and non-state arenas, by looking at, for example, how state officials enforced and talked about laws, the extent to which people conformed to laws or informal rules when dealing with state officials, villagers' perceptions of corruption and bribery, local definitions and interpretations of legal/illegal and moral/immoral binaries, everyday coping strategies, values and moral obligations, and the perceived role and image of the state in everyday life. We also explored community life and social relations by focusing on the role of society's cultural repertoires, moral codes, informal norms and 'non-monetary currencies' (i.e., trust, honour, respect, and reputation), and social hierarchies (i.e., age, gender, and social status) that explain the everyday social life of corruption. We also learned about local narratives and stories about corruption by following the everyday rumours and gossip centred around informal transactions between villagers and state officials. We regularly met and interacted with both people of influence and ordinary residents when we visited the village's social hotspots and life-cycle and socialising events. Given the first author's *svoi* status, our informants openly and freely reflected upon their understandings of what constitutes corruption and shared their stories and adventures involving their interactions with state officials. Because we met more than ten village members on a daily basis, it was quite difficult to keep track of the exact number of people with whom we spoke during our fieldwork trips. Thus, the narrative we provide in the empirical chapters in this book can be viewed as a collection of the voices of the hundreds of villagers we encountered during our daily visits to these social hotspots.

During our fieldwork, research participants were fully informed about the purpose and methods of our research project. In order to ensure maximum anonymity, we have changed the names of informants, villages, and *mahallas*, and provided only the most general information about the fieldwork sites. Our dual identities (two researchers with Uzbek and Swedish backgrounds) significantly shaped our access to participants, data, and fieldwork sites, social positions which require some reflection regarding how these characteristics influenced the fieldwork dynamics (Wasserfall 1993). Whilst acknowledging that there is no completely neutral or objective knowledge (Ritchie *et al.* 2013), we nevertheless attempted to avoid any obvious or conscious bias by seeking to remain as neutral as possible when collecting, interpreting, and presenting our data and analysis. During our fieldwork, we occupied multiple statuses (Merton 1972), experiencing both 'insider moments' with participants (May 2014) and assuming the position of the 'outsider within' (Zempi and Awan 2017). We were 'insiders' when we approached informants through a mutual contact or gatekeeper who enjoyed their trust. Being accepted as insiders allowed us to gain easy access to our research participants' everyday lives and experiences. At times, when we approached informants without a mutual contact or a proper introduction, we were 'outsiders', viewed as two strangers or spies (Simmons 2007) collecting information about people's experiences of corruption and illegal activities. We are aware that our fluid identities, sliding between the 'insider' and 'outsider' positions, may have influenced the content of our empirical data. We also accept that our gender (both authors are male) may have affected our interactions with female and male informants rather differently. However, given that we relied on various data collection strategies, we could cross-check and triangulate the different datasets. A more comprehensive description of the ethnographic project and its results can be found in previous publications (Urinboyev 2013, 2019, Urinboyev and Svensson 2013b, 2013a, 2014, 2017).

Book structure and chapter outlines

This book offers a socio-legal ethnography of (anti)corruption in the authoritarian regime context of Uzbekistan, investigating the role and meaning of corruption and informal/illegal practices in a political system undergoing a gradual transition from a tightly closed and repressive authoritarianism towards softer forms of authoritarianism akin to a hybrid political regime. In doing so, we focus on the role and meaning of corruption at different levels of society, covering developments in macro-, meso-, and micro level arenas of Uzbek society. This investigation is informed by socio-legal perspectives, starting from the premise that explanations of corruption in the context of authoritarian regimes cannot be reduced to 'black-and-white' perspectives. This implies that the situation on the ground is much more complex than conventional approaches assume, given that it is mediated by state officials and ordinary citizens and by their varied positionalities and power geometries within the governance system. The 'corruption experiences' of every kind of person—whether state officials responsible for implementing anticorruption measures, law enforcement actors, civil society activists, mid- and low-level state officials, local government officials, community leaders, religious actors, and ordinary citizens—are informed by a multiplicity of structural variables, power positions, and contextual and situational factors, such as age, gender, education, ethnicity, personal histories, beliefs and ideologies influencing morality, and people's views about a just and fair normative order in society. All of these varying experiences and perspectives enter into mutually transforming interactions, calling for a more careful analysis.

Based on these considerations, our socio-legal ethnographic approach was informed by the 'bottom–up' logic of ethnography. We observed the everyday experiences of the legal system (particularly anticorruption laws, policies, and programmes) as they unfolded in the lives of the aforementioned actors as we attempted to identify what issues come to the fore as most relevant and analytically significant for understanding the social life of corruption in Uzbekistan. Whilst Chapters 2–3 focus on the political environment, governance trajectories, and provide an overview of Uzbekistan's anticorruption legislation with the aim of equipping readers with the contextual knowledge and political and legal background of the country, we note that these two context-focused chapters were developed at the end of the data analysis and writing processes.

Chapters 4–6 comprise the main body of this book. Each of these chapters has a 'personality of its own' in the sense that we use different methods and datasets and focus on macro-, meso-, or micro-level processes in each chapter. More specifically, we provide a 'law in action/living law' analysis and present the ethnographic material (observations, informal interviews, and case studies) and analyse them by pinpointing key concepts, ideas, images, and discursive patterns shared across different case studies. Each of these empirical chapters focuses on diverse actors, social associations, institutions, or cases, such as (1) central-level political and business elites; (2) traffic police authorities; (3) a maternity hospital; (4) a prosecutor's office; and (5) village-level social practices, life-cycle events, actors, and norms. In this sense, each chapter represents a self-contained case study of an aspect, element, or constituent part of how (anti)corruption is interpreted, experienced, and negotiated in everyday life in Uzbekistan.

More specifically, Chapter 4 focuses on macro-level developments and presents the results of our 'law in action/living law'–grounded fieldwork conducted in Tashkent, informed by key informant interviews with lawyers, local corruption researchers, anticorruption experts, public prosecutors, members of Parliament, policymakers, and practitioners who design and enforce anticorruption laws and policies. These various datasets provide first-hand insights into the daily life of central-level institutions, anticorruption laws, policies, and initiatives, as well as how they are perceived, experienced, and renegotiated in different social arenas and everyday life situations. Based on our informal interviews and conversations with the aforementioned key informants, we provide reflections on 'how the law works in Uzbekistan', focusing on various corruption cases and conflicts of interest revolving around the informal and extra-legal practices of high-level state officials.

Chapter 5 represents a study of corruption within a meso-level arena and explores the multifarious meaning, logic, and morality of informal, illegal transactions that take place in the daily workings of three formal (state) associations in Uzbekistan: (1) regional traffic safety enforcement services, (2) a district maternity hospital, and (3) a district prosecutor's office. The chapter will illustrate that corruption has different meanings and logic on different levels of society and that we need to distinguish between the predatory practices of kleptocratic elites and high-level state officials, which have nothing to do with 'survival', and the informal coping strategies of low-level officials and ordinary citizens. Hence, the 'corruption experiences' of every kind of person are mediated by their varied navigation skills and positionalities within the governance system.

Chapter 6 focuses on the role and meaning of corruption in micro-level arenas of Uzbekistan. The chapter presents the fieldwork setting, the Shabboda village situated in the Fergana region of Uzbekistan. Here we specifically focus on three main social associations within the village that form the nitty-gritty of everyday life and social relations: the *mahalla* (neighbourhood community), the *urug'* (extended family/kinship group), and the *oila* (immediate family). We also examine the role of life cycle events such as weddings to describe the multifarious nature of informal transactions, and practices in Uzbek society. By doing so, we demonstrate the role of these associations and life-cycle events in creating, reproducing, and maintaining social norms and sanctions establishing moral and affective bonds amongst villagers and how these informal elements of social control shape people's behaviours when they engage in public administration, business, or wield some political or economic resources.

Finally, we offer our concluding remarks in the final chapter, bringing together the main empirical and theoretical findings from previous chapters and discuss them in relation to existing scholarly explanations for and conceptual approaches to (anti)corruption. We place the distinct theoretical framework (a hybrid compliance model for studying (anti)corruption in authoritarian regimes) developed in the Uzbek context in the broader corruption literature and socio-legal studies, and discuss its relevance and applicability to the study of (anti)corruption in similar socio-legal contexts.

References

Acemoglu, D., and Verdier, T., 2000. The choice between market failures and corruption. *American Economic Review*, 90 (1), 194–211.

Adams, L., Svensson, M., and Urinboyev, R., 2018. Everyday Life Governance in Post-Soviet Uzbekistan. *In*: D. Burghart and T. Sabonis-Helf, eds. *Central Asia in the Era of Sovereignty. The Return of Tamerlane? Boulder*, CO: Lexington, 487–508.

Adserà, A., Boix, C., and Payne, M., 2003. Are you being served? Political accountability and quality of government. *The Journal of Law, Economics, and Organization*, 19 (2), 445–490.

Al-Ramahi, A., 2008. Wasta in Jordan: A distinct feature of (and benefit for) Middle Eastern Society. *Arab Law Quarterly*, 22 (1), 35–62.
Andvig, J.C., Fjeldstad, O.-H., Weltzien, Å., Amundsen, I., Sissener, T.K., and Søreide, T., 2001. *Corruption. A Review of Contemporary Research*. Oslo: Norwegian Institute of International Affairs.
Augustine, D., 2019. Working around the law: Navigating legal barriers to employment during reentry. *Law & Social Inquiry*, 44 (3), 726–751.
Banakar, R., 2008. The politics of legal cultures. *Scandinavian Studies in Law*, 4 (23), 151–175.
Banerjee, R., 2016. On the interpretation of bribery in a laboratory corruption game: Moral frames and social norms. *Experimental Economics*, 19 (1), 240–267.
Barnes, T.D., and Beaulieu, E., 2019. Women politicians, institutions, and perceptions of corruption. *Comparative Political Studies*, 52 (1), 134–167.
Becker, G.S., and Stigler, G.J., 1974. Law enforcement, malfeasance, and compensation of enforcers. *The Journal of Legal Studies*, 3 (1), 1–18.
von Benda-Beckmann, F., 2002. Who's afraid of legal pluralism. *Journal of Legal Pluralism and Unofficial Law*, 47, 37–82.
Besley, T., 2006. *Principled Agents: The Political Economy of Good Government*. Oxford: Oxford University Press.
Bilz, K., and Nadler, J., 2009. Law, Psychology, and Morality. *In*: D.M. Bartels, C.W. Bauman, and L.J. Stitka, eds. *Psychology of Learning and Motivation: Moral Judgment and Decision Making*. San Diego, CA: Academic Press, 101–131.
Bogdanova, E., 2018. Obtaining redress for abuse of office in Russia: The Soviet legacy and the long road to administrative justice. *Communist and Post-Communist Studies*, 51 (3), 273–284.
Camargo, C.B., and Passas, N., 2017. Hidden agendas, social norms and why we need to re-think anti-corruption. *Basel Institute on Governance*, 22.
De Graaf, G., 2007. Causes of corruption: Towards a contextual theory of corruption. *Public Administration Quarterly*, 31 (1/2), 39–86.
De Sardan, J.-P.O., 1999. A moral economy of corruption in Africa? *The Journal of Modern African Studies*, 37 (1), 25–52.
Della Porta, D., and Tarrow, S., 2012. Interactive diffusion: The coevolution of police and protest behavior with an application to transnational contention. *Comparative Political Studies*, 45 (1), 119–152.
Diamond, L., Plattner, M.F., and Walker, C., eds., 2016. *Authoritarianism Goes Global: The Challenge to Democracy*. Baltimore, MD: John Hopkins University Press.
Dzmitryieva, A., 2021. Becoming a judge in Russia: An analysis of judicial biographies. *Europe-Asia Studies*, 73 (1), 131–156.
Ehrlich, E., 1912. Das lebende Recht der Völker der Bukowina. *In*: M. Rehbinder, ed. *Eugen Ehrlich, Recht und Leben*. Berlin: Duncker & Humblot, 43–60.
Ellis, J., ed., 2019. *Corruption, Social Sciences and the Law: Exploration Across the Disciplines*. Abingdon: Routledge.
Esarey, J., and Chirillo, G., 2013. "Fairer sex" or purity myth? Corruption, gender, and institutional context. *Politics & Gender*, 9 (4), 361–389.
Esarey, J., and Schwindt-Bayer, L.A., 2018. Women's representation, accountability and corruption in democracies. *British Journal of Political Science*, 48 (3), 659–690.

Ewick, P., and Silbey, S.S., 1998. *The Common Place of Law: Stories from Everyday Life*. London: University of Chicago Press.
Favarel-Garrigues, G., 2021. 'Vigilante shows' and law enforcement in Russia. *Europe-Asia Studies*, 73 (1), 221–242.
Freedom House, 2013. Freedom House, Nations in Transit 2013 – Uzbekistan [Online]. Available from https://www.refworld.org/docid/51efca3523.html [Accessed 11 Aug 2023].
Friedman, L.M., 1975. *The Legal System: A Social Science Perspective*. New York, NY: Russell Sage Foundation.
Fritsvold, E.D., 2009. Under the law: Legal consciousness and radical environmental activism. *Law & Social Inquiry*, 34 (4), 799–824.
Galtung, F., 1998. Criteria for sustainable corruption control. *The European Journal of Development Research*, 10 (1), 105–128.
Gans-Morse, J., 2020. Taxes, banking, and legal development in Russia: Lessons about institutional complementarities and the rule of law. *Demokratizatsiya: The Journal of Post-Soviet Democratization*, 28 (1), 47–75.
Geertz, C., 1973. *The Interpretation of Cultures*. New York, NY: Basic Books.
Gibbs, J.P., 1975. *Crime, Punishment, and Deterrence*. New York, NY: Elsevier.
Glencorse, B., 2014. 5 ways to beat global corruption. World Economic Forum [online]. *World Economic Forum*. Available from https://www.weforum.org/agenda/2014/11/five-ways-beat-global-corruption/ [Accessed 1 April 2020].
Graycar, A., and Prenzler, T., 2013. *Understanding and Preventing Corruption*. New York, NY: Palgrave MacMillan.
Griffiths, J., 1986. What is legal pluralism. *Journal of Legal Pluralism & Unofficial Law*, 24 (18).
Griffiths, J., 2003. The social working of legal rules. *The Journal of Legal Pluralism and Unofficial Law*, 35 (48), 1–84.
Groenendijk, N., 1997. A principal-agent model of corruption. *Crime, Law and Social Change*, 27 (3), 207–229.
Gupta, A., 1995. Blurred boundaries: The discourse of corruption, the culture of politics, and the imagined state. *American Ethnologist*, 22 (2), 375–402.
Haller, D., and Shore, C., eds., 2005. *Corruption: Anthropological Perspectives*. London and Ann Arbor, MI: Pluto Press.
Hasty, J., 2005. The pleasures of corruption: Desire and discipline in ghanaian political culture. *Cultural Anthropology*, 20 (2), 271–301.
Heidenheimer, A.J., and Johnston, M., 2011. *Political Corruption: Concepts and Contexts*. New Brunswick, CT and London: Transaction Publishers.
Hendley, K., 2020. Assessing the potential for renegades among Russian Millennial lawyers. *Demokratizatsiya: The Journal of Post-Soviet Democratization*, 28 (1), 143–175.
Hertogh, M., 2018. *Nobody's Law: Legal Consciousness and Legal Alienation in Everyday Life*. London: Palgrave Macmillan UK.
Heywood, P.M., 2018. Combating corruption in the twenty-first century: New approaches. *Daedalus*, 147 (3), 83–97.
Holmes, L., 2015. *Corruption: A Very Short Introduction*. Oxford: Oxford University Press.

Hunja, R., 2015. *Here are 10 Ways to Fight Corruption*. The World Bank [Online]. Available from https://blogs.worldbank.org/governance/here-are-10-ways-fight-corruption [Accessed 1 Apr 2020].

Huntington, S.P., 1968. *Political Order in Changing Societies*. New Haven, CT: Yale University Press.

ICG, 2007. Uzbekistan: Stagnation and Uncertainty [Online]. Available from http://www.crisisgroup.org/en/regions/asia/central-asia/uzbekistan.aspx [Accessed 14 Sept 2012].

Isabaeva, E., 2021. Transcending illegality in Kyrgyzstan: The case of a squatter settlement in Bishkek. *Europe-Asia Studies*, 73 (1), 60–80.

Ismailbekova, A., 2021. Native son Japarov: The embodiment of injustice? *Anthropology Today*, 37 (5), 14–17.

Jancsics, D., 2014. Interdisciplinary perspectives on corruption. *Sociology Compass*, 8 (4), 358–372.

Johnson, M., 2005. *Syndromes of Corruption: Wealth, Power and Democracy*. Cambridge: Cambridge University Press.

Kandiyoti, D., 2007. Post-soviet institutional design and the paradoxes of the Uzbek path. *Central Asian Survey*, 26 (1), 31–48.

Kaufmann, D., Kraay, A., and Mastruzzi, M., 2011. The worldwide governance indicators: Methodology and analytical issues. *Hague Journal on the Rule of Law*, 3 (2), 220–246.

Klitgaard, R., 1988. *Controlling Corruption*. Berkeley, Los Angeles, CA and London: University of California Press.

Klitgaard, R., 1998. International cooperation against corruption. *Finance & Development*, 0035 (001), 3–6.

Köbis, N., Jackson, D., and Carter, D.I., 2020. Recent approaches to the study of social norms and corruption. *In*: A.Mungiu-Pippidi and P.M. Heywood, eds. *A Research Agenda for Studies of Corruption*. Edward Elgar Publishing, 41–53.

Kostadinova, T., 2012. *Political Corruption in Eastern Europe: Politics After Communism*. Boulder, CO: Lynne Rienner Publishers.

Kovács, K., and Scheppele, K.L., 2018. The fragility of an independent judiciary: Lessons from Hungary and Poland—and the European Union. *Communist and Post-Communist Studies*, 51 (3), 189–200.

Krislov, S., Boyum, K.O., Clark, J.N., Schaefer, R.C., and White, S.O., 1972. Compliance and the law: A multidisciplinary approach. *Criminology*, 10 (2), 243–243.

Kubbe, I., 2017. Elites and corruption in European Democracies. *In*: P. Harfst, I. Kubbe, and T. Poguntke, eds. *Parties, Governments and Elites*. Wiesbaden: Springer, 249–279.

Kubbe, I., and Engelbert, A., 2017. *Corruption and Norms: Why Informal Rules Matter*. Basingstoke: Palgrave Macmillan.

Kubbe, I., and Engelbert, A., 2018. Corruption and the impact of democracy. *Crime, Law and Social Change*, 70 (2), 175–178.

Kubbe, I., and Varraich, A., 2019. *Corruption and informal practices in the Middle East and North Africa*. Abingdon: Routledge.

Kurkchiyan, M., and Kubal, A., eds., 2018. *A Sociology of Justice in Russia*. Cambridge: Cambridge University Press.

Langbein, L., and Knack, S., 2010. The worldwide governance indicators: Six, one, or none? *The Journal of Development Studies*, 46 (2), 350–370.
Lazar, S., 2005. Citizens despite the state: Everyday corruption and local politics in El Alto, Bolivia. *In*: D. Haller and C. Shore, eds. *Corruption: Anthropological Perspectives*. London and Ann Arbor, MI: Pluto Press, 212–228.
Ledeneva, A.V., 2013. *Can Russia Modernise? Sistema, Power Networks and Informal Governance*. Cambridge: Cambridge University Press.
Leff, N.H., 1964. Economic development through bureaucratic corruption. *American Behavioral Scientist*, 8 (3), 8–14.
Levitt, S., and Miles, T.J., 2008. Economic Analyses of Deterrence: Empirical. *In*: S. Durlauf and L. Blume, eds. *The New Palgrave Dictionary of Economics*. Cham: Palgrave MacMillan.
Leys, C., 1965. What is the problem about corruption? *The Journal of Modern African Studies*, 3 (2), 215–230.
Lloyd Bierstaker, J., 2009. Differences in attitudes about fraud and corruption across cultures: Theory, examples and recommendations. *Cross Cultural Management: An International Journal*, 16 (3), 241–250.
Lomnitz, C., 1995. Ritual, rumor and corruption in the constitution of polity in modern Mexico. *Journal of Latin American Anthropology*, 1 (1), 20–47.
Lopez-Claros, A., 2014. *Six Strategies to Fight Corruption*. The World Bank [Online]. Available from http://blogs8.extcc.com/futuredevelopment/six-strategies-fight-corruption [Accessed 1 Apr 2020].
Lu, Y., 2021. Negotiating the right to information: Citizen–government interactions in the implementation of the regulations on open government information in China. *Europe-Asia Studies*, 73 (1), 81–100.
Lührmann, A., and Lindberg, S.I., 2019. A third wave of autocratization is here: What is new about it? *Democratization*, 26 (7), 1095–1113.
Marat, E., and McCarthy, L.A., 2021. Justice, crime and citizenship in Eurasia: A socio-legal perspective. *Europe-Asia Studies*, 73 (1), 1–7.
Marat, E., and Sutton, D., 2021. Technological solutions for complex problems: Emerging electronic surveillance regimes in Eurasian cities. *Europe-Asia Studies*, 73 (1), 243–267.
Markowitz, L.P., 2008. Local elites, prokurators and extraction in Rural Uzbekistan. *Central Asian Survey*, 27 (1), 1–14.
Marquette, H., and Peiffer, C., 2015. *Corruption and Collective Action (Research Paper No. 32), Developmental Leadership Programme (DLP)*. Birmingham: University of Birmingham.
Mauro, P., 1997. *Why Worry About Corruption? Washington*, DC: International Monetary Fund.
May, R.A.B., 2014. When the methodological shoe is on the other foot: African American interviewer and White interviewees. *Qualitative Sociology*, 37 (1), 117–136.
McAdams, R.H., 2000a. An attitudinal theory of expressive law norms theory. *Oregon Law Review*, 79 (2), 339–390.
McAdams, R.H., 2000b. A focal point theory of expressive law. *Virginia Law Review*, 86 (8), 1649–1729.
McAdams, R.H., 2015. *The Expressive Powers of Law*. Cambridge, MA: Harvard University Press.

McCarthy, L.A., Gehlbach, S., Frye, T., and Buckley, N., 2021. Who reports crime? Citizen engagement with the Police in Russia and Georgia. *Europe-Asia Studies*, 73 (1), 8–35.
McMann, K.M., 2015. *Corruption as a last resort: Adapting to the market in Central Asia*. Ithaca, NY: Cornell University Press.
Méon, P.-G., and Sekkat, K., 2005. Does corruption grease or sand the wheels of growth? *Public Choice*, 122 (1), 69–97.
Merry, S.E., 1988. Legal pluralism. *Law & Society Review*, 22.
Merton, R.K., 1972. Insiders and outsiders: A chapter in the sociology of knowledge. *American Journal of Sociology*, 78 (1), 9–47.
Migdal, J.S., 2001. *State in Society: Studying How States and Societies Transform and Constitute One Another*. Cambridge: Cambridge University Press.
Migdal, J.S., Kohli, A., and Shue, V., eds., 1994. *State Power and Social Forces: Domination and Transformation in the Third World*. Cambridge and New York, NY: Cambridge University Press.
Moore, S.F., 1973. Law and social change: The semi-autonomous social field as an appropriate subject of study. *Law & Society Review*, 7 (4), 719–746.
Mullen, E., and Nadler, J., 2008. Moral spillovers: The effect of moral violations on deviant behavior. *Journal of Experimental Social Psychology*, 44 (5), 1239–1245.
Mungiu, A., 2006. Corruption: Diagnosis and treatment. *Journal of Democracy*, 17 (3), 86–99.
Mungiu-Pippidi, A., and Fazekas, M., 2020. How to define and measure corruption. *In*: A. Mungiu-Pippidi and P.M. Heywood, eds. *A Research Agenda for Studies of Corruption*. Cheltenham: Edward Elgar Publishing, 7–26.
Mungiu-Pippidi, A., and Hartmann, T., 2019. Corruption and development: A reappraisal. *Oxford Research Encyclopaedia of Economics and Finance*.
Mungiu-Pippidi, A., and Heywood, P.M., eds., 2020. *A Research Agenda for Studies of Corruption*. Cheltenham: Edward Elgar Publishing.
Nadler, J., 2004. Flouting the law. *Texas Law Review*, 83, 1399–1441.
Nuijten, M., 2003. *Power, Community, and the State: The Political Anthropology of Organization in Mexico*. London: Pluto Press.
Nuijten, M., and Anders, G., 2007. *Corruption and the Secret of Law: A Legal Anthropological Perspective*. Farnham: Ashgate.
Ostrom, E., 1998. A behavioral approach to the rational choice theory of collective action. *American Political Science Review*, 92 (1), 1–22.
Pani, N., 2016. Historical insights into modern corruption: Descriptive moralities and cooperative corruption in an Indian city. *Griffith Law Review*, 25 (2), 245–261.
Pardo, I., 1996. *Managing Existence in Naples: Morality, Action, and Structure*. Cambridge: Cambridge University Press.
Pardo, I., 2004. *Between Morality and the Law: Corruption, Anthropology and Comparative Society*. London: Ashgate.
Paternoster, R., 2010. How much do we really know about criminal deterrence? *The Journal of Criminal Law and Criminology*, 100 (3), 765–824.
Persson, A., Rothstein, B., and Teorell, J., 2013. Why anticorruption reforms fail—systemic corruption as a collective action problem. *Governance*, 26 (3), 449–471.
Pirie, F., 2006. Legal complexity on the Tibetan Plateau. *The Journal of Legal Pluralism and Unofficial Law*, 38 (53–54), 77–99.

Podrobno.uz, 2017. Popalis-: v Uzbekistane zaveli ugolovnye dela protiv 1566 chinovnikov, obviniaemykh v korruptsii [Online]. *Podrobno.uz*. Available from http://podrobno.uz/cat/proisshestviya/popalis-v-uzbekistane-zaveli-ugolovnye-dela-protiv-1566-chinovnikov-obvinyaemykh-v-korruptsionnykh-p/ [Accessed 20 Dec 2017].

Polese, A., 2008. 'If I receive it, it is a gift; if I demand it, then it is a bribe': On the local meaning of economic transactions in Post-Soviet Ukraine. *Anthropology in Action*, 15 (3), 47–60.

Polese, A., Kovács, B., and Jancsics, D., 2018. Informality 'in spite of' or 'beyond' the state: some evidence from Hungary and Romania. *European Societies*, 20 (2), 207–235.

Pozsgai-Alvarez, J., 2020. The abuse of entrusted power for private gain: Meaning, nature and theoretical evolution. *Crime, Law and Social Change*, 74 (4), 433--455.

Prasad, M., da Silva, M.B.M., and Nickow, A., 2019. Approaches to corruption: A synthesis of the scholarship. *Studies in Comparative International Development*, 54 (1), 96–132.

Rasanayagam, J., 2011. Informal economy, informal state: The case of Uzbekistan. *International Journal of Sociology and Social Policy*, 31 (11/12), 681–696.

Reyes, V., 2020. Ethnographic toolkit: Strategic positionality and researchers' visible and invisible tools in field research. *Ethnography*, 21 (2), 220–240.

Ritchie, J., Lewis, J., Nicholls, C.M., and Ormston, R., 2013. *Qualitative Research Practice: A Guide for Social Science Students and Researchers*. London: SAGE Publications.

Rivkin-Fish, M., 2005. Bribes, Gifts and Unofficial Payments: Rethinking Corruption in Post-Soviet Russian Health Care. *In*: D. Haller and C. Shore, eds. *Corruption: Anthropological Perspectives*. London and Ann Arbor, MI: Pluto Press, 47–64.

Roberts, S., 2005. After government? On representing law without the state. *The Modern Law Review*, 68 (1), 1–24.

Robinson, P.H., and Darley, J.M., 1995. *Justice, Liability, and Blame: Community Views and the Criminal Law. New Directions in Social Psychology*. Boulder, CO: Westview Press.

Rose-Ackerman, S., 1999. *Corruption and Government: Causes, Consequences, and Reform*. Cambridge and New York: Cambridge University Press.

Rothstein, B., 2011. *The Quality of Government: Corruption, Social Trust, and Inequality in International Perspective*. Chicago, IL: University of Chicago Press.

Rothstein, B., 2018. Fighting systemic corruption: The indirect strategy. *Daedalus*, 147 (3), 35–49.

Rothstein, B., and Torsello, D., 2013. Is corruption understood differently in different cultures? Anthropology meets political science. *QoG Working Paper Series, The Quality of Government Institute, Department of Political Science, University of Gothenburg*, 2013:(5), 1–27

Sampson, S., 2005. Integrity Warriors: Global Morality and the Anti-corruption Movement in the Balkans. *In*: D. Haller and C. Shore, eds. *Corruption: Anthropological Perspectives*. London and Ann Arbor, MI: Pluto Press, 103–130.

Schwertheim, H., 2017a. *Innovations in Anti-corruption Approaches: A Resource Guide*. Stockholm: International Institute for Democracy and Electoral Assistance.

Schwertheim, H., 2017b. Innovations in anti-corruption approaches: A resource guide. *International Institute for Democracy and Electoral Assistance*. Available from https://www.idea.int/gsod/files/IDEA-GSOD-2017-RESOURCE-GUIDE-ANTI-CORRUPTION.pdf [Accessed 22 Dec ember 2023].

Schwickerath, A.K., Varraich, A., and Smith, L.-L., eds., 2016. *How to Research Corruption? Conference Proceedings: Interdisciplinary Corruption Research Forum*. Interdisciplinary Corruption Research Network.

Scott, J.C., 1972. *Comparative Political Corruption*. Englewood Cliffs, NJ: Prentice Hall.

Şerban, M., 2018. Stemming the tide of illiberalism? Legal mobilization and adversarial legalism in Central and Eastern Europe. *Communist and Post-Communist Studies*, 51 (3), 177–188.

Shah, A., 2007. Tailoring the fight against corruption to country circumstances. *In*: A. Shah, ed. *Performance Accountability and Combating Corruption*. Washington, DC: World Bank, 233–254.

Simmons, M., 2007. Insider ethnography: Tinker, tailor, researcher or spy? *Nurse Researcher*, 14 (4), 7-–17.

Smart, A., and Hsu, C.L., 2007. Corruption or Social Capital? Tact and the Performance of Guanxi in Market Socialist China. *In*: D. Haller and C. Shore, eds. *Corruption and the Secret of Law: A Legal Anthropological Perspective*. Farnham: Ashgate, 167–190.

Solomon, P.H., 2004. Judicial power in Russia: Through the prism of administrative justice. *Law & Society Review*, 38 (3), 549–582.

Solomon, P.H., 2008. Judicial Power in Authoritarian States: The Russian Experience. *In*: T. Moustafa and T. Ginsburg, eds. *Rule by Law: The Politics of Courts in Authoritarian Regimes*. Cambridge: Cambridge University Press, 261–282.

Solomon, P.H., and Gadowska, K., 2018. Legal change in post-communist states: Contradictions and explanations. Introduction. *Communist and Post-Communist Studies*, 51 (3), 173–176.

Tamanaha, B., 2001. A non-essentialist version of legal pluralism. *Journal of Law & Society*, 27, 296-–321.

TI, 2007. *Global Corruption Report 2007: Corruption and Judicial Systems. Transparency International*. New York, NY: Cambridge University Press.

TI, 2016a. Corruption Perceptions Index 2016, Transparency International [Online]. Available from https://www.transparency.org/news/feature/corruption_perceptions_index_2016 [Accessed 23 Mar 2020].

TI, 2016b. How to stop corruption: 5 key ingredients. Transparency International [Online]. *www.transparency.org*. Available from https://www.transparency.org/news/feature/how_to_stop_corruption_5_key_ingredients [Accessed 1 Apr 2020].

TI, 2022. Corruption Perceptions Index 2022, Transparency International [Online]. Available from https://www.transparency.org/en/cpi/2022 [Accessed 26 Apr 2023].

Tittle, C.R., 1980. *Sanctions and Social Deviance: The Question of Deterrence*. New York, NY: Praeger.

Torsello, D., and Venard, B., 2016. The anthropology of corruption. *Journal of Management Inquiry*, 25 (1), 34–54.

Trevisani, T., 2022. The Moral Economy of Consensus and Informality in Uzbekistan. *In*: J. Buzalka and A. Pasieka, eds. *Anthropology of Transformation: From Europe to Asia and Back*. Cambridge: Open Book Publishers, 105–130.

Tyler, T.R., 2006. *Why People Obey the Law*. Princeton, NJ: Princeton University Press.

Urinboyev, R., 2013. *Living Law and Political Stability in Post-Soviet Central Asia. A Case Study of the Ferghana Valley in Uzbekistan*. (Ph.D. Dissertation, Lund Studies in Sociology of Law). Lund: Lund University.

Urinboyev, R., 2019. Everyday Corruption and Social Norms in Post-Soviet Uzbekistan. *GLD Working Paper No. 19. The Program on Governance and Local Development at the University of Gothenburg*. Gothenburg: University of Gothenburg.

Urinboyev, R., Polese, A., Svensson, M., Adams, L.L., and Kerikmäe, T., 2018. Political vs everyday forms of governance in Uzbekistan: The illegal, immoral and illegitimate politics and legitimacy in Post- Soviet Eurasia. *Studies of Transition States and Societies*, 10 (1), 50–64.

Urinboyev, R., and Svensson, M., 2013a. Living Law, Legal Pluralism, And Corruption in Post-Soviet Uzbekistan. *Journal of Legal Pluralism and Unofficial Law*, 45 (3), 372–390.

Urinboyev, R., and Svensson, M., 2013b. Corruption in a Culture of Money: Understanding Social Norms in Post-Soviet Uzbekistan. *In*: M. Baier, ed. *Social and Legal Norms*. Farnham: Ashgate, 267–284.

Urinboyev, R., and Svensson, M., 2014. Rethinking corruption in Post-Soviet Uzbekistan: Ethnography of "Living Law". *Eugen Ehrlich's Sociology of Law*, 207–235.

Urinboyev, R., and Svensson, M., 2017. Corruption, Social Norms and Everyday Life in Uzbekistan. *In*: I. Kubbe and A. Engelbert, eds. *Corruption and Norms: Why Informal Rules Matter?* Basingstoke: Palgrave, 187–210.

Vlassis, D., 2015. 3 key steps to end corruption. World Economic Forum [Online]. *World Economic Forum*. Available from https://www.weforum.org/agenda/2015/01/three-ways-to-end-global-corruption/ [Accessed 1 Apr 2020].

Wasserfall, R., 1993. Reflexivity, feminism and difference. *Qualitative Sociology*, 16 (1), 23–41.

Werner, C.A., 2000. Gifts, bribes, and development in Post-Soviet Kazakhstan. *Human Organization*, 59 (1), 11–22.

Wilson, S., 2020. Law enforcement and the politics of religious minority rights in Azerbaijan. *Demokratizatsiya: The Journal of Post-Soviet Democratization*, 28 (1), 177–198.

Wood, A.L., 1974. *Deviant Behavior and Control Sategies: Essays in Sociology*. Lexington, MA: Lexington Books.

World Bank, 2002. The New Anticorruption Home Page [Online]. *World Bank*. Available from http://www.worldbank.org/en/topic/governance/brief/anti-corruption [Accessed 19 June 2017].

World Bank, 2013. World Bank Governance Studies: Corruption [Online]. Available from http://web.worldbank.org/WBSITE/EXTERNAL/WBI/EXTWBIGOVANTCOR/0,,contentMDK:20725263~menuPK:1977002~pagePK:64168445~piPK:64168309~theSitePK:1740530,00.html [Accessed 19 June 2013].

World Bank, 2015. Spotlight 1: When corruption is the norm. *In*: *World Development Report 2015: Mind, Society, and Behavior*. Washington D.C: World Bank, 60–61.

Zaloznaya, M., 2020. A Law & Society take on legality in the former Soviet Union: An Introduction To The Special Issue. *Demokratizatsiya: The Journal of Post-Soviet Democratization*, 28 (1), 3–14.

Zempi, I., and Awan, I., 2017. Doing 'dangerous' autoethnography on Islamophobic victimization. *Ethnography*, 18 (3), 367–386.

Chapter 2

Political environment and governance trajectories in Uzbekistan

Introduction

This chapter examines the political environment and governance trajectories in Uzbekistan since the collapse of the Soviet Union. The analysis of these processes equips readers with contextual information and insights into the political economy of anticorruption reforms in an authoritarian regime context. Such information and insights prove instructive to understanding the legal environment and institutional context as well as the ethnographic material and various case studies in the chapters that follow. When examining these processes, we place special emphasis on (1) political, economic, and societal transformations in the country since the collapse of the Soviet Union; (2) governance trajectories and transition from heavily repressive to a softer form of authoritarianism; (3) the country's position on international indicators concerning corruption, the rule of law, and good governance; (4) the business environment and legal culture; and (5) political and economic conditions under which informal, illegal practices take place.

Uzbekistan under Islam Karimov, 1991–2016

The demise of the Soviet Union in 1991 paved the way for the rapid proliferation of Western-backed reform initiatives in the post-communist societies of Central and Eastern Europe, Russia, the South Caucasus, and Central Asia, reforms primarily focused on good governance, the rule of law, and democratisation (Ajani 1995, Alkon 2002, Gupta *et al.* 2002, Krygier 2019). The Soviet collapse was proclaimed by the Western world as a victory for freedom, a final triumph of democracy over communism, and proof of the superiority of the legal traditions of Western culture over socialist (Soviet) law based on a Marxist–Leninist ideology. A widespread euphoria proliferated in the 1990s, spurred by the notion that the introduction of Western-style legal systems and governance institutions would play a pivotal role in promoting the rule of law and democratisation in -the post-communist societies (Gleason 2001, Alkon 2002, Paggi 2009, White 2010).

DOI: 10.4324/9780429952968-2

Like other newly independent countries, after gaining independence in 1991, the political leadership of Uzbekistan proclaimed their strong commitment to promoting democracy, the market economy, and the rule of law, as well as its intention to break the stronghold of a clientelist culture and (Soviet-style) kleptocratic practices (Karimov 1992, 1993, 1997). In turn, these official proclamations were reflected in institutional and legal reconfigurations, which, amongst many other changes, included the establishment of a Western-style constitution, parliament, judiciary, human rights ombudsman, and anticorruption departments within law enforcement agencies. However, the unstable political situation in Central Asia in the 1990s (i.e., civil war in Tajikistan and ethnic conflicts in southern Kyrgyzstan) for various reasons left the government sceptical of genuine democratisation and market reforms. This scepticism rested on the concern that a rapid transformation of the economy would impact the lives of millions, likely resulting in political instability. Therefore, Uzbek authorities emphasised 'stability at any cost' and made it clear from the beginning that the 'big bang' or shock therapy approach to transition would be unsuitable for Uzbekistan (Ruziev *et al.* 2007). Instead, Uzbekistan proclaimed its preference for a gradualist approach, maintaining Soviet-era welfare policies and centralised control over the priority sectors of the economy (Spoor 1995). As such, preserving the stability of the economy and social and political order has since become an overarching rationale for rejecting all manner of economic and political reforms recommended by international institutions and for developing a strict border regime (Fumagalli 2007).

The Soviet legacy also profoundly impacted Uzbekistan's social policy strategies in the 1990s. Given that the former Soviet social welfare system provided relatively strong social protection and healthcare infrastructures, the general population of Uzbekistan likely expected the same treatment and conditions from the new Uzbek authorities. This issue carried important implications for the maintenance of security and stability in the country. Uzbek authorities were well aware that they might lose legitimacy and face social unrest if they failed to meet the expectations of the people. Given the high proportion of low-income groups and the country's dependence on the importation of consumption goods, any attempt at contracting social welfare benefits would affect millions, consequently leading to social unrest. Along the same vein, Uzbek authorities in the early years of independence remained primarily concerned with preventing dramatic output losses, maintaining strong social protections, and modernising the economy by strengthening the industrial sector (Ruziev *et al.* 2007). As a result, Uzbek authorities attempted to prevent social unrest and instability by devising social welfare policies targeting the most vulnerable population groups. The social welfare strategies adopted by Uzbek authorities during the early years of independence almost mirrored Soviet-era practices (Johnson 2007). Thus, the social protection policies of the 1990s were primarily pursued with the aim of 'buying off' the sympathy of the people and maintaining social order and political stability.

Notably, during the early years of transition, Uzbekistan achieved small but positive and persistent economic growth due to its favourable economic conditions, such as the dominance of its agricultural production, a low level of initial industrialisation, and its rich natural resource base (Zettelmeyer 1998). Uzbekistan suffered less from the transition depression than neighbouring Central Asian states and was amongst the first to report positive output growth, reported for the first time in 1996 (Spechler 2002, Ruziev *et al.* 2007). Interestingly, the cumulative decline in gross domestic product (GDP) between 1989 and 1996 was lowest in Uzbekistan when comparing all former Soviet republics. Uzbekistan also performed fairly well in terms of providing a social safety net, alleviating poverty, and limiting spending cuts to education and healthcare, especially in the mid-1990s (Pomfret 2000, Johnson 2007, Ruziev *et al.* 2007). Soviet-style centralised economic management and strong social protection measures appeared successful in the transition period, given that they prevented large output declines and served to maintain a reasonable living standard. Furthermore, the agricultural sector prevented an increase in unemployment by providing job opportunities in rural areas. As such, the continuation of Soviet-era welfare policies and centralised control over the economy considerably contributed to preserving political stability and security during the early years of independence.

However, the gradual reform strategy appeared to serve as a short-term remedy. Although the gradualist approach to transition contributed to the prevention of sharp output losses and a consequential rise in unemployment and social unrest during the early years of independence, by 2000, it became clear that the economy was simply stagnating (Ruziev *et al.* 2007). As Kandiyoti (2007 p. 44) notes, the partial market reforms that the government of Uzbekistan implemented in pursuit of stability paradoxically resulted in inefficient resource allocation and widespread corruption. Active government intervention created significant administrative barriers and a high tax burden, thereby causing high transaction costs for domestic businesses and a burgeoning informal economy (Rasanayagam 2011). The continuation of Soviet-style centralised economic planning and management created unfavourable conditions for the long-term prospects of the Uzbek economy, leading to macroeconomic distortions and the proliferation of informal economic practices. Simultaneously, the government adopted a series of severe punitive measures to liquidate or formalise informal economic activities (bazaars and petty cross-border trade), activities which provided an alternative means of survival for hundreds of thousands of people (Ilkhamov 2013). As a result, high tax and regulatory burdens expanded the informal economy, bringing additional pressure to public finances and resulting in higher tax rates, which again increased the incentives to evade taxes and escape via the informal economy.

In turn, these processes eventually led to a significant retrenchment of the welfare state and, subsequently, impoverishing the masses in Uzbekistan, particularly in rural areas of the country. In Uzbekistan, Kandiyoti (2007, p. 44) notes that the 'social contract between the state and its population is increasingly under strain and the state's limited capacity to provide social welfare and means of interest articulation to its citizenry exposes it to a crisis of legitimacy'. As Rasanayagam (2011) notes, in the Soviet Union, a clear vision of citizen and state was expressed in the official discourse and enacted in social and material provisions. However, in post-independence Uzbekistan, the formal state in this sense appeared 'absent' since the state retreated from social and material provisions. Whilst state institutions continued to maintain major social welfare programmes, the capacity of the state to provide a comprehensive package of social protection measures and employment opportunities became increasingly limited. This situation forced the population to increasingly turn to traditional methods of safeguarding their lifestyles and welfare within local neighbourhood communities, immediate families, and wider kinship ties. The family and the *mahalla,* thus, became the primary shock-absorbing structures of Uzbek society (Kandiyoti 1998, Dadabaev 2004, Urinboyev 2011).

Accordingly, the analysis of scholarly research indicates that very few Uzbeks reaped the rewards of its reported economic growth (Kandiyoti 1999, 2003, 2007, Abramson 2000, Ilkhamov 2001, 2004, Luong 2004, Wegerich 2006, Trevisani 2007, Markowitz 2008, Rasanayagam 2011). A growing number of Uzbek labour migrants in Kazakhstan, Russia, and Turkey provide clear evidence of the weakening nature of economic and social policies. Although the Uzbek economy has experienced above-average rates of growth—about 7–8% since 2004 (Ruziev *et al.* 2007 IMF 2012)—these indicators hardly reflect everyday life in Uzbekistan, where state salaries fail to secure survival and people are compelled to employ informal coping strategies to meet their livelihood needs. The more one moves from macro- to micro-level analyses of Uzbekistan's post-Soviet transition, the more complex and paradoxical the developmental outcomes appear. According to Ruziev *et al.* (2007), economic growth was not due to structural reforms but to a better agricultural harvest, large inflows of monetary remittances sent from abroad by Uzbek migrant labourers, and, more importantly, favourable world prices for the country's primary exports, including gold, cotton, natural gas, and oil. Instead, this energy-driven economic growth came at the expense of ordinary people in rural areas, where service interruptions, often including the absence of gas and electricity supplies to households during the cold winter months, have become customary over the years. Consequently, the growing gap between official assertions—which state that everything is perfect—and what is actually delivered has given rise to popular dissatisfaction in rural areas and compelled people to search for survival strategies that provide alternative sources of income and a social safety net.

These developments had significant repercussions for governance trajectories and state–society relations in Uzbekistan. The partial market reforms and the continued use of centralised management methods have resulted in a gradual intensification of surveillance at the expense of service delivery. The ruling regime aggressively pursued the policy of 'political stability at any cost', providing them with leverage to deploy coercive strategies and punitive sanctions as an exclusive means of social control. Under Islam Karimov, who ruled the country between 1989 and 2016, the government did not listen to the people, and there was no viable mechanism for a dialogue between the state and society. In addition, the mass media was used by the regime to manipulate people's minds. Within this system, all conflicts between the state and society were resolved primarily through the use of pressure, threats, and repressions. The presence of widespread police and security forces throughout the country clearly illustrated this trend. As a result, the saying '*och qornim—tinch qulog'im*' ('a hungry stomach is better than a worried ear') became commonplace in Karimov's Uzbekistan. As such, Karimov's government extracted resources, exercised strong social control, and foisted its ideology on ordinary people without providing anything in return. The ruling regime absolved itself from social welfare and service provision responsibilities without creating alternative welfare structures. As the state retreated from its social welfare obligations and failed to provide formal income-earning opportunities, citizens reacted to these changes by devising informal coping strategies based on unwritten sets of rules that did not conform to laws, escaped monitoring by state officials, and were mostly pervasive and informal in nature.

Consequently, international indicators of the rule of law and state capacity, such as the World Justice Project's Rule of Law Index, Freedom House's Democracy Index, and Transparency International's Corruption Perceptions Index, consistently portrayed Uzbekistan as a paradoxically 'strong–weak state'—that is, strong when it comes to using coercive strategies, yet weak when it comes to implementing the rule of law and good governance. These processes have also been confirmed within the scholarly literature on Karimov-era governance practices, demonstrating that Uzbekistan made little progress in introducing Western-style legal structures with many formal institutions of government merely achieving a showcase quality. As such, corruption permeated all levels of state and society, from daily interactions between ordinary citizens and low-level state officials to kleptocratic practices involving high-level state officials. The bulk of the extant research focuses on kleptocratic elites in the upper echelons of the state organisation (Ilkhamov 2007, 2017), authoritarianism and the persistence of Soviet-style governance (Fane 1996, Kubicek 1998, Melvin 2004), malfunctioning public administration structures (Melvin 2000, Ergashev *et al.* 2006), administratively commanded economic policies (Zettelmeyer 1998, Pomfret 2000, Kandiyoti 2007, Ruziev *et al.* 2007), clans and regional patronage networks (Luong 2002, Ilkhamov 2004, Collins 2006), inefficient post-Soviet agricultural reforms (Wegerich 2006, Trevisani 2007), corrupt law-enforcement agencies, and inadequate ways of dealing with corruption on the part of state authorities (Markowitz 2008). These studies argue that the struggles amongst various state actors to gain control over scarce resources have resulted in inefficient resource allocation and contradictory state policies, thereby rendering corruption and bribery part of the governance mode in Uzbekistan.

Another noteworthy feature of Karimov-era governance was the convergence of political, economic, and business elites. Given the excessive government control over all areas of the economy and society, it was nearly impossible to conduct business without resorting to informal and extra-legal practices. In their investigative report, 'A Dance with the Cobra: Confronting Grand Corruption in Uzbekistan', Lasslett *et al.* (2017) described three currencies of power in Uzbekistan which shaped the business environment: (1) personal connections and the networks to which you belong; (2) tributes (payments to secure loyalty or services), a widespread practice locally known as '*dolya*'; and (3) violence which involves the use of threats, fear, and coercion by law enforcement and the state's security services to keep the target audience and general population under control. Accordingly, many successful businesses were owned by or linked to high-level state officials. Some relationships took the form of patronage. Indeed, it was an open secret that high-level state officials (e.g., ministers, governors, public prosecutors, judges, state security service officials, heads of tax departments, or customs officials) frequently provided protection and privileges to businesses by establishing a monopoly over the provision of services or goods, winning various tenders, avoiding high taxes or fines, lowering customs duties and tariffs, and acquiring land in key areas amongst other actions.

Corrupt schemes and practices surrounding Gulnara Karimova, daughter of the late President of Uzbekistan, serve as a relevant example here. The investigative report by Lasslett *et al.* (2017) indicated that by 2003–2004, Karimova and her team had effectively established themselves as a racket in Uzbekistan's telecommunications sectors. Thus, any prospective investor interested in entering Uzbekistan's market had to pay one of Karimova's proxy companies an entrance fee (*dolya*), an illegal practice which violated Uzbekistan's law, international law, and foreign bribery legislation. As a result, three major international telecom brands—namely, Telia, VimpelCom, and MTS—had succeeded in entering Uzbekistan's market by the end of 2007, an outcome which would have been impossible without the stewardship of Gulnara Karimova. Allegedly, these corrupt schemes generated at least US$850 million for Karimova. In fact, the telecommunications sector was just one amongst many other sectors of Uzbekistan's economy controlled by the Karimova syndicate. A drastic turn to Gulnara Karimova's 'successful business practices' was an exposé by *Uppdrag granskning* (Sweden's leading investigative journalism TV show) in September 2012, which presented a number of revelations regarding Telia's (the Swedish telecom giant) corrupt and unethical business practices in Central Asia. The culmination of these revelations was the so-called 'Uzbekistan affair'—the 3G-licencing process in Uzbekistan, which provided solid evidence of how Telia, in an attempt to acquire a 3G licence in Uzbekistan, made extensive monetary transfers (over €200 million) to an offshore company, Takilant, a company linked to the late President Islam Karimov's family (Schoultz and Flyghed 2016). Takilant was 'nominally owned' by an assistant to Gulnara Karimova[1] (Lasslett *et al.* 2017), and reportedly earned over €200 million between 2007 and 2010 as a result of the licensing deal (Schoultz and Flyghed 2016). This corruption scandal sent shockwaves rumbling across Sweden, the European Union (EU), the United States, and Uzbekistan, eventually resulting in criminal charges against the former Telia chief executive officer (CEO) and two other senior officials for their involvement in the bribery scheme. As a result of legal proceedings against the company, Telia agreed to pay US$965 million to resolve charges relating to violations of the Foreign Corrupt Practices Act (FCPA). Telia's 'Uzbekistan affair' was not the only case in which foreign companies and business actors were involved in corruption scandals associated with Gulnara Karimova. Similarly, VimpelCom, the Amsterdam-based telecommunications company, also faced criminal charges for paying massive bribes to Gulnara Karimova in order to enter Uzbekistan's telecommunications market; as a result, the company agreed to pay US$835 million to settle US and Dutch charges (*The Guardian* 2016).

The abovementioned corruption scandals revolving around Uzbekistan's telecommunications sector appear to indicate that political, economic, and business elites are intertwined in mutually dependent relationships. The analysis of Gulnara Karimova's corrupt schemes shows the complicity of a myriad of high-level state institutions and actors (e.g., cabinet secretaries, government committees, ministries, the courts, sector regulators, and the security services). The corruption scandal revolving around members of the presidential family was just one case amongst many other corruption cases and purges that were part and parcel of the Karimov-era governance and business practices.[2]

Post-Karimov Uzbekistan, 2016–present: Authoritarian modernisation

The death of Islam Karimov, the first president of independent Uzbekistan, was announced on 2 September 2016. For many Western analysts, journalists,

1 It has now been established in the Swiss courts that Gulnara Karimova is the ultimate beneficiary and owner of Takilant. Indeed, Karimova has argued in Switzerland that she is the owner of Takilant in order to claim standing in asset recovery efforts.

2 See, for example, Bruce Pannier, 'Big Business In Uzbekistan Targeted In Wave of Arrests', RFE/RL, 12 March 2010; see also US Department of State, 'Uzbekistan: From A to Zeromax', 20 January 2010, Tashkent, http://www.wikileaks.ch/cable/2010/01/10TASHKENT27.html

business circles, and scholars writing about Uzbekistan, Islam Karimov's quarter-century rule proved politically, economically, and morally oppressive—the brutal suppression of free speech, the merciless fight against political opposition, the systematic abuse of human rights, the extremely high unemployment rate, rampant corruption, and the impossibility of doing ethical business in the country (March 2003, Rasanayagam 2011, Ilkhamov 2017, Buckley 2018). Domestically, however, Karimov enjoyed some degree of legitimacy as the first president of Uzbekistan, who succeeded in upholding political stability and interethnic peace in the 1990s when its neighbouring countries, Kyrgyzstan and Tajikistan, experienced violent ethnic conflicts and civil war.

Yet, the political climate shifted in Uzbekistan following the instalment of Shavkat Mirziyoyev as the president of Uzbekistan in December 2016. Given that Mirziyoyev served as Prime Minister for 13 years under Uzbekistan's first president, Islam Karimov, there was an expectation both inside and outside the country that he would naturally continue his predecessor's repressive authoritarian policies. Despite the dubious nature of the power transition and pessimistic predictions, Mirziyoyev emerged as a reform-oriented leader and initiated an ambitious reform programme under the umbrella of 'the state should serve its citizens, not vice versa'. This rested upon an understanding within the higher echelons of government that the political regime had already hit a dead end, and the only way to create a new leader's legitimacy and improve the economic and social situation was to attract foreign investments, best practices, and technologies. The opening up of the previously tightly closed country and the announcement of an ambitious reform programme produced widespread euphoria and optimism. Most discourse on Uzbekistan's post-Karimov governance trajectories, both domestically and internationally, welcomed Mirziyoyev's reformist agenda. In his inspirational reformist speeches, Mirziyoyev declared his intention to dismantle the Karimov-era governance practices, calling for the necessity of liberalising the economy; promoting good governance and the rule of law; developing an efficient, transparent, and accountable public administration system; and increasing the activity of citizens and locally elected officials (deputies of the *kengash* (local legislative body)) as agents of accountability. The most noteworthy feature of these post-Karimov developments was the establishment of the President's online 'virtual reception portal' and the President's reception houses (known as '*halq qabulhonalari*') in all regions of the country. These initiatives allowed ordinary citizens to report their grievances, submit complaints related to unlawful actions by state officials and institutions, and make policy recommendations to the President's Office.

In turn, these official proclamations were laid out in two documents—namely, a decree 'On the approval of the concept of administrative reform in the Republic of Uzbekistan' (No PF-5185, adopted on 8 September 2017) and a decree 'About the strategy of actions for further development of the

Republic of Uzbekistan' (PF-4947, adopted on 7 February 2017). More specifically, the 2017–2021 Strategy of Actions emphasised the following five main pillars of reforms: (1) improving the system of public administration; (2) ensuring the rule of law and further reforming the judicial system; (3) development and liberalisation of the economy; 4) development of the social sphere; and (5) ensuring security, religious tolerance, and interethnic accord, pursuant to a balanced and mutually advantageous and constructive foreign policy.

As a result of these initiatives, Uzbekistan under Mirziyoyev's leadership has undergone significant changes since 2017, notably: (1) strict state control over the economy has been reduced; (2) liberalisation of foreign exchange has been introduced; (3) law enforcement bodies' pressure on the business sector has decreased; (4) local mass media outlets (especially in online contexts) have become more vocal, and ordinary citizens have become less afraid of expressing their opinions on political issues; (5) the government freed 18 high-profile prisoners and removed nearly 16,000 people from a 17,500-strong security blacklist of potential extremists; (6) a number of officials in leadership positions at the National Security Service (notorious for corruption and/or repression) were either fired or jailed; (7) forced labour involving children, students, teachers, and doctors during the annual cotton harvest has been eliminated; and (8) Uzbekistan has improved its relations with neighbouring countries, established a dialogue with international institutions, and begun to market itself as open to the international community after its nearly three decades of isolationism.

Another notable change was the April 2023 referendum resulting in significant constitutional amendments, increasing the state's social protection support for vulnerable citizens, granting more rights to the accused, and establishing the separation of legislative and executive functions at the local government level. In its amended constitution, Uzbekistan has been proclaimed a 'social state' (welfare state), a legislative proposal from President Shavkat Mirziyoyev primarily aimed at restoring the social contract between the state and society. In terms of anticorruption measures, Uzbek authorities regularly report news of officials arrested on corruption charges. For example, in 2018, more than one thousand criminal cases were opened on suspicion of corruption. Most recently, in December 2023, the Uzbek government conducted a series of raids and corruption purges aimed at capturing corrupt state officials, which included dozens of high-ranking state officials such as a former minister, district governors, deputy regional governors, and tax officials amongst others. These corruption raids coincided with the visit of Qatar's Amir Sheikh Tamim, who attended the seventh International Anticorruption Excellence Award ceremony in Uzbekistan on 19 December 2023. The culminating point of this visit was the opening of the anticorruption monument, 'a twelve-metre metal composition in the form of an open hand pointing upward', symbolising honesty, purity of actions and thoughts, absolute zero tolerance for corruption, and a call to all countries of the world to unite in fighting against corruption (Gazeta.uz 2023).

Academic and policy circles have voiced mixed reactions to various post-Karimov developments. Some commentators provided rather optimistic accounts, asserting that the new Uzbek leadership's reform agenda promotes economic development and political liberalisation, thereby creating dialogue and trust between the state and citizens (Bowyer 2018, Sever 2018). In December 2019, *The Economist* posited the following: 'Shavkat Mirziyoyev...has astonished and delighted his citizens with his enthusiasm for reform. The question now is how far and how fast he will dare to go'.[3] However, other commentators called for more cautious optimism, stating that the post-Karimov developments in Uzbekistan may be a form of authoritarian modernisation mainly oriented towards promoting economic growth and effective governance and attracting foreign direct investment (Pannier 2017, Buckley 2018, Anceschi 2019, Wood 2019). Thus, they argue that current transformations in Uzbekistan cannot be viewed as a political reform project, but rather a transition from heavily repressive to a softer form of authoritarianism (akin to a hybrid political regime).

It has been more than seven years since Shavkat Mirziyoyev took over the leadership of Uzbekistan. Whilst the new government has made progress in many areas since 2016, the analysis of public policy developments indicates that Mirziyoyev's reform initiatives were mainly limited to economic policies. Although initial reform initiatives, such as virtual reception portals, seemed promising in the early stages, many turned out to be ineffective and paradoxical in the long run. Citizens' complaints are, for the most part, not handled by central or regional-level organisations, but rather are transferred to the same organisation or agency against which citizens filed a complaint. Economic and social inequality has further increased since 2017, with wealth growing amongst political elites and business actors who are well-connected to high-level state officials, and growing unemployment and social inequality amongst the population in general, especially in rural areas. There is a widespread perception within society that the government's economic modernisation and development programmes benefit the privileged few, rather than the whole country and ordinary citizens. One clear example is the Tashkent City mega-project, a large-scale construction project valued at US$1.3 billion. A report published on the openDemocracy website shows that a number of companies involved in the construction of Tashkent City were closely linked to Jahongir Ortiqhodjaev, the former mayor of Tashkent (Lasslett 2019). This construction project is just one example from a series of similar informal transactions and patron–client relations that are part and parcel of the governance mode and business climate in Uzbekistan. Thus, many features

3 https://www.economist.com/asia/2019/12/18/uzbekistan-holds-a-semi-serious-election

and the legacy of the Karimov-era political and administrative system remain intact.

Another area of concern was the steady surge in kleptocratic practices in the highest echelons of power. A series of journalistic investigations released by the *Ozodlik* (Radio Free Europe's Uzbek service) revealed the amalgamation of political elites and business circles in Uzbekistan.[4] These processes were particularly visible in *Ozodlik's* revelations concerning kleptocratic practices leading to the 'Sardoba' dam collapse[5] and the dubious energy-sector agreements connected to the oligarch Bakhtiyor Fozilov,[6] which led to serious energy shortages during the cold winter months throughout the country. These revelations sent shockwaves rumbling across Uzbekistan, given that the scale of corruption was unprecedented and impacted the entire population of the country. One possible inference is that the enduring structures of the Uzbek political system developed during the Karimov era continue to shape current governance trajectories. Despite Mirziyoyev's reformist intentions, it seems as though the old, entrenched governance practices persist, leading to a regression to past practices. As a result, these processes carry severe repercussions for state–society relations and significantly undermine the image and legitimacy of the state and its anticorruption agenda.

In addition, the situation surrounding media freedom has also gradually deteriorated and raised serious concerns both inside and outside the country. Whilst Uzbekistan experienced positive changes related to press freedom and political liberalisation during the initial years of Mirziyoyev's presidency, recent developments indicate a backsliding towards coercive strategies. Specifically, 2023 witnessed the highest number of arrests. In January 2023, Uzbek authorities detained seven journalists on extortion charges, the single largest raid targeting media workers since the incumbent president took office in 2016.[7] In July 2023, Olimjon Haydarov, a vocal critic of officials in the city of Qo'qon, was arrested on extortion charges, raising further alarms about the state of free expression.[8] The situation worsened in August 2023, when Abduqodir Mominov, a prominent blogger with the Ko'zgu YouTube channel boasting nearly 250,000 subscribers, received an 87-month (seven years and three months) jail sentence. He was found guilty of 'large-scale extortion' and 'violation of privacy with serious consequences', a charge increasingly used against bloggers critical of the government.[9] Adding to the crackdown, in August 2023, the Uzbekistan Interior Ministry issued an arrest

4 https://www.ozodlik.org/a/ozodlik-surishtiruvi-gaz-putin-eriell-mirziyoyev-fozilov-timchenko/32261934.html

5 https://www.youtube.com/watch?v=0mbHCTBMqns&ab_channel=OzodlikRadiosi

6 https://www.youtube.com/watch?v=D3TfzSYJ-TU&ab_channel=OzodlikRadiosi

7 https://eurasianet.org/uzbekistan-detains-seven-journalists-in-secretive-raids

8 https://eurasianet.org/uzbekistan-another-citizen-journalist-falls-prey-to-investigators

9 https://rus.ozodlik.org/a/32535417.html

warrant for Sanzhar Ikramov, a blogger likely based in Turkey. He operated a politically themed YouTube channel with over 200,000 subscribers, and his alleged crime dates back to 2011.[10] These events collectively paint a troubling picture of Uzbekistan's declining freedom of expression, freedom of assembly, and freedom of association despite earlier positive strides towards political liberalisation and media freedom.

Similarly, despite the establishment of the Anticorruption Agency in 2020 and the introduction of numerous anticorruption laws, policies, and programmes (e.g., Anticorruption Law, adopted on 4 January 2017), no significant success has resulted in reducing corruption. The newly established Anticorruption Agency, which has investigative authority over budgetary processes, public procurement, sales of state-owned assets, and other relevant areas, rarely investigates elite-level corruption and kleptocratic practices within the highest echelons of power, given that the agency is not fully independent and remains directly subordinate to the Presidential Administration. As Transparency International's Corruption Perceptions Index (TI 2024) indicates, Uzbekistan continues to remain amongst the most corrupt countries in the world. Accordingly, notwithstanding Uzbek authorities' anticorruption rhetoric, it should be noted that these measures primarily represent an attempt to curb petty corruption through instrumental (penalty) approaches, whilst the social basis and systemic roots of corruption remain unaddressed. As such, one of the key features of the Mirziyoyev-era anticorruption efforts is a primary focus on combating petty corruption, whereas high-level corruption remains largely intact. The return of several officials previously linked to large-scale corruption cases (e.g., the Swedish Telia scandal) to key government positions further undermined the legitimacy of anticorruption policies. Although Uzbek authorities continuously report news of officials arrested on corruption charges, these corruption raids are not a genuine campaign against corruption given their selective nature and focus on petty corruption. Rather, it is common practice to occasionally conduct various kinds of campaigns against corrupt officials who are rendered scapegoats. Along this vein, a policy report by the Open Society Foundations Eurasia Programme (Lewis 2016) argues that corruption charges associated with high-level state officials in authoritarian regimes such as Uzbekistan are largely driven by political manoeuvrings and power struggles within the political elite, rather than a genuine attempt to combat corruption. As one of our informants anecdotally noted, 'Anticorruption laws are usually adopted not to fight corruption, but to get rid of the competing corrupt officials'. In this respect, the reshuffling and imprisonment of several officials within the highest echelons of the Uzbek government over the last seven years clearly reflect such intra-elite conflicts, which have little to do with broader anticorruption efforts.

10 https://www.rferl.org/a/uzbekistan-freedom-of-speech-arrests-bloggers/32552409.html

Whilst Uzbekistan continues to experience robust annual GDP growth of about 5%, most of this growth stems from natural resource extraction, notably from the export of gold and natural gas, with productivity and employment rates remaining low. As a result, millions of Uzbek citizens are compelled to work abroad on a seasonal, temporary, or permanent basis in order to meet their livelihood needs. Examining growing economic and social inequality in the country, one possible inference would be that any hopes and trust of ordinary citizens placed on the reform agenda appear to have already evaporated. The current regime seems trapped in the expectations of the systemic reforms and economic modernisation they promised yet failed to deliver given their own reluctance to implement political liberalisation. The administrative reforms package, initially introduced via the President's decree 'On the approval of the concept of administrative reform in the Republic of Uzbekistan' (No PF-5185, 8 September 2017) and then further elaborated in 'Uzbekistan's New Development Strategy' (No PF-269, 21 December 2022), remains poorly implemented. The Karimov-era bureaucratic culture, organisational inertia, and kleptocratic practices continue to shape governance trajectories. As such, the majority of key management positions in the Uzbek government remain occupied by corrupt and incompetent officials reluctant to embrace the reform agenda. Thus, the selection and appointment of officials to high-level government positions are carried out primarily based on the principle of loyalty, rather than based on the principles of meritocracy through open recruitment processes. Such principles inevitably contribute to the proliferation of corruption, kleptocracy, and rent-seeking practices within state institutions. Given the gap between everyday reality and Mirziyoyev's reform rhetoric, the current government in Uzbekistan runs a similar risk of losing its legitimacy as its predecessor Karimov's regime did.

References

Abramson, D.M., 2000. Socialism's Bastard Children. *POLAR: Political and Legal Anthropology Review*, 23, 49–64.

Ajani, G., 1995. By chance and prestige: Legal transplants in Russia and Eastern Europe. *The American Journal of Comparative Law*, 43 (1), 93–117.

Alkon, C., 2002. The cookie cutter syndrome: Legal reform assistance under post-communist democratization programs. *Journal of Dispute Resolution*, 2002 (2), 327–366.

Anceschi, L., 2019. New Authoritarianism in Post-Karimov Uzbekistan. *In*: C. Frappi and F. Indeo, eds. *Monitoring Central Asia and the Caspian Area: Development Policies, Regional Trends, and Italian Interests*. Venice: Edizioni Ca' Foscari, 117–119.

Bowyer, A.C., 2018. *Political Reform in Mirziyoyev's Uzbekistan: Elections, Political Parties and Civil Society*. Washington, DC: Central Asia-Caucasus Institute & Silk Road Studies Program.

Buckley, N., 2018. Once-repressive Uzbekistan begins a post-Karimov opening [online]. *Financial Times*. Available from https://www.ft.com/content/6c37419c-0cbf-11e8-8eb7-42f857ea9f09 [Accessed 19 May 2018].

Collins, K., 2006. *Clan Politics and Regime Transition in Central Asia*. Cambridge: Cambridge University Press.

Dadabaev, T., 2004. Post-Soviet realities of society in Uzbekistan. *Central Asian Survey*, 23 (2), 141–166.

Ergashev, B., Iusupov, I., Pogrebniak, A., Korenev, I., Allaev, B., Gaibullaev, O., Usmanov, S., Gasanova, N., and Saifulin, R., 2006. Public administration reform in Uzbekistan. *Problems of Economic Transition*, 48 (12), 32–82.

Fane, D., 1996. Ethnicity and Regionalism in Uzbekistan: Maintaining Stability through Authoritarian Control. *In*: L. Drobizheva, R. Gottemoeller, C.M. Kelleher, and L. Walker, eds. *Ethnic Conflict in the Post-Soviet World: Case Studies and Analysis*. Armonk, NY: M.E. Sharpe, 271–302.

Fumagalli, M., 2007. Introduction: Stability, sovereignty, and the resilience of politics under authoritarian rule. *Central Asian Survey*, 26 (1), 1–6.

Gazeta.uz, 2023. Monument symbolizing fight against corruption presented in Tashkent [online]. *Gazeta.uz*. Available from https://www.gazeta.uz/en/2023/12/19/monument-symbolizing-fight-against-corruption-presented-in-tashkent/ [Accessed 28 December 2023].

Gleason, G., 2001. Asian values and the democratic transition in Central Asia. *Harvard Asia Quarterly*, 5 (1), 35–44.

Gupta, P., Kleinfeld, R., and Salinas, G., 2002. *Legal and judicial reform in Europe and Central Asia. World Bank Operations Evaluation Department*. Washington, DC: World Bank.

Ilkhamov, A., 2001. Impoverishment of the masses in the transition period: Signs of an emerging 'new poor' identity in Uzbekistan. *Central Asian Survey*, 20 (1), 33–54.

Ilkhamov, A., 2004. The limits of centralization: Regional challenges in Uzbekistan. *In*: P.J. Luong, ed. *The Transformation of Central Asia. States and Societies from Soviet Rule to Independence*. Ithaca, NY: Cornell University Press, 159–181.

Ilkhamov, A., 2007. Neopatrimonialism, interest groups and patronage networks: The impasses of the governance system in Uzbekistan. *Central Asian Survey*, 26 (1), 65–84.

Ilkhamov, A., 2013. Labour migration and the ritual economy of the uzbek extended family. *Zeitschrift für Ethnologie*, 138 (2), 259–284.

Ilkhamov, A., 2017. Grand corruption in Uzbekistan's telecommunication sector: Root causes and social costs. *In*: M. Laruelle, ed. *Constructing the Uzbek State: Narratives of Post-Soviet Years*. Boulder, CO: Lexington Books, 45–68.

IMF, 2012. *Republic of Uzbekistan and the IMF. Washington, DC:* International Monetary Fund.

Johnson, E.J., 2007. *Post-Soviet welfare provision: State or society?* Paper presented at the Annual Meeting of the American Political Science Association, Chicago, IL.

Kandiyoti, D., 1998. Rural livelihoods and social networks in Uzbekistan: Perspectives from Andijan. *Central Asian Survey*, 17 (4), 561–578.

Kandiyoti, D., 1999. Poverty in transition: An ethnographic critique of household surveys in Post-Soviet Central Asia. *Development and Change*, 30, 499–524.

Kandiyoti, D., 2003. The cry for land: Agrarian reform, gender and land rights in Uzbekistan. *Journal of Agrarian Change*, 3 (1–2), 225–256.

Kandiyoti, D., 2007. Post-Soviet institutional design and the paradoxes of the Uzbek Path. *Central Asian Survey*, 26 (1), 31–48.

Karimov, I., 1992. *Uzbekistan: The Road of Independence and Progress*. Tashkent: Uzbekistan.

Karimov, I., 1993. *Building the Future: Uzbekistan – Its Own Model for Transition to a Market Economy*. Tashkent: Uzbekistan.

Karimov, I., 1997. *O'zbekiston XXI asr bo'sag'asida: xavfsizlikka tahdid, barqarorlik shartlari va taraqqiyot kafolatlari (Uzbekistan on the Threshold of the Twenty First Century: Challenges to Stability and Progress)*. Tashkent: O'zbekiston.

Krygier, M., 2019. The challenge of institutionalisation: Post- communist 'transitions', populism, and the rule of law. *European Constitutional Law Review*, 15 (3), 544–573.

Kubicek, P., 1998. Authoritarianism in Central Asia: Curse or cure? *Third World Quarterly*, 19 (1), 29–43.

Lasslett, K., 2019. Uzbekistan Ltd: Private–public interests clash in flagship project [online]. *openDemocracy*. Available from https://www.opendemocracy.net/en/odr/uzbekistan-ltd/ [Accessed 31 March 2020].

Lasslett, K., Kanji, F., and McGill, D., 2017. *A Dace with a Cobra: Confronting Grand Corruption in Uzbekistan*. London: International State Crime Initiative.

Lewis, D.G., 2016. *Tackling Corruption in Uzbekistan: A White Paper*. New York, NY: Open Society Foundations.

Luong, P.J., 2002. *Institutional Change and Political Continuity in Post-Soviet Central Asia: Power, Perceptions, and Pacts*. Cambridge: Cambridge University Press.

Luong, P.J., ed., 2004. *The Transformation of Central Asia. States and Societies from Soviet Rule to Independence*. Ithaca, NY: Cornell University Press.

March, A.F., 2003. From leninism to karimovism: Hegemony, ideology, and authoritarian legitimation. *Post-Soviet Affairs*, 19 (4), 307–336.

Markowitz, L.P., 2008. Local elites, prokurators and extraction in Rural Uzbekistan. *Central Asian Survey*, 27 (1), 1–14.

Melvin, N.J., 2000. *Uzbekistan: Transition to Authoritarianism on the Silk Road*. Amsterdam: Harwood Academic.

Melvin, N.J., 2004. Authoritarian Pathways in Central Asia: A Comparison of Kazakhstan, the Kyrgyz Republic, and Uzbekistan. *In:* Yaacov Ro'i, ed. *Democracy and Pluralism in Central Eurasia*. London: Frank Cass, Cummings Centre Series, 127–128.

Paggi, L.A., 2009. Pretending Civil Society: Western NGO scripts and local actors in Post-Soviet Tajikistan. *The Harriman Review*, 16/17 (4/1), 22–33.

Pannier, B., 2017. Analysis: How High Should Hopes Be for Change in Uzbekistan? [online]. *Radio Free Europe/Radio Liberty*. Available from https://www.rferl.org/a/uzbekistan-mirziyoev-hopes-for-change-karimov-cotton-foreign-policy/28938193.html [Accessed 16 July 2018].

Pomfret, R., 2000a. The Uzbek model of economic development, 1991-99. *Economics of Transition*, 8 (3), 733–748.

Rasanayagam, J., 2011. Informal economy, informal state: The case of Uzbekistan. *International Journal of Sociology and Social Policy.*, 31 (11/12), 681–696.

Ruziev, K., Ghosh, D., and Dow, S.C., 2007. The Uzbek puzzle revisited: An analysis of economic performance in Uzbekistan since 1991. *Central Asian Survey*, 26 (1), 7–30.

Schoultz, I. and Flyghed, J., 2016. Doing business for a "higher loyalty"? How Swedish transnational corporations neutralise allegations of crime. *Crime, Law and Social Change*, 66 (2), 183–198.

Sever, M., 2018. *Judicial and Governance Reform in Uzbekistan*. Washington, DC: Central Asia-Caucasus Institute & Silk Road Studies Program.

Spechler, M.C., 2002. Free at last? Uzbekistan and Russia. *Problems of Post-Communism*, 49 (1), 63–67.

Spoor, M., 1995. Agrarian transition in former Soviet Central Asia: A comparative study of Uzbekistan and Kyrgyzstan. *The Journal of Peasant Studies*, 23 (1), 46–63.

The Guardian, 2016. VimpelCom pays $835m to US and Dutch over Uzbekistan telecoms bribes [online]. Available from https://www.theguardian.com/world/2016/feb/19/vimpelcom-pays-835m-to-us-and-dutch-over-uzbekistan-telecoms-bribes [Accessed 15 November 2020].

TI, 2024. Corruption Perceptions Index 2023, Transparency International [online]. Available from https://www.transparency.org/en/cpi/2022/index/uzb [Accessed 5 February 2024].

Trevisani, T., 2007. After the Kolkhoz: Rural elites in competition. *Central Asian Survey*, 26 (1), 85–104.

Urinboyev, R., 2011. Law, social norms and welfare as means of public administration: Case study of Mahalla Institutions in Uzbekistan. *The NISPAcee Journal of Public Administration and Policy*, 4 (1), 33–57.

Wegerich, K., 2006. 'A little help from my friend?' Analysis of network links on the Meso level in Uzbekistan. *Central Asian Survey*, 25 (1–2), 115–128.

White, B.T., 2010. Putting Aside the rule of Law Myth: Corruption and the case for juries in emerging democracies. *Cornell International Law Journal*, 43 (2), 307–364.

Wood, C., 2019. What are the Prospects for Reform in Uzbekistan? [online]. Available from https://thediplomat.com/2019/05/what-are-the-prospects-for-reform-in-uzbekistan/ [Accessed 27 March 2020].

Zettelmeyer, J., 1998. The Uzbek growth puzzle. Working paper of the International Monetary Fund. *International Monetary Fund*, WP/98/133.

Chapter 3

Anticorruption laws, policies, and initiatives in Uzbekistan

An overview of the legal and institutional environment

Introduction

The overview of the legal and institutional context outlined in this chapter reckons with the analysis of the political environment presented in the previous chapter. In that analysis, we examined Uzbekistan's governance trajectories in terms of Karimov era and post-Karimov era developments. In line with this approach, the evolution of Uzbekistan's anticorruption legislation can be provisionally divided into two periods: the first period covering 1991–2016 (the Karimov era) and the second period covering post-Karimov developments, from September 2016 until the present time. In this chapter, we aim to examine the anticorruption legal environment in Uzbekistan—that is, the laws, regulations, and bylaws (decrees, orders, resolutions, decisions, etc.)—alongside specific policies, programmes, initiatives, and institutional developments, covering Karimov-era and post-Karimov developments. Our analysis of the 'law in books' legal environment helps to contextualise the diverse interpretations, applications, and experiences of the law by a plethora of actors (law in action), whom we discuss in the empirical chapters presented later in this book. These actors span state officials responsible for implementing anticorruption measures, law enforcement officials, medium and low level state officials, local government officials, community leaders, religious actors, and ordinary citizens. In so doing, in this chapter we also aim to equip the reader with a contextual lens which proves instructive to understanding how different actors interpret, experience, and negotiate laws and legal changes in everyday Uzbek life.

Uzbekistan, like many modern independent states, regulates its anticorruption policies, initiatives, and programmes through a myriad of international and domestic laws. In 2008, Uzbekistan acceded to the UN Convention against Corruption (UNCAC), the only legally binding universal anticorruption instrument, adopted by the General Assembly of the United Nations on 31 October 2003. Uzbekistan regularly participates in

DOI: 10.4324/9780429952968-3

UNCAC's Implementation Review Mechanism (IRM),[1] a peer-review process that assists states' parties to effectively implement the Convention.[2] Since its accession, Uzbekistan adopted numerous laws, policies, and programmes with the aim of incorporating UNCAC's provisions and other related international anticorruption standards into its national legislation. In addition to UNCAC, Uzbekistan also joined the Anti-Corruption Network for Eastern Europe and Central Asia (ACN) in 2010, a global relations programme of the Organisation for Economic Co-operation and Development (OECD) tasked with promoting anticorruption reforms in Eastern Europe and Central Asia in accordance with international anticorruption standards. As a part of its ACN membership, Uzbekistan regularly participates in the Istanbul Anti-Corruption Action Plan, a sub-regional peer-review programme launched in 2003 under the aegis of OECD/ACN. By reviewing participating countries' anticorruption performance and continuously monitoring their implementation of recommendations, the Istanbul Anti-Corruption Action Plan supports ACN member-states' efforts to comply with UNCAC and other international standards and best practices.[3] At the national level, anticorruption law primarily relies on the following laws and bylaws (with their respective changes and amendments):

- Law of the Republic of Uzbekistan 'On Combating Corruption' (No. O'RQ-419, adopted 3 January 2017);
- Decree of the President of the Republic of Uzbekistan 'On Measures to Further Improve the System of Fighting against Corruption in the Republic of Uzbekistan' (No. PF-5729, adopted 27 May 2019);
- Resolution of the Cabinet of Ministers of the Republic of Uzbekistan 'On the Approval of the Regulation on the Procedure for Rewarding Persons Who Reported a Corruption Offence or Assisted in the Fight against Corruption' (No. 829, adopted 31 December 2020);
- Decree of the President of the Republic of Uzbekistan 'On Additional Measures of Improvement to the Anticorruption System' (No. PF-6013, adopted 29 June 2020);
- Law of the Republic of Uzbekistan 'On Public Procurement' (No. O'RQ-684, adopted 22 April 2021);

1 See 'Review of Uzbekistan's implementation of the United Nations Convention against Corruption' [online]. Available from https://www.unodc.org/documents/treaties/UNCAC/WorkingGroups/ImplementationReviewGroup/ExecutiveSummaries/V1604916e.pdf [Accessed 15 January 2024].

2 For more information on the IRM process, see https://www.unodc.org/unodc/en/corruption/implementation-review-mechanism.html [Accessed 10 December 2023].

3 For more information on ACN and the Istanbul Anti-Corruption Action Plan, see https://www.oecd.org/corruption/acn/istanbul-action-plan.htm [Accessed 08 November 2023].

- Decree of the President of the Republic of Uzbekistan 'On Measures to Create an Environment of Zero Tolerance for Corruption, to Drastically Reduce Corruption-Causing Factors in the Governance of State and Society, and to Increase the Participation of the Public in These Processes' (No. PF-6257, adopted 6 July 2021);
- Law of the Republic of Uzbekistan 'On Public Civil Service' (No. O'RQ-788, adopted 8 August 2022);
- Decree of the President of the Republic of Uzbekistan 'On Measures to Introduce a System for Rating the Effectiveness of Anticorruption Efforts' (No. PQ-81, adopted 12 January 2022);
- Resolution of the Cabinet of Ministers of the Republic of Uzbekistan 'On Additional Measures to Ensure Compliance with the Rules of Conduct by Public Civil Servants (Annex 1 "On the Code of Ethics for Public Civil Servants")' (No. 595, adopted 15 October 2022); and
- Law of the Republic of Uzbekistan 'On the Anticorruption Assessment of Normative Legal Acts and Their Drafts' (No. O'RQ-860, adopted 9 August 2023).

In addition to these legal documents, the following three drafts or forthcoming laws also deserve special mention:

- Draft Law of the Republic of Uzbekistan 'On Conflicts of Interest' (No. QL-922, under consideration in the Senate);
- Draft Law of the Republic of Uzbekistan 'On the Declaration of the Incomes and Property of Civil Servants';
- Draft Law of the Republic of Uzbekistan 'On the Public E-Registry of Persons Convicted of Corruption Offences'.

The aforementioned laws and bylaws interact, to varying degrees, with the Criminal Code (Law No. 2014-XII, adopted 1 April 1995, with accompanying amendments to date), the Code of Criminal Procedure (Law No. 2013–XII, adopted 1 April 1995, with accompanying amendments to date), the Administrative Liability Code (Law No. 2015–XII, adopted 1 April 1995, with accompanying amendments to date), and the Civil Code (Law No. 257-I, adopted 1 March 1997, with accompanying amendments to date). In addition, there are numerous laws pertaining to anticorruption activities, including laws focusing on (1) courts; (2) the prosecutor's office; (3) combating the legalisation of proceeds derived from criminal activities and the financing of terrorism; (4) business and entrepreneurship; (5) citizens' self-governance institutions; (6) public associations; (7) public funds; (8) trade unions, and other relevant laws adopted by the Parliament of Uzbekistan.

This complex legal architecture is supplemented by various bylaws (decrees, decisions, and resolutions) adopted by the President, the Cabinet of Ministers, various ministries and state agencies, and regional and district government bodies. When examining the anticorruption legislation, we must also consider the government's five-year development strategies and yearly anticorruption programmes. For instance, Uzbekistan's commitment to combat any form of corruption is a part of Uzbekistan's Development Strategy 2022–2026. Namely, Aim 84 of the strategy stipulates the following five main priorities: (1) enhancing systematic anticorruption preventive measures; (2) the anticorruption education of civil servants and the population; (3) collaboration with civil society organisations and strengthening and supporting public oversight; (4) the use of information technologies and artificial intelligence in anticorruption efforts; and (5) enacting legislation free from corruption loopholes. It is also worthwhile considering the speeches of the President during government meetings, speeches which provide the necessary contextual background and prove helpful in analysing and predicting the direction of forthcoming legal changes. For instance, on 14 December 2016, during a joint session of Parliament, President Shavkat Mirziyoyev stated, 'We must take decisive measures to counter and prevent corruption in our society [...] and ensure that the punishments set forth by laws are actually carried out'.[4] Following his speech, on 2 February 2017, the President signed the Resolution 'On Measures to Implement the Provisions of the Law of the Republic of Uzbekistan "On Combating Corruption"',[5] approved by the State Programme on Combating Corruption for 2017–2018, which established the Republican Interagency Commission on Combating Corruption (Anticorruption Commission) under the General Prosecutor's Office.[6]

Notably, Uzbekistan's specialised anticorruption institutional framework comprises the following institutions: (1) the National Anticorruption Council of the *Oliy Majlis* (Parliament) of the Republic of Uzbekistan, (2) the Committee on Judicial Legal Issues and Anticorruption of the Legislative Chamber of the *Oliy Majlis* (Parliament) of Uzbekistan, and (3) the Anticorruption Agency of the Republic of Uzbekistan. These specialised institutions primarily carry out legislative, preventive, monitoring, and analytical work, whilst investigative and operational functions are fulfilled by law enforcement agencies. In this regard, the General Prosecutor's Office,

4 A joint session of the Parliament of Uzbekistan. Available from https://president.uz/oz/lists/view/89 [Accessed on 22 Feb 2024].

5 Resolution of the President of Uzbekistan, 'On Measures of the Implementation of the Law of the Republic of Uzbekistan "On Combating Corruption", №ПП-2752, adopted 2 February 2017.

6 The Anticorruption Commission was chaired by the Prosecutor General and consisted of 43 representatives from various organisations, such as the General Prosecutor's Office, the Ministry of Internal Affairs, the Ministry of Justice, the State Security Service, the Customs Committee, the Supreme Court, and non-governmental organisations (NGOs). However, the Commission was disbanded in June 2020 following the establishment of the Anticorruption Agency of the Republic of Uzbekistan.

the Ministry of Internal Affairs, the State Security Service, the Ministry of Justice, and the Department on Combating Economic Crimes under the General Prosecutor's Office 'work on the ground', developing and implementing practical measures to prevent and combat corruption (as stipulated in Article 7 of the Anticorruption Law).

The National Anticorruption Council is headed by the Chairperson of the Senate of the *Oliy Majlis* (Parliament) of the Republic of Uzbekistan. This council consists of 48 members, which include heads of ministries and departments, as well as representatives of civil society institutions. The National Anticorruption Council organises the implementation of state anticorruption programmes and coordinates the activities of the bodies and organisations operating in the sphere of anticorruption. The council also facilitates joint activities carried out by the mass media, non-governmental organisations, civil society institutions, and citizens related to preventing and fighting corruption and organises measures to raise the legal consciousness and legal culture of the population. The National Anticorruption Council also drafts proposals for sociological, scientific, and other research projects in order to understand the state, trends, and causes of corruption, as well as assesses and monitors the effectiveness of anticorruption measures. Based on these findings, it develops proposals for improving legislation on combating corruption. Decisions made by the National Anticorruption Council are mandatory and must be implemented by all state institutions, management bodies, public associations, and other organisations.

The Committee on Judicial Legal Issues and Anticorruption of the Legislative Chamber of the *Oliy Majlis* (Parliament) of Uzbekistan conducts parliamentary oversight on the development and implementation of internal anticorruption programmes in government bodies and state agencies. The Committee also conducts anticorruption scrutiny of existing legislative acts to identify provisions and norms that create the favourable conditions for abuses. Based on its assessment, the Committee then prepares proposals aimed at improving anticorruption legislation.

The Anticorruption Agency was established on 29 June 2020, in accordance with the Decree (No. PF-6013, adopted 29 June 2020) of the President of the Republic of Uzbekistan 'On Additional Measures to Improve the Anticorruption System in the Republic of Uzbekistan'. The Agency has a special mandate to formulate and implement state policy aimed at preventing and combating corruption. This agency is directly subordinate to the President of the Republic of Uzbekistan and accountable to the Senate and the Legislative Chamber of the *Oliy Majlis* (Parliament). As stated on its website,[7] the key goals and objectives of the Anticorruption Agency are to:

7 https://anticorruption.uz/en/about [Accessed 15 September 2023].

- conduct a systematic analysis of the corruption situation in the country;
- identify areas, institutions, norms, and practices most prone or vulnerable to corruption;
- implement state and other programmes aimed at eradicating the causes and conditions of corrupt offences;
- create a culture of zero intolerance towards all forms and manifestations of corruption by shaping the legal culture and legal awareness of citizens;
- coordinate the work of ministries and departments related to preventing and combating corruption;
- introduce an anticorruption control system to government agencies and institutions, state-owned enterprises, and enterprises with a state share in authorised capital, including banks;
- introduce and maintain the effective functioning of the system for the declaration of the assets and incomes of state officials;
- organise sociological, scientific, and other research on the state, trends, and causes of corruption and the effectiveness of anticorruption measures;
- develop international cooperation related to preventing and combating corruption; and
- ensure openness and transparency of activities to prevent and combat corruption.

In addition, the Agency is also empowered to (1) conduct an analysis of the results of the investigation of corruption crimes (especially those cases which made media headlines); (2) request, receive, and examine materials related to the spending of budgetary funds, the sale of state-owned assets, public procurement, the implementation of investment projects, and the implementation of state programmes; (3) consider appeals from individuals and legal entities on corruption issues and take measures to restore their infringed rights and protect legitimate interests; (4) conduct administrative investigations into cases of corrupt offences; and (5) submit statutory notices, obligatory for consideration, on the suspension of execution or cancellation of decisions of executive authorities, economic management bodies, and their officials in the case of revealing signs of corruption.

Uzbekistan's anticorruption legal regime: Main phases of development

The analysis of Uzbekistan's trajectories since 1991 indicates two distinct periods in its development of an anticorruption legal environment: (1) Karimov-era governance characterised by a tightly closed and repressive authoritarian regime reluctant to acknowledge governance problems and challenges, including rampant corruption; and (2) post-Karimov governance marked by the transition from a tightly closed to softer forms of authoritarianism, manifesting as an authoritarian modernisation project aimed at promoting economic liberalisation and bureaucratic efficiency (including measures to combat medium and petty corruption).

Based on these considerations, we now examine the development of anticorruption legislation in accordance with the above timeline. More specifically, we demonstrate that anticorruption legislation remained underdeveloped until the end of 2016, essentially generic and mainly regulated by the Criminal Code, the Code of Criminal Procedure, and the Administrative Liability Code. The Karimov era was thus characterised by the development of general legislation that avoided the use of the term 'corruption' in legislation, instead focusing on malfeasance. During that period, legal initiatives primarily focused on good governance, increasing transparency, and combating malfeasance amongst public officials. This primarily reflected the reality that the government under President Karimov was reluctant to admit the ubiquity of corruption, viewing corruption as an insignificant problem caused by the dishonesty of individual state officials. With the ascendancy of Mirziyoyev to the presidency in December 2016, Uzbekistan openly acknowledged the sheer magnitude of corruption in the country, a key paradigm shift in official government rhetoric, leading to the adoption of many anticorruption laws, bylaws, policies, and state programmes.

1991–2016: Karimov-era anticorruption legal environment

During the Karimov era, no specific anticorruption law existed. Rather, the national anticorruption legal framework was generic and relied heavily on the Constitution, the Criminal Code, the Code of Criminal Procedure, the Administrative Liability Code, the Civil Code, and other laws and regulations. Institutionally, no specific anticorruption agency existed. Uzbekistan's institutional framework for combating corruption comprised the Office of the Prosecutor General, the Ministry of the Interior, the National Security Service, the Ministry of Justice, the Ministry of Finance, and other public authorities including their specialised units.[8]

During the Karimov era, the anticorruption legal framework was largely underdeveloped due to the reluctance of the government to acknowledge the persistence and massive scale of corruption. This tendency became visible in basic legal matters, such as the ambiguous definition of a state (public) official (civil servant), what constituted an abuse of public office or power, and the definition and types and forms of bribery, none of which were adequately laid out. For example, the Criminal Code, the main legal document covering corrupt offences and establishing the criminal liability of bribery

8 Uzbekistan country report (CAC/COSP/IRG/I/4/1/Add.41). UNCAC Implementation Review Group, Vienna, 14–16 November 2016. Available from https://www.unodc.org/unodc/en/corruption/IRG/session7-resumed.html [Accessed on 10 Jan 2024].

of state-salaried employees (Article 211 and Paragraph 1 of Article 213), interchangeably used two terms, 'officials' and 'responsible officials', to refer to state-salaried employees or public officials. Simultaneously, Article 15 of the Administrative Liability Code also contained an additional definition of 'official', which was inconsistent with the definition provided in the Criminal Code. These definitional problems largely resulted from a lack of uniform law related to public or civil service. Labour relations in state institutions were regulated by the Labour Code and a number of sector-specific laws (e.g., laws on courts, tax, customs, etc.) and bylaws adopted by ministries and state agencies.

Many other shortcomings and inconsistencies existed in the Karimov-era anticorruption laws. Specifically, the following shortcomings were noted in UNCAC's country report, which reviewed Uzbekistan's corruption-related legal framework until 2016:[9] (1) non-property-related advantages and favours were not treated as bribes; (2) the promise, offering, and soliciting of bribes were not treated as corrupt offences; (3) the bribery of a foreign official or an official from an international organisation was not designated a criminal offence; (4) private sector–related corrupt offences were not fully covered; (5) trading in influence was not viewed as an illegal act; (6) a system for the mandatory declaration of the income and property of civil servants was absent; (7) illicit enrichment was not viewed as a criminal offence; (8) clear provisions concerning the powers of law enforcement bodies in relation to investigating corrupt offences were lacking; and (9) legal protection of whistleblowers was weak.

Consequently, these shortcomings, definitional gaps, and ambiguities created many inconsistencies and confusion, rendering it difficult to understand the functions and duties of officials and to what extent acts committed by an 'official' or a 'responsible official' constituted an 'abuse of public office or entrusted power' for private gain. The existence of definitional ambiguities and inconsistencies provided wide leverage and flexibility for law enforcement bodies (more generally, for Karimov's authoritarian regime) when occasionally implementing various anticorruption campaigns and raids. As noted in the policy report by the Open Society Foundations Eurasia Programme (Lewis 2016), the Karimov-era anticorruption campaigns were selective and largely driven by political manoeuvrings and power struggles within the political elite, rather than representing a genuine attempt to combat corruption.

Information regarding the magnitude and forms of corruption was largely inaccessible and secretive. Surveys on corruption conducted by *Ijtimoiy Fikr* (Public Opinion Centre) were dubious and offered a highly optimistic picture

9 *Uzbekistan country report* (CAC/COSP/IRG/I/4/1/Add.41). UNCAC Implementation Review Group, Vienna, 14–16 November 2016. Available from https://www.unodc.org/unodc/en/corruption/IRG/session7-resumed.html [Accessed on 10 Jan 2024].

of the corruption situation in the country. According to Uzbekistan's 2014 progress report and update prepared under the Istanbul Anti-Corruption Action Plan, in 2013, the Chamber of Commerce and Industry of Uzbekistan and the General Prosecutor's Office conducted an anonymous survey asking more than 10,000 entrepreneurs whether and how they experienced corruption when doing business. However, Uzbek authorities refused to make the survey results public, stating that the findings were intended for internal use only. As such, Uzbek authorities maintained a complete blackout of corruption-related information.

All in all, the Karimov-era legal framework was characterised by a lack of specialised anticorruption legislation. Instead, corruption offences and informal and illegal economic activities and practices were primarily regulated through provisions stipulated in the Criminal Code and other laws indirectly concerned with corruption offences.

2016–present: The post-Karimov era and the explosive growth in anticorruption legislative activity

The most distinctive feature of the post-Karimov era is the progressive opening up of Uzbekistan to the outside world. Unlike Karimov's regime, Mirziyoyev's government recognised the ubiquity of corruption and declared its intention to combat any form of corruption as an integral part of the governance reform agenda. Coming on the heels of these reform declarations, Mirziyoyev's government adopted numerous laws aimed at promoting the rule of law and combating corruption. As a result, since 2017, more than 40 legislative acts have been adopted laying out the legal and institutional basis and leading to the formation of specialised anticorruption legislation and an institutional framework.

The most notable development lay in the adoption of the Law of the Republic of Uzbekistan, 'On Combating Corruption' (No. O'RQ-419, adopted 3 January 2017). Consisting of six chapters and 34 articles, this newly adopted anticorruption law determines the primary parameters and directions of Uzbekistan's anticorruption policy and legislative framework. The law introduces definitions of 'corruption', 'corrupt offence', and 'conflict of interest', as well as the basic principles of countering corruption, including the role of citizens, openness, and transparency, and the importance of a systematic approach to preventing and combating corruption. The law defines three main directions of Uzbekistan's anticorruption policy: (1) developing anticorruption norms in Uzbek society by improving the legal culture and legal consciousness of citizens and public officials; (2) developing a comprehensive corruption prevention system in the fields of public administration, business, public procurement, and public services provided to citizens, as well as introducing anticorruption expertise and the assessment of laws and measures to prevent conflicts of interest; and (3) developing effective measures to identify and combat corruption offences by enhancing the capacity and performance of law enforcement authorities in this area. The law made it mandatory for civil servants to notify their supervisor or law enforcement agencies about corrupt offences, and strengthened the rights and protection of whistleblowers.

Another key legal document is the Law of the Republic of Uzbekistan, 'On Anticorruption Expertise and the Assessment of Normative Legal Acts and Their Drafts' (No. O'RQ-860, adopted 9 August 2023). This recently adopted law supplements the Anticorruption Law and describes the procedures for conducting expert assessments of normative legal acts and their drafts. According to the law, the following entities are authorised to scrutinise anticorruption in the context of normative legal acts: (1) the Anticorruption Agency; (2) the Ministry of Justice and its territorial units; (3) the legal units of state bodies and organisations that develop normative legal acts and their drafts; and (4) state agencies and organisations assigned to facilitate the implementation of the respective normative legal acts. The Anticorruption Agency can conduct an assessment of normative legal acts either on its own initiative or upon instruction from the *Oliy Majlis* (the Parliament) and the President. Furthermore, an anticorruption assessment can be conducted in relation to any normative legal act (and its draft) when acts of legal violations emerge resulting from studies and inspections. Moreover, an *ad hoc* anticorruption assessment may also be initiated by the Anticorruption Agency in response to certain cases and situations. This may take place when a draft normative legal act leads to heated discussions and debates in the media and social networks given various corruption risks and factors.

In addition to the above, Uzbekistan's Parliament adopted numerous laws and bylaws relevant to the state's anticorruption reform intentions in the post-Karimov era. In this regard, the adoption of the following laws and bylaws further contributed to the development of a specialised anticorruption legal framework:

- Law of the Republic of Uzbekistan 'On Administrative Procedures' (No. O'RQ-457, adopted 10 January 2019);
- Law of the Republic of Uzbekistan 'On Public Procurement' (No. O'RQ-684, adopted 22 April 2021);
- Law of the Republic of Uzbekistan 'On the Dissemination of Information and Ensuring Access to Legal Aid' (No. O'RQ-443, adopted 8 September 2017);
- Law of the Republic of Uzbekistan 'On Public Control' (No. O'RQ-474, adopted 13 April 2018);
- Law of the Republic of Uzbekistan 'On the Protection of Victims, Witnesses, and Other Participants in the Criminal Process' (No. O'RQ-515, adopted 16 July 2019);

- Decree of the President of the Republic of Uzbekistan 'On Measures to Radically Enhance the Role of Civil Society Institutions in the Process of the Democratic Renewal of the Country' (No. PF-5430, adopted 5 May 2018); and
- Decree of the President of the Republic of Uzbekistan 'On the Fundamental Improvement of the System of Raising Legal Awareness and Legal Culture in Society' (No. PF-5618, adopted 10 January 2019).

Whilst these laws do not explicitly focus on anticorruption, they provide the legal basis for the protection of private property and business entities, as well as offering legal tools for public control over the actions and decisions of state institutions and officials. According to news circulating in the Uzbek media, Uzbekistan's Parliament is preparing a new edition of the law 'On Administrative Procedures'.[10] This new version includes several principles of administrative procedures with direct relevance to anticorruption, such as the 'prohibition of arbitrariness', the 'prohibition of the abuse of authority', and 'not allowing the denial of the application of the law'.

In addition to the aforementioned legislative initiatives, the Uzbek government has implemented numerous anticorruption measures, programmes, initiatives, and campaigns over the last seven years. The full list is quite long; thus, we mention only those measures and activities which garnered more media headlines:

- Since 1 July 2019, state institutions must periodically conduct an assessment of corruption risks in connection with the implementation of the tasks and functions assigned to it. This assessment must be conducted in accordance with the methodological framework outlined in the Law of the Republic of Uzbekistan 'On Anticorruption Expertise and the Assessment of Normative Legal Acts and Their Drafts' (No. O'RQ-860, adopted 9 August 2023).
- The Anticorruption Agency, in collaboration with the United Nations Development Programme (UNDP) Office in Uzbekistan, created an electronic system (e-anticor.uz) for assessing and rating the efficiency of the fight against corruption. This e-platform aims to analyse and eliminate the shortcomings of measures taken to combat corruption in state institutions, including local government bodies (https://e-anticor.uz/oz/ratings).
- An internal anticorruption control system or department (compliance control) has been established in more than 100 state institutions.

10 The Law "On Administrative Procedures" is being adopted in a new version. Available from: https://yuz.uz/uz/news/mamuriy-tartib-taomillar-togrisidagi-qonun-yangi-tahrirda-qabul-qilinmoqda [Accessed on 11 Jan 2024].

- The number of ministries and agencies has been reduced, from 61 to 28, in order to optimise the public administration system and reduce the duplication of functions amongst various state bodies. However, recent changes show a development in the opposite direction (new state agencies and ministries are being established).
- The Anticorruption Agency annually conducts an assessment on the level of openness of the activities of state agencies and organisations, publishing its results on the electronic platform (https://e-anticor.uz/) and in the media.
- An automated case allocation system (electronic allocation of cases amongst judges) was introduced in all courts in Uzbekistan in 2018. Moreover, judicial decisions issued by courts are published on the website of the Supreme Court (www.sud.uz). In 12 pilot courts, it is also possible to watch live or recorded broadcasts from the courtroom via the Internet. These actions are intended to reduce corruption and arbitrary decisions in the judicial system.
- As of 1 September 2019, new programmes and courses on anticorruption have been introduced into the curricula at educational institutions. Anticorruption topics have also been included in the curricula of general secondary and vocational educational institutions. The Anticorruption and Crime Prevention Centre under the Law Enforcement Academy of the General Prosecutor's Office regularly provides anticorruption training to civil servants. Thus far, various educational institutions have conducted over 500 corruption prevention educational activities.
- Throughout the country, 'Anticorruption Weeks' are held annually from November to December, including on 9 December, International Anticorruption Day. This activity aims to increase social awareness and the involvement of society in the fight against corruption.
- Anticorruption forums are held annually in Tashkent, with the participation of national and international experts, civil society representatives, and the media. These forums aim to inform the general public and international actors about anticorruption initiatives in Uzbekistan, as well as to determine the direction for future reforms and serve as venues for exchanging experiences and best practices.

Future prospects, challenges, and uncertainties

In this chapter, we described two major phases in Uzbek anticorruption legislation, specifically focusing on laws, policies, programmes, and initiatives shaping the current anticorruption legal environment in the country. That said, we caution that we have refrained from attempting to provide an exhaustive review of Uzbekistan's post-Soviet legal developments. Instead, we aimed in this legal chapter to provide the context for our socio-legal approach. Our approach relies on an analysis of how law is interpreted and applied in state and non-state arenas, as well as on our ethnographic 'thick description' (Geertz 1973) of informal practices and coping strategies revolving around the daily experiences of civil servants, school teachers, traffic police officers, healthcare workers, law enforcement officials, community leaders, and ordinary citizens. Only after gathering the first-hand ethnographic material did we return to a review of the black-letter law, with the aim of linking our fieldwork-based insights and experiences to concrete legislative initiatives, policy developments, and legal changes.

As we show in this chapter, Uzbekistan's anticorruption laws and policies represent complex pieces of legislation developed gradually following the collapse of the Soviet Union, but which gained momentum in late 2016 following the reformist agenda of the newly installed president. Thus, these legal developments reflect the emergence of a specialised anticorruption legal framework in a political environment transitioning from a tightly closed and repressive authoritarian regime towards softer forms of authoritarianism. Many commentators referred to these developments as an example of authoritarian modernisation, developments observed in many hybrid political regimes that are neither clearly democratic nor conventionally authoritarian (Diamond 2002, Levitsky and Way 2010). Such developments are primarily geared towards promoting economic growth and governance effectiveness rather than achieving a full-scale political liberalisation (Pannier 2017, Buckley 2018, Anceschi 2019, Wood 2019). This selective reform agenda is visible in the emergence of two parallel, yet contradictory legislative and policy tendencies—one fairly liberal and one fairly restrictive—resulting in uncertainty in and delays to anticorruption reforms.

One poignant example of these tendencies emerges in the unreasonable delay and uncertainty in the adoption of the law 'On the Declaration of the Incomes and Property of Civil Servants'. According to the State Anticorruption Programme 2021–2022 (Decree No. PF-6257, adopted 6 July 2021), the Uzbek government was expected to introduce a new system for the declaration of the income and property of civil servants beginning on 1 January 2022. According to this new legislative initiative, civil servants and their family members (spouses and children) were subject to mandatory income and property declarations. More specifically, the income and property declarations of civil servants and their family members were intended to occur in two stages:

- the first stage encompasses the President, members of Parliament (both the Legislative Chamber and the Senate), members of the Cabinet of Ministers, members of public administration bodies (ministries and regulatory bodies), and heads (governors) of local state authorities (both regional and district governments) and their deputies;
- the second stage includes other civil servants (excluding auxiliary, technical, and service employees).

These measures were outlined in the draft law 'On the Declaration of the Incomes and Property of Civil Servants', prepared by the Anticorruption Agency in November 2020. In August and September 2021, the draft law was further developed in consultation with the General Prosecutor's Office, the State Security Service, the Ministry of Internal Affairs, the State Tax Committee, the Supreme Court, the State Services Development Agency, the Ministry of Economic Development and Poverty Reduction, the Ministry of Finance, and the Central Bank. On 10 November 2021, after conducting a thorough legal assessment, the Ministry of Justice concluded that the draft law met the legislative requirements and sent it to the Presidential Administration for further processing. On 13 November 2021, the Presidential Administration forwarded the draft law to the Cabinet of Ministers for further consideration. However, since then, the Cabinet of Ministers has delayed its processing for unknown reasons and has yet to submit the draft law to the Legislative Chamber of the *Oliy Majlis* (Parliament).

Another pertinent example emerges from the Draft Law of the Republic of Uzbekistan 'On Conflicts of Interest' (No. QL-922, under Senate consideration). In fact, Uzbekistan's legislative bodies introduced provisions concerning the prevention of conflicts of interest in the Law of the Republic of Uzbekistan 'On Combating Corruption' (No. O'RQ-419, adopted 3 January 2017). However, these provisions remain rather generic and do not provide specific details nor procedures on how to prevent and resolve conflicts of interest. Currently, liability for conflicts of interest is limited to disciplinary sanctions. Therefore, further substantive regulations are required in order to prevent and properly address any conflict of interest arising from the fulfilment of formal public duties.

Whilst Uzbekistan established the Anticorruption Agency in line with UNCAC provisions, the prospects for the Agency's success in effectively combating corruption remain opaque. This is because the Agency is not fully independent and operates under the direct subordination of the President. As a result, the Anticorruption Agency is torn between everyday political realities and its 'controlled or selective' focus on medium and petty corruption. As such, the institutional arrangement of anticorruption law enforcement serves as an intriguing case and provides a shortcut to exploring the relationship between formal anticorruption policies and how things work in real-life situations (that is, law in action).

As we demonstrate in the chapters that follow, the recent drastic boom in anticorruption legislation does not necessarily translate into favourable outcomes. Rather, these anticorruption efforts focus primarily on medium and low-level (petty) corruption, whilst Uzbekistan witnessed an uptick in elite-level corruption and kleptocratic practices. As noted in ACN/OECD's 2019 report, the international community welcomes Uzbekistan's anticorruption laws and policies, but these reform initiatives, absent a systematic priority- and results-based approach, remain merely declarative, implemented 'tick-by-tick' or in order to achieve a higher anticorruption rating, whilst the real meaning of anticorruption measures may be overlooked or lost.[11] These processes will be illustrated in the subsequent empirical chapters.

References

Anceschi, L., 2019. New Authoritarianism in Post-Karimov Uzbekistan. *In*: C. Frappi and F. Indeo, eds. *Monitoring Central Asia and the Caspian Area: Development Policies, Regional Trends, and Italian Interests*. Venice: Edizioni Ca' Foscari, 117–119.

Buckley, N., 2018. Once-repressive Uzbekistan begins a post-Karimov opening [online]. *Financial Times*. Available from https://www.ft.com/content/6c37419c-0cbf-11e8-8eb7-42f857ea9f09 [Accessed 19 May 2018].

Diamond, L.J., 2002. Thinking about hybrid regimes. *Journal of Democracy*, 13 (2), 21–35.

Geertz, C., 1973. *The Interpretation of Cultures*. New York, NY: Basic Books.

Levitsky, S. and Way, L.A., 2010. *Competitive Authoritarianism: Hybrid Regimes after the Cold War*. New York, NY: Cambridge University Press.

Lewis, D.G., 2016. *Tackling Corruption in Uzbekistan: A White Paper*. New York, NY: Open Society Foundations.

Pannier, B., 2017. Analysis: How High Should Hopes Be for Change in Uzbekistan? [online]. *Radio Free Europe/Radio Liberty*. Available from https://www.rferl.org/a/uzbekistan-mirziyoev-hopes-for-change-karimov-cotton-foreign-policy/28938193.html [Accessed 16 July 2018].

Wood, C., 2019. What are the Prospects for Reform in Uzbekistan? [online]. Available from https://thediplomat.com/2019/05/what-are-the-prospects-for-reform-in-uzbekistan/ [Accessed 27 March 2020].

11 ACN/OECD Report 2019, Anti-corruption reforms in Uzbekistan: 4th round of monitoring of the Istanbul Anti-Corruption Action Plan. Available from https://www.oecd.org/corruption/acn/OECD-ACN-Uzbekistan-4th-Round_Monitoring-Report-2019-ENG.pdf [Accessed on 12 Jan 2024].

Chapter 4

Law, society, and corruption in Uzbekistan

A socio-legal analysis of macro-level developments

Introduction

During our decade of fieldwork in Uzbekistan, we observed the commonplace and more or less taken-for-granted activities that signal the key features of social structures, norms, and interactions. Our fieldwork strategy also included the collection of statements and discourses amongst ordinary citizens and low-level state officials that can stand for broader public policy developments. In this regard, we present several statements below which we came across during our fieldwork:

> *Laws work only when they are needed. Only those laws that match the interests of the state, people at the top or law enforcement authorities are enforced without any delay. But when it comes to the freedom and rights of ordinary people and society, laws are rarely enforced.*
>
> (Salima, 38, female, lawyer)

> *'Laws do not regulate the state and society. Laws are mainly used to deceive society. If the rules of the game are not within the framework of the laws, the energy of the nation will not focus on development, but on cheating each other, corruption, and creating monopolies. We are making more and more powerful and numerous laws, but the situation is becoming more and more controversial. Because the laws do not work.'*
>
> *(Odil, 43, male, state official)*

> *'Each nation has its own quality. The quality of Uzbek society is that we have fully mastered living by unwritten rules.'*
>
> *(Shuhrat, 52, male, anti-corruption expert)*

> *In Uzbekistan, people dream of two contradictory things: no corruption at all and having a powerful acquaintance who can solve any problem.*
>
> (Ozod, 45, male, social media activist)

DOI: 10.4324/9780429952968-4

The above statements appear to shed light on people's views of the image and role of law in everyday life—the idea that state law remains distant and alien to ordinary people's livelihoods and daily needs. Such statements provide us with clues to the existence of a plethora of informal rules and practices (living law) in Uzbekistan which dominate everyday life and help individuals 'get things done'. The statements can also be examined through the lens of socio-legal perspectives on legal compliance, which we presented in the introductory chapter. In this respect, the legislative boom in Uzbekistan's anticorruption efforts reminds us of the instrumental perspective on legal compliance. Here, legislators and policymakers view legal changes as a panacea, seeking to obtain compliance by applying legal sanctions, assuming that changing the incentive mechanisms (rewards and punishments) shape and control people's behaviours (Krislov *et al.* 1972, Gibbs 1975, Paternoster 2010). The development of specialised anticorruption legislation and institutions in Uzbekistan since 2017 (as shown in Chapter 3) clearly reflects the principal–agent model. This model relies on the assumption that the best way to combat corruption is to improve institutional and legal configurations, thereby preventing and reducing corruption by increasing the surveillance and severity of penalties for corrupt practices (Klitgaard 1988, Groenendijk 1997, Besley 2006).

At a glance, one would expect that such explosive growth in anticorruption legislation would significantly reduce the level of corruption in Uzbekistan. However, as we show in various chapters in this book, in Uzbekistan, the state and its legal system lack legitimacy in the eyes of citizens given its failure to ensure the rule of law. Thus, the normative perspective on legal compliance states that people are more likely to obey the law when they view the law as generally just and moral and/or those enforcing the law provide models of legitimate moral authorities (Tyler 2006, Bilz and Nadler 2009). Viewed from this perspective, it is unlikely that the adoption of numerous anticorruption laws will produce the expected outcomes. In this regard, despite the explosive growth in anticorruption legislation, the analysis from Transparency International's Corruption Perceptions Index (CPI) demonstrates that no 'breaking point' has occurred in Uzbekistan's position on CPI since 2017.[1] Instead, a slow development on a steady trajectory towards less corruption in Uzbekistan has taken place since 2012. This trajectory, however, began well before the onset of post-Karimov-era reforms and, therefore, cannot be solely explained by Mirziyoyev's anticorruption measures.

Based on these considerations, in this chapter we aim to examine the daily life and operation of law in macro-level arenas and central-level state institutions. In undertaking this task, we review the outcomes of legal and institutional reforms adopted since 2017 by analysing them through the lens of

1 https://www.transparency.org/en/countries/uzbekistan

a law in action/living law–grounded socio-legal approach. We also rely on our fieldwork data collected in Tashkent, based on key informant interviews with lawyers, local corruption researchers, anticorruption experts, public prosecutors, members of the Parliament, policymakers, and practitioners who design and enforce anticorruption laws and policies. In analysing 'how the law works' and its implications for (anti)corruption, we provide empirical examples focusing on the following issues and processes: (1) relations between business elites and state officials occupying key positions; (2) corruption and the business environment; (3) nepotism and conflicts of interest and their impact on governance and the rule of law; and (4) the culture of informality and why it persists in everyday life. Examining these various processes and issues provides first-hand insights into the daily life of central-level institutions, anticorruption laws, policies, and initiatives and how they are perceived, experienced, and renegotiated in different social arenas and everyday situations. These strategies provide reflections on 'how the law works in Uzbekistan', focusing on various corruption cases and conflicts of interest revolving around the informal practices of high-level state officials.

The convergence of public administration system and the business sector

According to Article 13 of the Law of the Republic of Uzbekistan, 'On Public Civil Service' (No. O'RQ-788, adopted 8 August 2022), civil servants are prohibited from engaging in business activities. Specifically, civil servants should not carry out activities that could harm them and should not hold other positions preventing them from fulfilling their official duties. A civil servant may not, under any circumstances, receive personal benefits that cannot be obtained through and/or from their official position. Moreover, civil servants must inform their superiors about their participation in the authorised capital of commercial organisations and take measures to prevent conflicts of interest. In addition, similar norms are stipulated in other laws, such as the Law of the Republic of Uzbekistan 'On the Prosecutor's Office' (No. 257-II, adopted 7 November 2001), 'On Internal Affairs Bodies' (No. O'RQ-407, adopted 18 March 2017), 'On Courts' (No. O'RQ-703, adopted 29 July 2021), and other similar laws.

However, in practice, despite these clearly formulated legal provisions, civil servants are actively involved in business activities, visible in two main forms. First, due to this prohibitive norm, civil servants do not directly engage in business activities but still generate additional income by 'patronising or roofing' (*kryshovanye*) a certain businessman. Second, civil servants register their business activity in the name of others and manage it on their behalf. The prevalence of such practices results in widespread corruption in formal state institutions. There are several reasons leading to the convergence of public administration and the business sector:

- there is an ambiguity or contradiction in many normative-legal acts, and civil servants have wide discretionary power in interpreting and applying laws and regulations;
- low salaries and weak social protections for civil servants result in many feeling compelled to supplement their meagre salary by engaging in entrepreneurial activities;
- Civil servants' labour rights remain precarious, whereby they can lose their jobs at any time for unforeseen reasons. Therefore, many civil servants attempt to secure an additional source of income in case they are fired.
- Business actors strive to become 'under the patronage' of civil servants. In some cases, a single act or decision from a civil servant may create an opportunity for an entrepreneur not to fulfil the requirements stipulated by law or create additional privileges for the entrepreneur.
- A system for the declaration of the incomes and assets of civil servants (including their spouses and children) has not yet been introduced. Paragraph 4 of the Decree of the President of the Republic of Uzbekistan (No. PF-6257, adopted 7 July 2021) states that, from 1 January 2022, the incomes and assets of civil servants, heads and deputies of organisations, state enterprises, and institutions with a state share of more than 50% would be subject to mandatory declaration. As discussed in Chapter 3, the draft version of the law 'On the Declaration of the Incomes and Property of Civil Servants' is currently with the Cabinet of Ministers and has not yet been submitted to the Legislative Chamber of the *Oliy Majlis* (Parliament) for final consideration. This situation demonstrates that the introduction of the declaration system is being delayed because this law may create an 'inconvenience' for certain high-level officials.

In Uzbekistan, reports of civil servants using their authority to grant illegal benefits to their close family members or to persons close to them often appear in the mass media (e.g., Kun.uz, Daryo.uz, etc.) and on social media platforms (e.g., Twitter/X, Telegram or Facebook). For example, on 26 April 2018, Jahongir Ortiqkhojaev, the head of the state unitary enterprise 'Tashkent City' and the founder of well-known Uzbek enterprises such as 'Artel' and 'Imzo', was appointed to the post of mayor of Tashkent[2] (he was fired from the mayoral position on 16 January 2023). According to the information provided at Orginfo.uz, Ortiqkhojaev is the founder of 11 enterprises, seven of which had closed and four operating enterprises (when he was mayor of Tashkent).[3] In addition, according to the information provided

2 https://uzlidep.uz/news-of-uzbekistan/1679
3 Details about the enterprises linked to Jahongir Ortiqkhojaev can be searched and found at https://orginfo.uz/

by the chairman of the State Tax Committee,[4] the Artel network of enterprises, Akfa enterprises, were granted tax benefits and the unofficial owner of these enterprises was Ortiqkhojaev.

Serving as another poignant example, a criminal case was initiated in 2021 against the former deputy governor of the Jizzakh region, Akram Rakhmonkulov. According to Gazeta.uz,[5] the tender for a construction project (with a budget of 292.1 billion Uzbek soum) was awarded to three companies (Qurlish Taminoti, J-Quruvchi, and Abduvohid Qurilish Tamir). The deputy governor, Akram Rakhmonkulov, was the chairman of the tender commission. Interestingly, Akram Rahmonkulov himself was the former head and owner of Qurlish Taminoti from 1998 to 2010 (he later transferred the ownership to his son), one of the companies awarded the tender. The other two companies (J-Quruvchi and Abduvohid Qurilish Tamir) also belonged to close relatives of Rahmonkulov. Another relevant example is a case connected to My Flower Limited Liability Company (LLC), which won a tender associated with urban forestry in Jizzakh city in November 2020. Later, it turned out that a 50.80% share of the LLC belonged to Salieva Nargiza Ergashevna, the daughter of regional governor Saliev Ergash.[6]

According to media reports, some business elites succeeded in receiving tax benefits[7] even though their activities were not at all related to the strategic activities of the state (e.g., Meros Pharm LLC, Akfa Dream World LLC, Akfa Extrusions LLC, Asosiy biznes LLC, Oziq ovqat standart karton LLC, etc.). Ordinary business entities cannot obtain such privileges, implying that there is some kind of 'hidden policy' in granting tax benefits without clearly formulated criteria.

Despite the fact that civil servants are legally prohibited from engaging in business activities, certain state officials seem to be 'above the law' and engage in business practices. According to Qalampir.uz, an online magazine,[8] Rakhmatov Murtaza Akhmedovich, a member of the Senate, served as the head of the Association of Cotton Textile Clusters of Uzbekistan. Rakhmatov was the founder of the BCT and TCT clusters in Uzbekistan and unofficially their leader. This example indicates that, behind every successful business entity, an influential civil servant 'operates in the shadows'.

As we see from the examples above, there is a close convergence between the public administration system and the business sector. This pattern, leading to corruption and conflicts of interest, will persist in Uzbekistan as long

4 https://qalampir.uz/news/akfa-artel-va-uzairways-tanka-si-borlarga-berilgan-imtiyezlar-yuki-kimning-buynida-53504 [Accessed 12 Jan 2024].

5 https://www.gazeta.uz/uz/2021/01/22/jizzakh/

6 https://www.gazeta.uz/uz/2020/12/25/jizzax/

7 https://www.gazeta.uz/uz/2022/05/30/tax-incentives/

8 https://qalampir.uz/news/uzbekiston-pakhta-tuk-imachilik-klasterlari-uyushmasiga-rais-saylandi-29591

as the civil service remains unregulated. Given the vested interests of high-level political elites, it is unsurprising that the adoption of two key normative legal acts—that is, the Draft Law of the Republic of Uzbekistan 'On Conflicts of Interest' (No. QL-922, under Senate consideration) and the Draft Law of the Republic of Uzbekistan 'On the Declaration of the Incomes and Property of Civil Servants'—has been delayed for unknown reasons.

Corruption and the business environment

Since 2017, Uzbek legal authorities have adopted numerous laws aimed at protecting the rights of entrepreneurs. Notable legislative initiatives include the law 'On the Representative for the Protection of the Rights and Legal Interests of Business Entities (Business Ombudsman) under the President of the Republic of Uzbekistan' (No. O'RQ-440, adopted 30 August 2017), the law 'On Investments and Investment Activities' (No. O'RQ-598-son, adopted 27 January 2020), and a number of amendments made to the law 'On Guarantees of the Freedom of Entrepreneurial Activity' (No. O'RQ-328, adopted 3 May 2012). Despite these positive legal developments, when doing business in Uzbekistan, it is necessary to distinguish between the law in books and street norms (law in action). There is a saying widely circulated within the Uzbek business sector: 'If you don't have a person at the top, they will eat you'. Thus, when discussing 'how the law works' in the field of entrepreneurship and its implications for an (anti)corruption environment, it is necessary to distinguish between three categories or groups of entrepreneurs and business actors.

The first category is entrepreneurs doing big business. Such entrepreneurs are close to the higher echelons of the government and engage in large and profitable business activities. For example, by a decision of the President of the Republic of Uzbekistan in 2017, the state's share in 'Uzmetkombinat' Joint-Stock Company (JSC) (74.1%) was transferred to the 'SFI Management Group' enterprise with no tender process.[9] According to information from an open source, the SFI Management Group belongs to Fattoh Shodiev, a Kazakhstan-based billionaire of Uzbek origin, the beneficiary of 25 offshore companies in the last 14 years. Similarly, in 2018, the state's share in the Almalyk Mining and Metallurgical Plant was transferred to the SFI Management Group.[10] Journalistic investigations carried out by the Anhor.uz editorial office[11] found that 'Uzmetkombinat' JSC allegedly sold a rather large number of construction materials (fittings) to companies working on

9 https://tj.sputniknews.ru/20170928/uzbekistan-struktura-milliardera-shodieva-poluchila-upravlenie-metkombinat-1023448880.html
10 https://sfi.uz/almalyikskiy-gmk.html
11 http://www.anhor.uz/vzglyad-iznutri/tashkent-city

the construction of 'Tashkent City' and 'Olmazor City' at below-market prices. Thus, the situation appears legitimate when looking at the formal sale contract. But, when details were cross-checked and further investigated, it became clear that construction materials were illegally sold to other business entities at the market price. Many similar examples exist connected to big businesses revolving around the business empire of Jahongir Ortiqkhojaev, the former mayor of Tashkent. Thus, through lobbying, large business entities succeed in ensuring the adoption of favourable laws and decisions giving a 'legal' tone to their activities.

The second category is entrepreneurs engaged in medium-level business. This group includes entrepreneurs who cannot make large sums of money but are well-connected to influential state officials. These entrepreneurs provide material and non-material benefits to state officials in exchange for their patronage or roofing (*kryshovanye*), such as when they experience problems with the tax office, customs clearance, or any other problem they encounter in their daily business. For instance, according to information from the General Prosecutor's Office,[12] in the first half of 2022, 1785 officials were prosecuted in 1429 criminal cases, causing nearly 700 billion soums in losses to the state budget. In 2021, 2804 officials were prosecuted in 2345 criminal cases, with losses amounting to 900 billion soum. Specifically, in July 2022, according to Daryo.uz news,[13] two employees from the Tashkent State Tax Department were caught taking bribes. In another case, an employee of the State Tax Inspectorate of the Khorezm Region, Khanka District, was caught accepting a bribe of US$5000 from an entrepreneur in return for illegally reducing the entrepreneur's tax by 720 million soums.[14] Similarly, in May 2022, the investigator of the Uchtepa District prosecutor's office of Tashkent city was caught receiving a bribe of US$50,000 from a businessman in exchange for giving them relief in a criminal case.[15] These instances are unsurprising given that entrepreneurs operate under conditions of an opaque legal environment and legal uncertainty, inciting them to find 'common ground' with state officials to solve their problems.

The last category is entrepreneurs not falling within the two previous categories—that is, entrepreneurs who attempt to conduct their activities based on procedures established by law and, in case of problems, they attempt to solve them using legal mechanisms or appealing to the President through social networks. For example, a video of a young entrepreneur's appeal to the President and the people was published on the Kun.uz news agency

12 https://www.gazeta.uz/ru/2022/07/28/gen-stat/
13 https://daryo.uz/k/2022/07/28/toshkent-shahar-soliq-boshqarmasi-pora-bilan-qolga-tushgan-xodimlar-yuzasidan-malumot-berdi/
14 https://www.gazeta.uz/uz/2022/02/17/khorezm/
15 https://uznews.uz/posts/55406

website under the heading 'I lost more than US$600,000 in one day. Houses built by entrepreneurs in Tashkent were demolished'. The item was widely circulated on social networks in 2018.[16] In this video appeal, the businessman, Muhammadbabur Khojaev, expressed his grievance, stating that a three-story residential building (under construction) in the Mirzo Ulugbek District of Tashkent city was demolished under the supervision of the city's mayor, Jahangir Ortiqkhojaev. During the investigation, it became clear that some experts assessed the documents serving as the basis for the construction of this residential building as legal, whilst other experts stated that they were illegal. However, in any case, according to Uzbekistan's legislation, an illegal device can be dismantled only on the basis of a court order. Thus, we can see that an illegal act was committed against an entrepreneur who did not have a 'patron', and his property was destroyed. Many similar examples exist. Here, we can provide the case of the illegal confiscation of land belonging to Ismail Panjiev, a businessman in the city of Karshi in the Karshkadarya Region[1] or the case of an entrepreneur in the Surkhondarya province who set himself on fire in response to his café being demolished.[17]

Nepotism, informal governance networks, and conflicts of interest

In Uzbekistan, the principles of openness and transparency are loosely articulated and applied in the personnel policy of the civil service. The existence of such legal loopholes leads to the prevalence of nepotism, cronyism, and localism (*mahalliychilik*) in state institutions. When appointing an individual to a position in the civil service, the knowledge, qualifications, experience, and suitability of the person for a position are not the most decisive factors. Instead, appointments are based on how loyal an individual is to the person or superior appointing them to that position. In other words, the principle of 'loyalty' (*sadoqat*) is the main criterion when making appointments. In most cases, officials place people they trust around them, attempting to easily manage one or another area through them. This, in turn, leads to the emergence of *komanda* (teams or groups) in a specific area. *Komanda* can take various forms:

1) The principle of *mahalliychilik* (localism, shared origin, or territory) involves an official appointing persons from their territory (shared region, district, or village) to the relevant positions.

16 https://kun.uz/news/2018/11/23/bir-kunda-600-ming-dollardan-ortik-mablag-jukotdim-toskentda-tadbirkor-kuraetgan-ujlar-buzib-taslandi
17 https://asr.uz/51525/

2) The principle of *qon* (blood or kinship/nepotism) involves cases when an official appoints their close relatives and extended family members to relevant positions. This is also known as *urug'-aymoqchilik* (clanism/kinship).
3) The principle of *tanish-bilish* (cronyism or networks/contacts) involving cases when an official appoints persons with whom they studied, previously worked, and/or know well.

So long as these three principles prevail in the selection and appointment of personnel, the rule of law is not fully ensured within society. Legally, these three principles are unlawful and contradict a number of normative legal acts in Uzbekistan. According to Article 121 of the Labour Code of the Republic of Uzbekistan (No. O'RQ-798, adopted 30 April 2023), persons who are closely related or related through marriage (parents, brothers, sisters, sons, daughters, husband, and wife as well as in-laws) cannot work together in the same state organisation if the fulfilment of their job duties depends on the direct subordination or the control of one of them to the other. Exceptions to this rule may be established by the Cabinet of Ministers of the Republic of Uzbekistan. Conflict of interest issues are also addressed in Article 21 of the Anticorruption Law (No. O'RQ-419, adopted 3 January 2017) as well as in the Resolution of the Cabinet of Ministers of the Republic of Uzbekistan 'On Additional Measures to Ensure Compliance with the Rules of Conduct by Public Civil Servants' (No. 595, adopted 15 October 2022). The most detailed provisions on conflicts of interest are provided in Article 19 of the Law of the Republic of Uzbekistan 'On Public Civil Service' (No. O'RQ-788, adopted 8 August 2022):

> A conflict of interest is the personal (direct or indirect) interest of a civil servant that affects or may affect the proper performance of their official duties, and the personal interest of citizens, society or a state body. It is a situation where a conflict between rights and legal interests occurs or may occur. In the event of a conflict of interest, a state civil servant must immediately notify their superior or a higher state body in writing. The head of the state body or higher-ranking state body who receives information about the existence of a conflict of interest must take timely measures to eliminate this conflict. The procedure for preventing and resolving conflicts of interest is determined by law.

In line with these legal provisions, an internal anticorruption control system or department (compliance control) has been established in more than 100 state institutions in Uzbekistan.

As shown above, state officials as well as their superiors who have violated the requirements to prevent or eliminate conflicts of interest are liable in accordance with the law. However, Uzbekistan's current legislation does not consider a conflict of interest a crime, viewing it as an instance of administrative liability.[18] There have been intense discussions amongst lawmakers, law enforcement agencies, and the general public about the necessity of criminalising conflict of interest cases causing considerable damage and/or losses to the state and society. The Decree of the President of the Republic of Uzbekistan 'On Combating Corruption' (No. PF-6257, adopted 6 July 2021) mentions the government's intentions to introduce criminal liability for officials involved in a conflict of interest. Under this decree, the Anticorruption Agency would be granted the authority to file a motion to suspend the contract, order, and other documents related to the conflict of interest or to file a lawsuit to declare it invalid. The decree also stipulated that the Law 'On the Regulation of Conflicts of Interest' to be adopted 1 January 2022, would introduce criminal liability for conflicts of interest in the fields of public procurement, tax incentives, land allocation, and the privatisation of state assets. Thus far, however, the plans envisaged in the decree remain declarative, and the draft law on conflicts of interest (No. QL-922) has not been adopted.

Consequently, these processes carried severe repercussions for state–society relations, leading to the proliferation of conflicts of interest within the public sector. Examples of conflicts of interest are innumerable. In this chapter, however, we discuss the details of only one case that caused massive economic, social, and humanitarian costs to Uzbek society. The case in point is a conflict of interest revolving around several high-level state officials, which eventually resulted in the collapse of the Sardoba dam. Gazeta.uz published a detailed account of the tragedy related to the Sardoba reservoir.[19] According to this account, on 1 May 2020 at 05:55, the Sardoba reservoir burst, and evacuation of the population began immediately. As a result, six people died and roughly 70,000 residents left their homes, whilst thousands of houses were destroyed. The disaster affected the entire population of the Sardoba District and caused billions of dollars in damage to the state budget.

This human-made natural disaster sent shockwaves across the entirety of Uzbekistan. Whilst the Sardoba disaster deeply affected the entire country, Uzbekistan's political and legal authorities decided to investigate and hear the criminal case around the Sardoba dam collapse in a closed court session without revealing the details to the public. In justifying this decision, Uzbek authorities referred to part 1 of Article 19 of the Code of Criminal Procedure (Law No. 2013–XII, adopted 1 April 1995), stating that the criminal case was directly related to state secrets. According to the conclusion of

18 For example, administrative liability exists to allow for conflicts of interest in public procurement relations. According to Article 1758 of the Code of Administrative Responsibility, the nonreporting of affiliations and conflicts of interest in the process of public procurement in accordance with the procedure established by the legislation on public procurement will result in a fine of 20 to 30 times the amount of the base calculation.

19 https://www.gazeta.uz/uz/2022/05/01/sardoba/#

the investigation carried out as a part of the criminal case, the following factors were identified as cause for the collapse of the reservoir dam: (1) errors and omissions in project documents, (2) errors and defects in construction, and (3) errors and defects in the dam's use and operation. Based on conclusions from the investigation and trial, more than 40 individuals deemed responsible for the design and construction of the Sardoba water reservoir were sentenced to imprisonment and fines.[20]

We now return to the issue of conflicts of interest (nepotism) around the construction of the Sardoba reservoir. In May 2017, three high-level state officials presented the Sardoba dam construction project to the President, namely (1) Ochilboy Ramatov, the former head of 'Uzbekistan Railways' (now the first deputy prime minister), (2) Shavkat Hamroev, the deputy minister of agriculture and water resources management (now minister of water resources), and (3) Abdugani Sanginov, the chairman of 'Uzbekgidroenergo'.[21] The order for the construction of the Sardoba reservoir was made by Uzbekgidroenergo, the state-owned joint-stock company established on 18 May 2017, by a Decree of the President of Uzbekistan. The main contractor in the construction of the Sardoba reservoir was an enterprise, 'Uztemiryolqurilishmontaj' (under Uzbekistan Railways), which, in turn, subcontracted the reservoir construction to more than ten companies. The value of the hydraulic infrastructure was 1.3 trillion soums (US$404 million). According to Gazeta.uz,[22] Topalang HPD Holding was one of the main subcontractors involved in the construction of the Sardoba reservoir. The director of Topalang HPD Holding was Islam Abduganievich Abdurahmanov, the son of Abdugani Sanginov, the chairman of Uzbekgidroenergo. Both 'Uzbekgidroenergo' and Topalang HPD Holding—the former a state-owned enterprise and the latter a private enterprise—had the same legal address: 22 Navoi Street, Tashkent city. This example indicates that the father was the head of the ordering enterprise, and the son was the head of the subcontracting enterprise, an obvious example of nepotism in the public procurement process. Neither Abdugani Sanginov, the chairman of Uzbekgidroenergo, nor his son Islam Abduganievich Abdurahmanov was held responsible for the errors and defects in the reservoir's construction, let alone for the conflicts of interest in the construction of the strategic project, despite the serious security implications for both the state and society.

Consequently, these processes resulted in strong dissatisfaction and criticism within Uzbek society regarding the conflict of interest and non-transparent investigation of the Sardoba dam collapse. Although authorities promised a transparent investigation and appropriate punishment for those responsible,

20 https://www.gazeta.uz/uz/2022/09/20/sardoba/
21 https://www.gazeta.uz/uz/2020/05/05/reservoir/
22 https://www.gazeta.uz/uz/2020/05/05/reservoir/

only low-level officials were held accountable for the disaster, whilst high-level officials escaped any consequences. Given the aforementioned conflict of interest in the public procurement process, speculation circulated that the dam's construction was linked to a powerful family with members in both government and business, further fuelling public criticism.[23] In response to allegations of a sluggish and non-transparent investigation, officials even suggested the possibility that various animals, including rodents, foxes, and catfish, might be responsible for the dam's collapse.[24] This explanation was met with public scepticism and sarcasm, with many believing the explanation was an attempt to shield high-level corrupt officials who might have played a role in the catastrophe.

Culture of informality and unwritten rules

As shown in the previous section, a culture of informality and operating through unwritten rules has become something of the norm within Uzbekistan's public administration system. The prevalence of such a culture can be explained by the nonexistence or weakness of legal norms regulating various relationships in society. As a result, a vacuum or gap is filled and regulated by informal or unwritten norms. Even more so, if a relevant legal norm regulates certain social relations and processes, its participants may prefer to communicate relying on unwritten rules convenient to them. Of course, some exceptions exist in Uzbekistan's legal system, allowing the use of unwritten rules and norms in situations when legal norms cannot regulate certain relations. For example, in Uzbekistan's legislation, local customs and traditions can be used in the regulation of civil relations. According to Part 2 of Article 6 of the Civil Code of the Republic of Uzbekistan (Law No. 163-I, adopted 21 December 1995), in the absence of relevant norms in the civil legislation, local customs and traditions are used to regulate these relations. The Civil Code also deals with relations between business entities. According to it, a rule of conduct that has arisen and is widely used in any field of business activity and not provided for by law—regardless of whether it is written in any document or not—is considered a business practice.

During more than a decade of our fieldwork in Uzbekistan, we observed that informality has become commonplace in everyday life (Urinboyev and

23 Ozodlik Filmi. *Sardoba: Omon qolganlar hikoyasi* 2021. Available from: https://www.youtube.com/watch?v=zGvpUftemlk&ab_channel=OzodlikRadiosi [Accessed 9 Feb 2024].

24 Daryo. 2020. '*Zoologlar ko'rsichqon va tulkilarning Sardoba to'g'onining yemirilishiga ta'sirini o'rgandi*' [Zoologists studied the effect of rats and foxes on the erosion of the Sardoba dam], Daryo.uz, 6 June 2020, https://daryo.uz/2020/06/06/zoologlar-korsichqon-va-tulkilarning-sardoba-togonining-yemirilishiga-tasirini-organdi, accessed 5 September 2023.

Svensson 2013). Unwritten rules mould people's behaviours in both state and non-state arenas, regardless of whether they lie in accordance with existing legislation or not. Several factors contribute to this tendency.

First, a gap exists between the state and society due to the state's incapacity to valorise its laws and policies. Quite often, especially after the onset of the reform agenda in the post-Karimov period, Uzbekistan's political and legal authorities have adopted laws and made decisions quickly which are largely irrelevant to real life and without assessing social change and dynamics. As a result, many newly adopted laws remain on paper without being implemented in practice. In such situations, people resort to the unwritten rules and practices convenient to them. Thus, the existence of a gap between law in books and law in action led to the further proliferation of informal and nonlegal practices in society. Whilst these practices may benefit the participants involved, they carry repercussions for both the state and society. We empirically demonstrate these processes in subsequent chapters.

Second, the legislative boom observed in Uzbekistan since 2017, especially visible in the adoption of a large number of bylaws, has created contradictions, inconsistencies, and instability in the legal system. One notable feature of the Mirziyoyev era governance is the practice of adopting more bylaws, acts, and decrees (*qonun osti hujjatlari*) than laws. The legal framework has been largely enacted through decrees, producing an unstable legal environment because decrees can be easily overwritten with new directives. For instance, at a government meeting in February 2021, the President raised concerns about the poor implementation of laws. Between 2017 and 2021, more than 2000 bylaws (decrees, decisions, and orders) were adopted by the President, although more than 600 bylaws remained unimplemented.[25] This reality indicates that the President adopted more than 2600 bylaws during a four-year period. To this, we must also add the large number of bylaws adopted by the Cabinet of Ministers, the laws adopted by the Parliament, and the decisions adopted by ministries and local government bodies. In this respect, questions linger regarding how and to what extent a civil servant can grasp all these legal documents, which constantly change due to the adoption of new bylaws. Naturally, under such conditions, many state officials, who are unable or unwilling to catch up with the latest legal developments, often resort to informal norms and practices in their daily work. For example, in July 2022, the Ministry of Justice announced that it had overturned 422 government decisions through the 'regulatory guillotine' method. Notably, many of these documents were revoked given the presence of the same norms as documents subsequently adopted or because norms conflicted with the

25 https://daryo.uz/k/2021/01/18/mamlakatda-tort-yilda-2-mingdan-ziyod-qarordan-600-tasining-ijrosi-bajarilmagan-shavkat-mirziyoyev/

norms in documents later adopted.[26] Such examples demonstrate that the excessively high number of bylaws (ten, 20, or more than 50 documents to regulate a particular field) result in inconsistencies and contradictions between them, potentially leading to misunderstandings, corruption, and informalities in practice.

Third, political and legal authorities in Uzbekistan often fail to ensure the equality of all before the law and, instead, selectively apply the principle of the inevitability of punishment. Noncompliance with the principle of the inevitability of punishment may entice individuals to engage in informal and illegal practices. This implies that the impunity of an official or ordinary citizen who has committed an act contrary to the norms of the law in a certain case (e.g., the conflict of interest in the Sardoba dam case discussed above) may send a signal to the general public that 'one can easily bend laws and avoid punishment if they are well-connected'. One poignant example of these processes can be observed in the higher echelons of the government. For example, in August 2019, at the government level, the President ordered the governors (*hokims*) of the Fergana, Kashkadarya, and Khorezm regions to apologise to the people for their erroneous interpretation and implementation of centrally designed policies and laws at the regional and district levels, which led to people's dissatisfaction.[27] As a result, the governors of these three regions publicly apologised for their misconduct. Ironically, a year later, instead of being dismissed from his position, Shukhrat Ganiev, the governor of the Fergana Region, was promoted and appointed to the post of Deputy Prime Minister.[28] This case illustrates how the law and punishment are not applied equally to everyone. Ironically, a state official like Shukhrat Ganiev, who continuously failed to ensure the proper implementation of central government laws and policies in regions, was promoted to a higher position instead of being fired or punished. In such cases, the informal norms of loyalty to the President prevail over existing laws concerning the ethical codes and duties of civil servants. Witnessing such patterns, other officials also tend to act against the law with the assumption that 'they can escape punishment'. Ordinary people as well who see how state officials who break the law go unpunished then attempt to do the same. Against the backdrop of such situations, a culture of informality and social behaviour geared towards circumventing the law, using informal mechanisms and channels and thereby easily achieving one's goals, emerges and proliferates in Uzbek society.

The selective, contextual, and temporal enforcement of laws is a common pattern in many authoritarian regimes (Diamond 2002, Hendley

26 https://www.gazeta.uz/uz/2022/07/25/documents/

27 https://qalampir.uz/news/video-fargona-viloyati-%D2%B3okimi-khalk-dan-uzr-suradi-6957

28 https://www.gazeta.uz/uz/2020/09/25/ganiyev/

2010, Diamond *et al.* 2016, Şerban 2018, Kubal 2019, Zaloznaya 2020). Authoritarian regimes intentionally create loopholes, contradictions, and ambiguities in the legislation, enticing both state officials and ordinary citizens to engage in informal and illegal practices and transactions (Schenk 2018, Lemon and Antonov 2020, Epkenhans 2021). Given the weakness or ambiguity of formal rules and mechanisms, individuals may engage in illegal behaviours either intentionally or unintentionally given a lack of knowledge and experience. This may appear as a process of 'artificially instilling a feeling of guilt' into citizens' minds. As such, the ruling regime does not take timely measures against persons deemed 'artificially guilty' but accumulates their 'guilts' as *kompromat* (compromising material). Only when these persons commit acts contrary to the opinion of the government do the representatives of the authoritarian government use the *kompromat* against them, representing a hostage-taking governance strategy (Migdal 2001). It is this feeling of fear which prevents state officials and citizens from opposing an authoritarian regime, making it much easier to control citizens and society in general. Such actions are impossible in a well-established legal system, with formal relations and citizens who comply with the rules set by the government.

Implications for (anti)corruption

The abovementioned tendencies led to the further disjuncture between the state and society in Uzbekistan. Our fieldwork observations demonstrate that ordinary people in Uzbekistan do not expect the state to play an important role in their lives. Many people we encountered mentioned the existence of a wide gap between 'the beautiful words and promises of the government' and what happens in practice. This is clearly illustrated in the words of one of our interviewees:

> Such a picture has been formed today—the government continues to adopt laws, and people also continue doing their own work, relying not on the government and its laws, but on the unwritten rules and norms they have created in society.

Accordingly, during our fieldwork, we encountered three types or categories of people in relation to corruption. The first type consists of those who like and benefit from the existence of rampant corruption. The second type consists of those who acknowledge the necessity of completely eliminating corruption, but they make pragmatic choices and engage in corrupt and illegal practices to reach their own personal objectives. The third type consists of people who want to eliminate corruption completely, and they themselves do not engage in corruption at all. However, based on our daily observations and conversations in various social settings and arenas, we noted that today in Uzbek society relatively few people fall into the third category. Most of those we encountered belong to the first or second category. The second type or category of individuals offers a paradox: on the one hand, they criticise the corrupt society, whilst, on the other hand, when they need it, they try to solve cases suiting their interests through informal means. One possible reason for this is the fact that corruption is so deeply rooted in the state system and society that people are often confused when attempting to solve one or another issue. Therefore, they resort to corruption to solve their problems. It is for this reason that we argue that corruption 'is not always a matter of black and white' (De Graaf 2007, p. 43); its meaning and function may differ depending on the different levels and orders of society and dynamics at play in macro-, meso-, or micro-level arenas. These multilevel dynamics, or as we term 'multilevel orders of corruption', call for further empirical investigations, such as a socio-legal ambition, which we explore in various chapters in this book.

References

Besley, T., 2006. *Principled Agents: The Political Economy of Good Government*. Oxford: Oxford University Press.

Bilz, K. and Nadler, J., 2009. Law, psychology, and morality. *In*: D.M. Bartels, C.W. Bauman, and L.J. Stitka, eds. *Psychology of Learning and Motivation: Moral Judgment and Decision Making*. San Diego, CA: Academic Press, 101–131.

Daryo, 2020. Zoologists studied the effect of rats and foxes on the erosion of the Sardoba dam (in Uzbek) [online]. *Daryo.uz*. Available from https://daryo.uz/2020/06/06/zoologlar-korsichqon-va-tulkilarning-sardoba-togonining-yemirilishiga-tasirini-organdi [Accessed 5 September 2023].

De Graaf, G., 2007. Causes of corruption: Towards a contextual theory of corruption. *Public Administration Quarterly*, 31 (1/2), 39–86.

Diamond, L.J., 2002. Thinking about hybrid regimes. *Journal of Democracy*, 13 (2), 21–35.

Diamond, L.J, Plattner, M.F., and Walker, C., eds., 2016. *Authoritarianism Goes Global: The Challenge to Democracy*. Baltimore, MD: John Hopkins University Press.

Epkenhans, T., 2021. Authoritarian governance and ambiguous religious policy: An uncertain future for covenantal pluralism in Tajikistan. *The Review of Faith & International Affairs*, 19 (4), 85–97.

Gibbs, J.P., 1975. *Crime, Punishment, and Deterrence*. New York, NY: Elsevier.

Groenendijk, N., 1997. A principal–agent model of corruption. *Crime, Law and Social Change*, 27 (3), 207–229.

Hendley, K., 2011. Varieties of legal dualism: Making sense of the role of law in contemporary Russia. *Wisconsin International Law Journal*, 29 (3), 233–259.

Klitgaard, R., 1988. *Controlling Corruption*. Berkeley, Los Angelos, CA and London: University of California Press.

Krislov, S., Boyum, K.O., Clark, J.N., Schaefer, R.C., and White, S.O., 1972. Compliance and the law: A multidisciplinary approach. *Criminology*, 10 (2), 243–243.

Kubal, A., 2019. *Immigration and Refugee Law in Russia*. Cambridge: Cambridge University Press.

Lemon, E. and Antonov, O., 2020. Authoritarian legal harmonization in the post-Soviet space. *Democratization*, 27 (7), 1221–1239.

Migdal, J.S., 2001. *State in Society: Studying How States and Societies Transform and Constitute One Another*. Cambridge: Cambridge University Press.

Ozodlik Filmi. Sardoba: Omon qolganlar hikoyasi, 2021. Available from: https://www.youtube.com/watch?v=zGvpUftemlk&ab_channel=OzodlikRadiosi [Accessed 9 Feb 2024]

Paternoster, R., 2010. How much do we really know about criminal deterrence? *The Journal of Criminal Law and Criminology (1973–)*, 100 (3), 765–824.

Schenk, C., 2018. *Why Control Immigration? Strategic Uses of Migration Management in Russia*. Toronto: University of Toronto Press.

Şerban, M., 2018. Stemming the tide of illiberalism? Legal mobilization and adversarial legalism in Central and Eastern Europe. *Communist and Post-Communist Studies*, 51 (3), 177–188.

Tyler, T.R., 2006. *Why People Obey the Law*. Princeton, NJ: Princeton University Press.

Urinboyev, R. and Svensson, M., 2013. Living law, legal pluralism, and corruption in Post-Soviet Uzbekistan. *Journal of Legal Pluralism and Unofficial Law*, 45 (3), 372–390.

Zaloznaya, M., 2020. A law & society take on legality in the Former Soviet Union: An introduction to the special issue. *Demokratizatsiya: The Journal of Post-Soviet Democratization*, 28 (1), 3–14.

Chapter 5

Corruption, informality, and coping strategies in meso-level arenas

Introduction

Having explored the meaning, logic, and forms of corruption in macro-level arenas and central-level state institutions, in this chapter we move on to examine meso-level arenas. Here, we present a socio-legal analysis of the multifarious meanings, logics, and moralities of informal and nonlegal practices and transactions emerging in the daily workings amongst mid- and low-level state officials and civil servants. In doing so, we aim to understand the role of contextual, situational, and spatial factors in shaping the meanings of and logics to corruption. Our central argument in this chapter is that corruption carries different meanings and logics at different levels of society and we must, therefore, distinguish between the predatory practices of kleptocratic elites and high-level state officials, which have nothing to do with 'survival', and the informal coping strategies of low-level officials and ordinary citizens. This implies that the situation on the ground is much more complex than conventional approaches (e.g., economistic and legal centralistic perspectives) assume, as it is moulded by the daily interactions and negotiations between state officials and ordinary citizens. Thus, the 'corruption experiences' across individuals are mediated by their varied navigational skills and positionalities within the governance system.

Based on these considerations, in this chapter, we explore the everyday experiences of the legal system through case studies from mid- and low-level state officials operating in the following three public institutions in Uzbekistan: (1) regional traffic safety enforcement services; (2) a district maternity hospital' and (3) a district-level prosecutor's office. Before presenting these case studies, we first describe Uzbekistan's socio-legal context informing the meanings of corruption.

DOI: 10.4324/9780429952968-5

Understanding corruption in a legally pluralistic context

During the first period of our ethnographic fieldwork in Shabboda,[1] a village located in rural Ferghana in Uzbekistan, we attended a *nikoh toi* (a wedding ceremony) arranged by a local farmer. A *nikoh toi* normally begins at five o'clock in the morning with *nahor oshi* (a morning pilaf[2] feast) at the groom's house. Joyful sounds of *karnay* and *surnay* (traditional Uzbek musical instruments) extend far beyond the house and signal to the entire *mahalla* (local community) that the wedding ceremony has begun. At the threshold of the house, the head of the family himself greets each guest upon arrival by shaking hands or embracing, after which the guests are politely offered seats at the guest tables. Each guest gives a *toyana* (gift such as a carpet or cash) whilst shaking hands with the head of the family. The singer sings traditional Uzbek songs whilst the guests enjoy their table laden with bread, various candies, fruits, nuts, platters of pilaf, pots of tea, locally produced beverages, and a bottle of vodka. Guests leave the table as soon as they finish their pilaf, and tables are hurriedly cleared to welcome new arrivals. During this specific *nikoh toi*, we sat at a nicely decorated table with the *oqsoqol* (the leader of the *mahalla)* and *mahalla* residents, eating pilaf and talking about the role and importance of weddings in the lives of Uzbeks. Spontaneously, the *oqsoqol* began to share an anecdote related to weddings:

> There is an anecdote widely circulated in Uzbek society. Three men—an American, a Japanese, and an Uzbek—met in a restaurant for dinner. After some drinks, they all started boasting about their countries and cultures. The American said arrogantly that life in the United States is very good; every month, he earns US$10 000, enough to buy a new car. The Japanese man laughed sarcastically and said that the United States is nothing compared to Japan's hi-tech society, where robots carry out all tasks. He added that he earns US$15,000 a month and has a robot at home which does all the housework. When it was the Uzbek's turn to describe his country, he modestly said that the majority of people in Uzbekistan earn US$200 a month, but can spend more than US$10,000 a month. The Uzbek man also added that even poor people in Uzbekistan are able to invite up to 1000 guests to their weddings, whilst in the United States and Japan, only rich people can afford such events. These stories left both the American and Japanese men wondering how Uzbeks could spend more than they earned and arrange such expensive weddings when the average monthly salary does not exceed US$200.

1 The name of the village has been changed to protect the anonymity of our informants.
2 Pilaf is a festive Uzbek rice.

The last phrase was accompanied by loud laughter and nodding, demonstrating *mahalla* residents' awareness of the 'getting things done' philosophy slyly hinted at in the anecdote. This anecdote indicates that there is a plethora of 'hidden' informal transactions in Uzbek society, which are widespread but enigmatic to outsiders. Different versions of this anecdote exist, yet all provide us with clues to the existence of informal rules and practices ('living law') in Uzbekistan dominating everyday life and helping individuals 'get things done'.

These patterns were often confirmed during our ethnographic fieldwork in Uzbekistan. Particularly during our Karimov-era fieldwork (covering developments between 2009 and 2016), we conducted observations in various 'informal economy hotspots' in order to observe informal and nonlegal practices and transactions involving state officials and ordinary citizens. One of our frequently visited sites was a foreign currency black market, markets which exist in all parts of Uzbekistan. During our visits, we were always welcomed by an army of *valyutchiki* (money changers) who immediately offered their currency exchange services. What struck us was that there were usually several police officers present in the black market areas; none of them, however, bothered with illegal transactions, thereby de facto 'decriminalising' the illegal practices of all parties involved in such currency exchanges. This resulted from the fact that the official exchange rate was completely theoretical, meaning that it would be impossible to exchange currency at the official rate set by the national central bank. The official currency exchange option was accessible only to the privileged few, well-connected with high-level state officials. As such, the black market was the only available source for ordinary people to buy and sell foreign currencies. Police officers also benefited from the black market transactions since money changers regularly provided them with a *dolya* (share) for ignoring their illegal practices. These practices were part and parcel of everyday life in the Karimov-era Uzbekistan.

In addition, a large-scale shadow economy centred around the taxi sector, one of the most notable features of the Karimov-era livelihood strategies. In the absence of viable income-earning opportunities, many people resorted to the informal taxi sector, which provided an alternative means of survival (*cf.* Olma 2021). During our fieldwork in Tashkent (the capital city of Uzbekistan), we noticed that almost anybody could work as a taxi driver, colloquially known as a *bombila* (i.e., taxi drivers working without a licence/outside the law). There were no fixed taxi stands, and one need not order a taxi. Waving your hand whilst standing along a roadside was sufficient to find a taxi within a minute. This ultra-liberalisation of the taxi sector did not interest the traffic police nor any other police officers, officials who are supposed to manage street codes or take an interest in combating shadow transactions. Instead, the informal taxi sector provided informal income-earning opportunities for traffic police officers and tax officials who received a monthly *dolya* (share) from taxi drivers for ignoring their informal economic activities. We often observed taxi drivers shaking hands with policemen, who would sometimes stop them for breaking traffic rules, but, rarely, if ever, for working illegally as taxi drivers. Drivers generate income by working informally for people who need to be driven from one place to another. In turn, policemen generate income by fining and receiving cash when these drivers break traffic codes.

The above examples clearly illustrate the gap between the 'law in books' and 'law in action', demarcating the boundaries of legality and assuming that law enforcement officials operate in accordance with state law. However, these officers did not seem interested in keeping the social and political order for which they were hired. Not only did they not comply with state law, but they also turned a blind eye when coming across illegal transactions that, at least in theory, damage the state and, indirectly, its citizens. Through our observations, we noted that state law was rarely followed and enforced in everyday life in both urban and rural areas of Uzbekistan. In fact, many other competing 'informal legal orders' existed, influencing social behaviour and everyday life more effectively than the laws of the state. Both ordinary individuals and state officials seemed to ascribe to parallel or alternative moral orders (Wanner 2005, Stepurko *et al.* 2013, Urinboyev *et al.* 2018). Wherever we looked—at institutions such as bazaars, banks, hospitals, schools, universities, and villages—we observed the existence of a multitude of informal rules governing economic and social relations. The laws and policies of the state simply existed 'on paper', whilst, in practice, informal rules and practices were quite an omnipresent phenomenon. We have thus concluded that some kind of 'social contract' existed between the state and society under which people tacitly accepted an authoritarian regime, repressive measures, and kleptocratic practices. In return, the state ensured political stability and tolerated large-scale informal and illegal economic practices, which generated informal income-earning opportunities for both low-level state officials and ordinary citizens.

Another relevant observation was an incident we experienced in May 2009 whilst travelling by taxi from Tashkent to the Ferghana Valley. Only one route reaches the Ferghana Valley via a mountain pass called Kamchik. Since Kamchik is the only route connecting the Ferghana Valley to the rest of Uzbekistan, it remained heavily guarded during the Karimov era, with many checkpoints where traffic police and border officials stopped cars and checked passports. When we reached the pass, the driver asked us to unfasten our seat belts since it was uncommon at that time for individuals to use seat belts at all. At least the traffic police did not impose any fines for driving without seat belts fastened.[3] Thus, any use of seat belts by the driver or passengers could represent a clear signal that there was a foreigner or non-native

3 Seat belt use was not mandatory in Uzbekistan until 2010.

in the car, possibly easily attracting the attention of the traffic police, who always sought justification to stop cars. In requesting that we not use our seat belts, the driver was actually attempting to avoid any unnecessary attention from the police. However, out of concern for his own personal safety, the foreigner (Måns Svensson, the Swedish author of this book) did not unfasten his seat belt. As the driver predicted, our car was soon stopped by the traffic police. As usual, they checked the driver's documents. Due to the presence of a foreign citizen in the car, the police also wanted to check the car's boot. The foreigner, suspicious of the actions of the police, demanded that he be present whilst they checked the boot. Attempting to avoid a conflict with a foreign citizen, the policeman decided not to check the boot and politely asked the foreigner to sit in the car. Instead, the policeman ordered the driver to follow him to his small office to discuss some minor details in his car documents. Upon return, the driver angrily reported having to pay 15 000 *soum*[4] (about US$8 using the 2009 exchange rate) for this 'lack of respect' demonstrated by the foreigner. Not wanting the driver to pay for the consequences of his actions, the foreigner later reimbursed the driver for the costs incurred.

This observation provides useful insights into the nexus between corruption, social norms, and hierarchies in Uzbekistan. The power of the traffic police is rarely challenged in Uzbekistan, and ordinary people always show maximum deference when they interact with the police. Unlike in Western liberal democratic societies, when stopped by the police, citizens in Uzbekistan exit their cars and hand over their documents to the police officer, addressing him as 'commander'. Thus, the relations between the traffic police and citizens remain highly hierarchical. As we will demonstrate in the next chapter, such hierarchical relations between citizens and state officials can also be observed in everyday life situations, such as weddings, where 'people of influence' get the best tables. As a foreigner, the Swedish author of this book was unaware of Uzbekistan's local social norms and hierarchies (or 'living law' in Ehrlich's (1912) terms). By demanding to witness the boot inspection, the foreigner *de facto* challenged the undiscussed authority of the Uzbek policeman, who then decided to retaliate by extorting money from the driver who was driving that same foreigner. According to Uzbekistan's legislation, the foreigner's actions were entirely legal. However, from a 'living law' perspective, his actions were inconsistent with prevalent social norms and hierarchies, resulting in the indirect imposition of a fine. Certainly, the incident described represented a clear instance of corruption since the police officer forcibly extorted money from the driver. However, what struck us was that corruption was triggered by the foreigner's failure to show due respect to the policeman.

4 The *soum* is the national currency of Uzbekistan.

Accordingly, one possible inference from the above empirical examples is that we must consider the multifaceted meanings, logics, and moralities of informal transactions to better understand the social context informing the meanings of corruption and bribery. When measuring corruption in societies such as Uzbekistan, emphasis should also be placed on the recalcitrant complexity of local social life and hierarchies, which assign cultural and functional meanings to informal transactions perhaps different from those in the West. An extensive literature argues for the necessity of contextualising the so-called 'corrupted' practices and situations within a ritual form and the emotional valence of the transaction (Werner 2000, Gupta 2005, Haller and Shore 2005, Polese 2008). Such an understanding suggests that corruption should not only be viewed as instances of illegality and personal venality as assumed by the principal–agent model, but also as manifestations of power relations, hierarchies, status contestations, and coping strategies. We, therefore, argue that international legal definitions of corruption (as stipulated in the UNCAC or those put forward by the World Bank and TI) are Western-centric. Thus, those uniform definitions become problematic when dealing with local categories and needs, and with multifaceted meanings of power relations and exchange in different, non-Western cultural settings such as those in Uzbekistan.

Empirical case studies

In this section, we present three case studies to further elaborate this book's central narrative that, in contexts of authoritarian regimes, the analysis of (anti)corruption should extend beyond economic-based or legal centralistic approaches. Instead, such analyses should deal with the multiple forms of normative ordering, everyday power relations, conflicts, contradictions, social sanctions, and norms constituting the basic social fabric ('living law') of society. Thus, we must focus on pluralistic legal orders/focal points shaping citizen's behaviour as a lens through which to understand the emergence, explanation, persistence, and ubiquity of corruption. In suggesting this, we argue that corruption carries different meanings and logics at different levels of society depending upon contextual, situational, and spatial factors. Empirically, these processes are illustrated through three case studies, focusing on (1) a regional traffic safety enforcement service; (2) a district maternity hospital' and (3) a district-level prosecutor's office. These case studies illustrate how things get done and how they are perceived by mid- and low-level state officials, and their implications for understanding corruption in a meso-level context.

Case study 1: Pluralistic legal orders and legal (non-) compliance in traffic safety enforcement

The first case study focuses on informal and extra-legal practices in the realm of traffic safety enforcement. In constructing this narrative, we rely on the views and experiences of Dilshod, a traffic police officer, whose daily life involves the enforcement of traffic safety rules. We note that the account provided by Dilshod primarily reflects the Karimov-era state of affairs, given that we interviewed him in 2012. The level of corruption in the traffic safety enforcement system in the post-Karimov period has significantly diminished, a positive change largely resulting from the introduction of digital tools and technologies. Yet, despite the post-Karimov changes, the patterns described in this case study remain relevant and provide useful insights into the social life of corruption in meso-level arenas. Below, Dilshod, the true 'author' speaks in the first person, and we provide our comments to explain and analyse the empirical material.

Dilshod asks, 'How should I feed my kids when the state does not pay me any salary?'

> It is not so easy to work as a traffic policeman in Uzbekistan. We have to communicate with more than a hundred people on a daily basis, and we do not have fixed working hours. If you want to get a job with the traffic police, you have to pay a bribe of around US$6000–7000 to top officials in the traffic police. The biggest problem is, actually, that we do not get paid any salary for our work. The official monthly salary for traffic policemen is 900,000 *soum*,[5] but, in fact, we do not receive any salary. In rare cases, we might receive 10% of this salary, 100,000 *soum*. Of course, you may wonder how we survive. Here is the reality for you: instead of paying our salary, our administration provides us with traffic tickets, which we may sell to drivers to earn a salary.[6] We usually sell these tickets to drivers who drive without having their seat belt fastened and/or drive cars which do not meet technical safety standards. The price of one traffic ticket is 12,500 *soum*. So, we earn our salary by selling traffic tickets to drivers. Since we do not receive any salary, we are not required to return ticket receipts or submit reports to our administration and can keep the revenues we make from the ticket sales.
>
> This is not the end of the story. Our bosses give us the order (i.e., set the quota) to sell at least 20 tickets per day. However, drivers do not violate traffic rules every day. How can we sell 20 tickets per day? If I do not sell 20 tickets per day, I might get a warning from the administration or even lose my job. Under these circumstances, we are under severe pressure to find drivers to sell the tickets to. There is also an informal monthly payment called a *gruz* (burden), which we have to pay directly into our

5 The *soum* is the national currency of Uzbekistan. In June 2012, US$1 equalled 2700 *soum* (black market rate).

6 The expression 'to sell tickets to drivers' is slang widely used amongst traffic policemen in Ferghana, meaning 'to impose a fine on drivers'.

> bosses' pockets. The amount of this monthly payment ranges from 50,000 to 100,000 *soums*. We must make this payment if we want to keep our job. These circumstances compel us to sell tickets even to drivers who act legally. Ordinary people do not know about these problems and, therefore, hate us. It is politics. We cannot openly talk about these problems.
>
> I know many people look upon traffic police as the most corrupt profession in Uzbekistan. Since we do not receive any salary from the state for our work, the money we earn through selling tickets is completely legal. I am also an ordinary man, just like everybody else: I have a family, kids to feed! Instead of giving us a salary, our bosses force us to earn our salary through selling tickets to drivers. So, tell me, how should I feed my kids when the state does not pay me any salary? Had I received a normal salary, I would not bother selling tickets to law-abiding drivers.

There are three main issues requiring elaboration from this case study. First, the case above illustrates the existence of a shared language amongst traffic policemen serving to reconstruct the meaning and application of traffic laws. When describing his informal practices, the traffic policeman tends to use the expression 'selling tickets to drivers' rather than saying 'imposing a fine on drivers'. This expression also reveals that the traffic police view traffic tickets as a commodity for earning an income rather than as a means to enforce state traffic laws. Thus, the linguistic representation reveals the existence of pluralistic legal orders traffic police officers must navigate in their daily lives. This case is also useful in its ability to elucidate the local context of informal transactions, illustrating how the absence of formal income-earning opportunities influences the moral code and the legal culture of the traffic police.

Second, the traffic policeman's morality and reasoning are guided by unwritten rules. Dilshod did not seem to take into account the fact that imposing and pocketing fines was somehow illegal, at least normatively. Rather than an 'objective' morality, we discuss here the perceptions of morality (Gill 1998, Werner 2000, Wanner 2005) in two specific contexts. One is when certain actions, considered illegal by state morality, help a citizen survive (Rasanayagam 2011, Blundo and De Sardan 2013, Jávor and Jancsics 2016, Urinboyev *et al.* 2018). The other stemming directly from this is the case when the individual and state moralities do not overlap. Thus, in Dilshod's case, we can see that the state itself induces its citizens to engage in extra-legal practices. Therefore, as Dilshod claims, his illicit practices are completely legal since he receives no salary from the state for his arduous work. Accordingly, Dilshod's extra-legal practices are driven by the 'norms of adaptation/coping strategy', which are not comparable to the kleptocratic intentions of the high-level traffic police officials, who force low-level officials such as Dilshod to 'sell tickets to drivers'. However, from a legal positivist perspective, both these practices fall within the interpretation of corruption adapted from Western moral and juridical codes. Such an interpretation is quite normal and legitimate in the context of Western welfare states, where public authorities provide a formal means of survival. However, is it appropriate to interpret the low-level policeman's actions as illicit in the context of Uzbekistan, where the state fails to provide even a basic salary to traffic police? In light of these problems, one conclusion could be that informal practices allow low-level state officials such as traffic police officers to cope with uncertainty in the absence of decent salaries.

Third, it is also necessary to acknowledge that corruption carries different meanings and logics within different levels of society and that there is a difference between masses of low-level officials, on the one hand, and the smaller group of kleptocratic elites (as discussed in Chapter 4), on the other. During our interview, the traffic policeman expressed concerns about his working conditions and criticised the unreasonable demands of his administration. He frequently mentioned that he must follow unwritten rules of his organisation in order to keep his job. In this light, the elite-level corruption and kleptocratic practices described by scholars such as Ilkhamov (2004) and Lasslett (2020) are not the same as the everyday 'getting things done' practices of low-level traffic police officers.

Case study 2: Informal financing of the healthcare sector

The second case study focuses on Umida, a midwife at a maternity hospital in Fergana. This case illustrates the role of informal and extra-legal practices as a 'making-ends-meet' strategy under the opaque economic conditions. As we show below, noncompliance with the law (i.e., corruption) is not solely driven by greed or personal venality, but is also caused by the state's legal ideals and economic policies, which hardly reflect the realities of everyday life.[7] As a result, healthcare professionals like Umida straddle between legality and illegality in their daily working lives. Although the material presented in this case study largely reflects the state of everyday life under President Karimov (1991–2016), it should, however, be noted that our recent fieldwork observations indicate that similar informal practices are still commonplace in maternity hospitals.

Umida, summarised her situation, stating, 'I will not be able to feed my kids if I follow the law and refrain from accepting informal payments.'

> I know maternity hospitals are often criticised for being one of the most corrupt places in Uzbekistan. But those people and organisations who label us 'corrupt' are unaware of the serious problems we face in our daily working lives. I think all problems are connected to the state and system. During the Soviet era, the state provided everything for hospitals,

7 https://www.ozodlik.org/a/24944189.html

and physicians received a good salary. But, after independence, the state significantly reduced its financing for hospitals. There is a serious shortage of medical equipment. Hospitals are overcrowded. Electricity and gas cuts are rather common. The state does not supply us with the necessary medicaments.

By law, all maternity hospitals are state-owned in Uzbekistan, which means giving birth in a hospital must be free of charge. But this law is rarely enforced in practice. Almost everyone pays for maternity services. Of course, we accept their payment informally through handshakes. Often, people themselves slip money into our pocket. Such informal payments are called *suyunchi* [literally 'joy' in English], where the father or relatives of the newborn baby give cash [or sometimes expensive gifts] to the midwife and nurses who deliver the baby. In addition to *suyunchi*, some people give us chocolate, cognac or flowers as an expression of gratitude for our hard work. *Suyunchi* is usually given after the birth of a child. The amount of *suyunchi* varies from one individual to another, ranging anywhere from between 50,000 to 500,000 *soum*. If it is an uncomplicated vaginal birth, people give us *suyunchi* of around 50,000 to 100,000 *soum*. In cases of complicated vaginal births or C-sections, we receive a much larger *suyunchi*, approximately 300,000 to 500,000 *soum*.[8]

I know my actions are illegal based on the law, but real-life circumstances force me to accept *suyunchi* from patients. Law and real life are completely different things. You will understand what I mean after I explain my work conditions. First, it is rather difficult to get a job at a maternity hospital. For instance, if you want to work as a nurse at our hospital, you must pay a bribe of at least US$500 to top health officials. Second, our salaries are extremely low. A midwife's monthly salary is 280,000 *soum*, around US$100, and a nurse's salary is 180,000 *soum* (US$65). Isn't it frustrating when you pay a US$500 bribe in order to get a job with a US$100 salary? Our salary is exceptionally low, but I have to feed my kids. I studied for seven years to become a midwife, but I do not receive a sufficiently high salary to live on from the state. Due to my good education, I believe I should earn more money than people who sell potatoes at the bazaar. I, too, have my own dreams, so I want to have a good salary. Everything is expensive at the bazaar. For example, one kilo of meat costs 17,000 *soum* and one sack of flour is 60,000 *soum*. I must buy clothes for my kids. So, you see, it is impossible to survive on my 280,000 *soum* salary. Since the state does not compensate me properly, I have a full right to supplement my salary through *suyunchi*. I do not force

8 We should clarify here that the *suyunchi* rates mentioned reflect the reality in June 2012. At that time, US$1 equalled 2700 *soum* (black market rate); currently (as of January 2024), US$1 equals about 12,400 *soum*.

> anyone to give *suyunchi*, but people themselves voluntarily reward me. This is the only way to feed my kids and I do not see any other alternatives. I will not be able to feed my kids if I follow the law. Therefore, it is quite understandable that we expect people to reward us for our efforts.

To what extent are the stories of the midwife and traffic policeman comparable? To our minds, they are comparable given their 'making-ends-meet' character. The professional sphere, the amounts of informal payments, ways of bending the law, and other details may vary. But, the contextual factors, moral reasonings, and substance are similar. Given this connection, there are two main issues we must emphasise.

First, the midwife's story demonstrates that the gap between the law, which states that maternity services should be free of charge, and the actual delivery of services (the lack of state financing for hospitals and low salaries) forced maternity hospital workers to frantically search for informal coping strategies helping them survive in the absence of decent salaries.[9] As the midwife asserts, she would not be able to feed her children if she followed the law. Seemingly, since Uzbek authorities fail to secure the basic needs of citizens, state officials like the midwife and traffic policeman feel no moral obligation to comply with the law. According to the midwife's moral code, her informal practices are completely 'legal', and she has a full right to reap the benefits of her good education. Subsequently, informal transactions interpreted as corrupt in Western moral and juridical codes could be regarded as morally acceptable practices (i.e., the focal point for behaviour) according to the 'living law' of maternity hospitals in Uzbekistan. This example illustrates the existence of dual competing notions of morality in Uzbekistan, since the actions and working practices of hospital workers are shaped more by the 'living law' rather than the state law.

Second, as seen in the traffic policeman's case, the midwife's story indicates that kleptocratic practices amongst high-level state officials (as discussed in Chapter 4) should be distinguished from the informal practices of ordinary citizens and low-level officials, which have different meanings ('to get things done'). Thus, the midwife's informal practices significantly differ from the predatory practices of kleptocratic elites, such as the corrupt practices and schemes of Gulnara Karimova, the daughter of the late president of Uzbekistan (Lasslett *et al.* 2017) or the Sardoba dam collapse case involving high-level state officials (as described in Chapter 4). However, both transactions are illicit according to the Western-centric perspective. This leads us to conclude that, when studying corruption in a social setting such as Uzbekistan, we should analytically distinguish between functional

9 https://www.ozodlik.org/a/25061151.html

redistributive informal transactions and more predatory transactions where resources move from the weak to the strong.

Case study 3: Informal alliances between law enforcement bodies and the business sector

The third case study focuses on Abdulla, an employee in the district prosecutor's office. The material presented in this case reflects developments in the post-Karimov period (2017–2023), specifically showing how two bylaws adopted by the President triggered new forms of corruption and extra-legal practices in meso-level arenas. The primary rationale for presenting this case study is that it not only describes the local governance dynamics and power struggles at the meso-level but also illustrates the 'legal production of corruption' manifested in the daily practices of law enforcement bodies. It shows how corruption is not just a free choice triggered by the personal venality of meso-level state actors but an adaptive strategy amongst state officials constrained by conflicting demands and expectations from central-level elites.

As Abdulla reflected, 'New laws adopted after 2016 are forcing us to resort to illegal and corrupt practices'.

> I have been working in the *prokuratura* (prosecutor's office) system since 2014. Until 2017, my daily work duties were determined according to the Law of the Republic of Uzbekistan, 'On the Prosecutor's Office' (No. 257-II, adopted 29 August 2001). According to this law, our main tasks are to ensure the rule of law, protect the constitutional system of the country, protect the rights and freedoms of citizens, protect the legal interests of the society and state, fight against, investigate and prevent crimes, and ensure the authority of the prosecutor in court. This law also gives us a broad array of authority and supervisory powers. Our supervisory powers extend to nearly all state bodies and officials, as well as to enterprises and organisations, regardless of their legal status. This means we can check the legality of their decisions and activities. We can even recall or file a protest against (unlawful) decisions of the *hokim* (governor).
>
> But, in 2017, our working life considerably changed after the adoption of two decrees of the President about the sectoral governance system. As a result of these decrees, a system of sectoral management of regions and districts was introduced in all regions of Uzbekistan. Each region (which, in turn, consists of districts) was divided into four sectors or territorial zones. In turn, the *hokim* (governor), the prosecutor, the head of internal affairs (police), and the head of the tax office were assigned as the heads of these four sectors. This means each region and district in Uzbekistan consists of four sectors/territories and is governed by four state officials: Sector 1 by the *hokim* (governor), Sector 2 by the prosecutor, Sector 3 by the police chief, and Sector 4 by the tax office head.

According to the President's decree, the head of each sector must be multifunctional and resolve all socioeconomic problems in the territory of their sector. In case the local population's problems and concerns are unresolved, sector leaders are punished or may be dismissed from their positions. This means the performance of the prosecutor, the police chief or the head of the tax office is not measured by how well they ensure the rule of law, reduce crime or collect taxes, but is instead assessed by indicators which have nothing to do with our job duties, such as job creation and poverty reduction. As a result of the sector system, we do not perform our duties and tasks stipulated in the law 'On the Prosecutor's Office'; instead, we have become a part of the local government (*hokimiyat*). It is funny and unbelievable, but prosecutors are now responsible for social protection, poverty reduction, and job creation in their sector. At university, we were educated to be lawyers, prosecutors or judges. But, we received no social policy training.

In addition, the central government does not allocate any specific funding for the needs of the sector. Thus, we must solve local problems by whatever means we can. The central government does not care whether we have a budget, but they keep giving us orders. The problem here is that the local government's budget is in the *hokim's* hands. Since 2017, all *hokims* have fallen under the President's protection. The President often repeats that no *hokim* can be arrested or imprisoned without his approval, even if the *hokim* engages in corruption. The *hokim* knows this and uses the local budget as it suits their interests. The heads of other sectors (the prosecutor, police chief, and head of the tax office) depend on the *hokim* since they do not have a separate budget to solve people's problems. During late-President Karimov's reign, prosecutors could file a protest against a *hokim's* unlawful decisions and orders; but, nowadays, prosecutors refrain from doing so. If we go against a *hokim* and protest their decision, they can limit our access to the local budget. So, the *prokuratura* (the prosecutor's office) are no longer independent and they subordinate to *hokims* (governors), who control the local government's budget.

Of course, many prosecutors want to maintain their pride and independence from *hokims*. How do we do this? Being pressured to solve people's socioeconomic needs, we usually look for sponsors. We often ask local businessmen and entrepreneurs to finance the needs of our sector. This could include, for example, road asphalting, economic support to needy households or addressing irrigation problems. In turn, we must ignore illegal activities perpetrated by businessmen when they act outside the law, or provide support and protection (*kryshovanye*) when they experience problems with the tax office or need a low-interest rate loan from the bank. Thus, the sector system forces us to close our eyes when businessmen break the law, making us accomplices to economic crimes.

Shavkat Mirziyoyev, after being elected President of Uzbekistan in December 2016, turned his attention to local governance problems. President Mirziyoyev frequently talks about the necessity of delegating additional power, responsibilities, and resources to local governmental bodies. More than 200 laws related to local governance have been passed since 2017, with many of these legislative pieces taking the form of Presidential decrees and orders to local governments. As a former *hokim* (governor), Mirziyoyev has a vision or belief that '*hamma sohani o'z egasi bo'lishi kerak*', which translates as 'each sphere should have its own owner or responsible official'.[10] Based on this understanding, he adopted two decrees in 2017 and 2019,[11] resulting in the establishment of a new local governance system throughout Uzbekistan—the sectoral management of regions and districts—each region and district is divided into four geographic sectors or territorial zones led by a *hokim* (governor), public prosecutor, chief of police, and head of the tax office. Through this sector management strategy, Mirziyoyev assigns the state law enforcement apparatus—namely, the prosecutor's office, the Ministry of Internal Affairs (police), and the State Tax Service—as the ultimate authorities in one territorial division of each region, but practically subordinate to the *hokim* who controls resources and access to the local budget.

Heads of sectors—the *hokim*, prosecutor, police chief, and head of the tax department—must be multifunctional and address and solve all issues of local importance in the territory of their sector, essentially assuming the broad list of local governmental functions. For example, public prosecutors, whose professional task is to ensure the rule of law, crime prevention, and human rights, are now also tasked with implementing state social welfare policies. However, assigning social welfare and job creation functions to sector leaders raises numerous questions about their capacity and leads to informality and frustrations. Several cases emerged in which the prosecutors were punished for their failure to resolve socioeconomic issues in their sector, even though these tasks were unrelated to their functions and duties stipulated in the law 'On the Prosecutor's Office'. For instance, the prosecutor of the Chilonzor district of Tashkent city was dismissed for not preventing damage to trees, whilst the *hokim* (governor) of the Surkhondarya Region insulted the prosecutor of the Angor district for failing to create jobs, reduce poverty, and attract foreign investment.

As a result, this 'authority' of sector leaders without resources can lead to corrupt and illegal practices. On the one hand, sector leaders must live up

10 https://president.uz/oz/lists/view/3864

11 The Decree of the President of the Republic of Uzbekistan 'On Priority Measures to Ensure the Rapid Socioeconomic Development of the Regions' (No. PQ-3182, adopted 8 August 2017) and the Decree of the President of the Republic of Uzbekistan 'On Additional Measures to Further Improve the Activities of the Sectors for the Comprehensive Socioeconomic Development of the Regions' (No. PQ-4102, adopted 8 January 2019).

to the demands and expectations of the central government by solving local socioeconomic issues without relying on state funding. On the other hand, in order to finance and resolve people's daily economic needs, they must enter into informal relations and alliances with local economic and business elites. Given the absence of government funding, sector leaders often enter into informal agreements or alliances with local business elites who have the money necessary to finance the needs of each sector. Of course, business elites also expect the prosecutor, police chief, or head of the tax office to reciprocate by serving as their patron when they encounter legal problems. As a result, local governance is organised through the sector management system, which generates widespread corruption, extra-legal practices, and conflicts of interest. Thus, the tasks and responsibilities assigned to sector leaders without adequate economic resources compel them to invent various extra-legal solutions.

The multifarious meanings of and logics to corruption in meso-level arenas

The empirical material presented in this chapter indicates that neither international legal definitions of corruption presented by UNCAC, the World Bank or TI nor nation-state laws regarding corruption (e.g., Uzbekistan's highly publicised Anticorruption Law) reckon with the multifarious meanings of and logics to informal and extra-legal practices in authoritarian contexts such as Uzbekistan. Thus, our observations and the case studies presented above demonstrate the existence of alternative moralities or informal legal orders shaping social behaviour vis-à-vis state law. Our empirical data show that the informal and extra-legal practices in meso-level arenas serve as 'palliative' mechanisms, making up for the incapacity of the state to finance the infrastructure of welfare systems. Although Uzbekistan's political leadership positions the country as a 'social state' (that is, a welfare state) under the new Constitution,[12] our findings show that the state does not have sufficient funding to run the system. As a result, the people of Uzbekistan have created alternative informal means of sustaining the welfare infrastructure, as we described in the three case studies presented here. The informal and extra-legal practices and transactions described in the case studies could thus be regarded as forms of an 'informal welfare system', given that this system in place maintains, for example, the sector management, healthcare, and traffic enforcement systems.

Whilst the government of Uzbekistan may appear to implement ambitious anticorruption measures, our results demonstrate such measures have precious little impact on everyday life, particularly in regions and districts where local

12 https://cabar.asia/en/will-constitutional-reform-lead-to-a-new-uzbekistan

elites' actions and decisions are driven by informal norms and practices. When observing local-level interactions in Uzbekistan, it becomes difficult to experience the state or its laws as an ontically coherent entity. What one confronts instead is an enormous degree of informal exchange and reciprocity in money, material goods, and services carried out through uncodified, but socially reproduced informal rules—that is, through the 'living law'. Both regular people and public officials increasingly rely on informal and extra-legal coping strategies. From this perspective, the apparent resilience of informal and extra-legal transactions and practices in Uzbekistan resides in its embeddedness in informal forms of coping strategies and might be viewed as a reaction to the state's unrealistic expectations and disregard for local needs and concerns.

Thus, the results presented in this chapter can be summarised as follows. First, anticorruption laws, policies, and initiatives should be sensitive to local categories, practices, and moral codes (i.e., 'how things get done' and how they are perceived by the various salient actors). Second, informal and extra-legal transactions are deeply embedded in coping strategies, particularly in authoritarian regime contexts where the central government imposes unrealistic demands on local actors. And third, any discussion of corruption must be contextualised. If these are not taken into consideration, informal transactions that are not corrupt run the risk of being labelled as illicit. Our analysis demonstrates that informal transactions considered corrupt from the legal centralistic or economistic-based perspectives have little to do with abuse. Instead, they represent a rational and pragmatic way of 'getting things done'. Therefore, anticorruption measures are not simply a matter of getting people to obey state law. They are, more importantly, about understanding the 'living law' and promoting socioeconomic change.

References

Blundo, G., and De Sardan, J.-P.O., 2013. *Everyday Corruption and the State: Citizens and Public Officials in Africa*. London: Zed Books.

Ehrlich, E., 1912. Das lebende Recht der Völker der Bukowina. *In*: M. Rehbinder, ed. *Eugen Ehrlich, Recht und Leben*. Berlin: Duncker & Humblot, 43–60.

Gill, M.S., 1998. India: running the world's biggest elections. *Journal of Democracy*, 9 (1), 164–168.

Gupta, A., 2005. Narrating the State of Corruption. *In*: D. Haller and C. Shore, eds. *Corruption: Anthropological Perspectives*. London and Ann Arbor, MI: Pluto Press, 173–193.

Haller, D., and Shore, C., eds., 2005. *Corruption: Anthropological Perspectives*. London and Ann Arbor, MI: Pluto Press.

Ilkhamov, A., 2004. The Limits of Centralization: Regional Challenges in Uzbekistan. *In*: P.J. Luong, ed. *The Transformation of Central Asia. States and Societies from Soviet Rule to Independence*. Ithaca, NY: Cornell University Press, 159–181.

Jávor, I. and Jancsics, D., 2016. The role of power in organizational corruption: an empirical study. *Administration & Society*, 48 (5), 527–558.

Lasslett, K., 2020. *Behind the Entrepreneurial Veil: State Aid and Elites in Uzbekistan*. Newtownabbey, Northern Island: UzInvestigations (a civic initiative administered by Ulster University in partnership with the Uzbek Forum for Human Rights), No. 3.

Lasslett, K., Kanji, F., and McGill, D., 2017. *A Dance with a Cobra: Confronting Grand Corruption in Uzbekistan*. London: International State Crime Initiative.

Olma, N., 2021. Driving in the Shadows. Rural–urban Labour Migrants as Informal Taxi Drivers in Post-socialist Tashkent. *In*: R. Turaeva and R. Urinboyev, eds. *Labor, Mobility and Informal Practices in Russia, Central Asia and Eastern Europe: Power, Institutions and Mobile Actors in Transnational Space*. London: Routledge, 36–50.

Polese, A., 2008. 'If I receive it, it is a gift; if I demand it, then it is a bribe': On the Local Meaning of Economic Transactions in Post-Soviet Ukraine. *Anthropology in Action*, 15 (3), 47–60.

Rasanayagam, J., 2011. Informal economy, informal state: The Case of Uzbekistan. *International Journal of Sociology and Social Policy*, 31 (11/12), 681–696.

Stepurko, T., Pavlova, M., Gryga, I., and Groot, W., 2013. Informal payments for health care services–Corruption or gratitude? A study on public attitudes, perceptions and opinions in six Central and Eastern European countries. *Communist and Post-Communist Studies*, 46 (4), 419–431.

Urinboyev, R., Polese, A., Svensson, M., Adams, L.L., and Kerikmäe, T., 2018. Political vs everyday forms of governance in Uzbekistan: The illegal, immoral and illegitimate politics and legitimacy in Post- Soviet Eurasia. *Studies of Transition States and Societies*, 10 (1), 50–64.

Wanner, C., 2005. Money, morality and new forms of exchange in postsocialist Ukraine. *Ethnos*, 70 (4), 515–537.

Werner, C.A., 2000. Gifts, bribes, and development in Post-Soviet Kazakhstan. *Human Organization*, 59 (1), 11–22.

Chapter 6

The social life of corruption in micro-level arenas

Introduction

In the previous chapter, we examined the multifarious meanings, logics, and moralities of extra-legal and informal transactions and practices ('corruption' from a legal standpoint) in meso-level arenas in Uzbekistan. To do so, we offered case studies of the everyday experiences amongst mid- and low-level state officials. Our analysis of these case studies demonstrated that corruption carries different meanings and logics at different levels of society depending upon contextual, situational, and spatial factors. In our analysis, we highlighted the existence of multiple moralities or multiple 'focal points' coordinating and shaping individuals' behaviours vis-à-vis state law. Thus, we argued that anticorruption measures are not simply a matter of changing incentive mechanisms and increasing the severity of punishment; rather, such measures are, more importantly, about understanding and reckoning with these multiple 'focal points' vying to influence social behaviour.

Armed with this understanding, in this chapter we move down one level—towards micro-level arenas—and probe the ways in which informal or illegal practices ('corruption' from a legal standpoint) not only mirror kleptocracy and individual greed (Chapter 4) or coping strategies (Chapter 5), but also reflect society's informal norms and 'non-monetary currencies', such as respect, prestige, social status, solidarity, trust, and kinship norms constituting the basic social fabric ('living law') of society. By doing this, we demonstrate that people engage in informal or illegal transactions not simply to satisfy their economic needs, but also to also fulfil their family and kinship obligations, socialise and maintain membership in their community, avoid gossip and social sanctions, improve or preserve their social status and reputation, and secure additional moral and affective support from those around them. As such, we argue that economic-based attempts or legal centralistic approaches to address corruption should be complemented with socio-legal perspectives that reckon with the role of society's informal norms and non-economic motivations. Thus, informal and illegal transactions that would be labelled corruption from a state law perspective may very well

DOI: 10.4324/9780429952968-6

be considered morally acceptable practices according to society's informal norms and moral codes.

Based on the above considerations, in this chapter, we show how the personal, the social, and the economic are interwoven and how private and professional life are shaped by informal norms of multiple social associations leaving little room for individual choice. This implies that the state and its laws are rarely the primary source of social control in Central Asian societies; as such, the state may face enormous resistance from other (formal and informal) social associations. These associations coexist, interact, and struggle with one another over material and non-material issues, attempting to impose their own norms and social control on socioeconomic relations. The more the focus moves from economic-based explanations and legal centralistic approaches to socio-legal ethnographic analyses of everyday life, the more it becomes clear that informal and extra-legal transactions are deeply embedded in the social norms, traditions, moral codes, and affective logics constituting the basic social fabric of society. Thus, anticorruption interventions should extend beyond top–down, legal centralistic approaches; we must include a bottom-up perspective and gain an in-depth understanding of micro-level 'legal orders' ('living law').

Empirically, this chapter relies on our extended ethnographic fieldwork in the Fergana Valley of Uzbekistan, conducted between 2009 and 2023, in a village we call Shabboda. In exploring the aforementioned questions and processes, we focus on daily interactions, negotiations, conflicts, discourses, and life-cycle events in the realm of the *mahalla* (neighbourhood community), *urug'* (extended family or kinship group), and *oila* (immediate family)—three key social associations in the Fergana Valley that shape the nitty-gritty details of everyday life and social relations. By focusing our attention here, we highlight the role of these associations in creating, reproducing, and maintaining social norms and moral and affective bonds that shape villagers' behaviours when they engage in public administration, business or wield some political or economic resources.

Fieldwork context: Shabboda village

Shabboda, where we conducted fieldwork, is a village (*qishloq*) in the Fergana Valley of Uzbekistan, with a population of more than 18,000 people. Administratively, Shabboda comprises 28 *mahalla* (neighbourhood communities). In turn, each *mahalla* contains 150 to 300 immediate families (*oilalar*), consisting of around 20 to 30 *urug'* (extended families or kinship groups). The income-generating activities of the village residents comprise multiple sources, ranging from cucumber and grape production, remittances, raising livestock for sale as beef, and informal trade to construction work, daily manual labour, fruit-picking jobs, and brokerage.

The *guzar* (village meeting space), *masjid* (mosque), and *choykhona* (teahouse) serve as the main public places in the Shabboda village. Typically, it is possible to find 10 to 15 male residents sitting in these social spaces in the morning, afternoon, or evening. Women's socialising and information exchange activities typically take place either in the streets or inside the household. Daily conversations and interactions in these social spaces fulfil important social and administrative functions in the village's everyday life. On the one hand, these daily interactions create and maintain a sense of community and solidarity amongst the villagers. On the other hand, they also serve as a site for establishing local politics and norms of conduct. Since villagers meet regularly (often daily) in these social spaces and attend most of the socialising events together, they are entwined in relationships of mutual dependence. Having a common residence and meeting and interacting daily produces a general expectation that residents will help their neighbours and co-villagers whenever assistance is needed. Villagers who ignore or fail to comply with these norms often face social sanctions, such as gossip, ridicule, a loss of respect and reputation, humiliation, and even exclusion from community events. Thus, money is not everything in the Shabboda village: upholding one's honour, respect, prestige, and reputation are all equally important. Whilst observing villagers' daily conversations at the *choykhona* and *guzar*, we learned a great deal about the role of social norms and 'non-monetary currencies' in shaping people's social behaviours and decisions. These became visible in villagers' frequent use of various folk sayings emphasising the importance of reputation, status, respect, and honour. Villagers often referred to the following folk sayings in daily-life situations:

> *Pul ketsa-ketsin obro', or-nomus ketmasin.* [Better to lose wealth than one's reputation and honour.]
> *Uyat—o'limdan qattiq.* [Shame is greater than death.]
> *Nomussiz yurmoqdan nomusli o'lmoq yaxshi.* [It is better to die with honour than to live without it.]
> *Joningni fido qilsang qil, nomusingni fido qilma.* [Better to sacrifice your life rather than your honour.]
> *Yigitning moli bo'lguncha, ori bo'lsin.* [A man should have his honour rather than wealth.]
> *Lafz—puldan qimmat.* [Keeping one's word or promise is more valuable than having money.]
> *Mol talashma, or talash.* [Seek honour, not wealth.]

Another key social arena rendering visible the role of society's informal norms and 'non-monetary currencies' emerges during life-cycle events (weddings, circumcisions, and funerals). Weddings are the most important life-cycle event in Shabboda, in which villagers invest a great deal of their time, energy, resources, reputations, and socioeconomic status. This stems from the fact that wedding ceremonies in Shabboda (and generally in Uzbekistan) are not considered a family event, but the concern of the entire community:

they are open to all community residents, and attended by an average of 400 to 500 guests. Given their collective nature, wedding ceremonies exhibit key features of social norms, hierarchies, status contestations, and gender divisions: men and women sit separately at different guest tables during the wedding feast and the 'best tables' are often reserved for people of influence such as local government officials, prosecutors, police, highly educated people, successful businessmen, and wealthy relatives and friends. If people of influence dance during the wedding party, a crowd of people hurriedly line up to give money to the dancing person. However, if the dancing person does not belong to the people of influence category, very few people approach the dancing person with a money offering.[1] This is the most central characteristic of the wedding, during which it is possible to compare one's social status and prestige to that of others. As each wedding ceremony is subject to intense public discussion and gossip in the *mahalla*, weddings are transformed into a display of a family's wealth, power, and social status. The local norms of gift exchange are maintained and reproduced through intense social interactions. Since information networks in the *mahalla* are quick and comprehensive, a person can simply elevate their socioeconomic status in the village by expending more on wedding feasts and gift-giving than others. Thus, weddings exhibit micro-level normative order, status contestations, and power geometries in Uzbek society.

Daily conversations in Shabboda primarily revolve around economic problems, remittances, gas and electricity cuts, and life-cycle events. Many of the villagers we encountered were of the opinion that the state should cater to their needs and have a 'presence' in their daily lives by providing employment opportunities and access to public goods and services. However, through our observations of villagers' lives over the last 14 years, we found that the role and legitimacy of the state diminished significantly. Because the state in contemporary Uzbekistan no longer provides jobs and all-encompassing social welfare services, many villagers we met stated that the state was virtually absent from their everyday lives. Many complained about unaffordable healthcare costs, unemployment, inflation, and declining public services. Given these economic realities, many households in Shabboda heavily relied on migrant remittances, sent by their male members (husband or sons) working in the Russian Federation and Kazakhstan. In addition to remittances, villagers increasingly relied on social safety nets and mutual-aid practices within their extended family and *mahalla* networks. These practices served

1 This tradition is called *pul qistirish* (giving money). The amount of money that guests give depends on the age, social status, and occupation of the dancing person. By giving money, a person can pay their respects and express loyalty to the person who is dancing. This is the most central aspect of the wedding where it is possible to observe how social status and reputation are translated into hard cash. All of the money collected during the dancing is given to the singer and musicians performing as payment for their efforts.

as a shock-absorbing institution for many villagers, enabling them to meet their basic needs and gain access to public goods, services, and social protection unavailable from the state. These community-based mutual-aid practices created strong moral and affective bonds, enabling villagers not only to meet their livelihood needs, but also to provide space for participation in everyday life and social interactions.

Thus, very few villagers reaped the rewards of independence. In the villagers' views, most of these economic problems resulted from widespread corruption in the upper echelons of the government. As seen in other contexts (Gupta 1995, Lazar 2005), the topic of corruption remained at the centre of village talk, a lens via which villagers imagined the role of the state and reflected upon their daily experiences with state institutions. Wherever we went and with whomever we talked, our interlocutors quickly brought up the subject of corruption. Stories and anecdotes from informal transactions involving the traffic police were most common. We, therefore, observed that petty, everyday corruption existed as an open secret in Shabboda, since villagers openly talked about situations in which they had given bribes to state officials.

Villagers also had their own interpretation of good and bad corruption. When they talked about corrupt state officials, they usually referred to those who used their 'oily position' to enrich themselves rather than sharing some of their wealth with the *mahalla* and members of the village. If a state official remained accountable and generous towards their community, they were not viewed as a corrupt official. But, as soon as the official distanced themselves from the people and showed no accountability towards locals, they were perceived as the 'other'—a representative of the kleptocratic elite. This is where locals drew a boundary between 'good corruption' and 'predatory practices' (*harombo'rlik*). As such, villagers knew that almost all state officials were corrupt and 'eat' on a regular basis. Because the state was 'absent' from everyday life and since its officials charged with enforcing the rule of law were themselves breaking the law, the villagers felt that they, too, had no moral obligation to act in accordance with state law. They were of the opinion that state officials should 'steal with a conscience' (*insof bilan o'g'rilash*) and share part of their accumulated wealth and political influence with their wider community.

The case of Tursunboy, a village member and director of a state-owned factory, serves as a relevant example here. Tursunboy was one of the richest residents in the village, such that his family owned fancy houses, expensive cars, more than a hundred hectares of land, and many other properties state officials could not legally afford in contemporary Uzbekistan. It was an open secret in the village that he would not have accumulated so much wealth without engaging in corrupt practices. Despite this understanding, he remained loved and respected by many people there. In the villagers' views, unlike many other greedy and selfish state officials, Tursunboy was not a self-centred official precisely because he shared his income with both his family and the wider community. This allowed him to be known locally as *taqsir*, a title historically used to address highly respected state officials, wealthy individuals, and religious leaders. When poor families found themselves unable to afford an urgent medical procedure or had nothing to eat during the cold winter months, rather than asking the local government and social welfare office for help, agencies actually responsible for addressing such issues, they usually visited Tursunboy's house to ask for assistance. At six in the morning, it was normal to see four or five people standing outside Tursunboy's house, waiting to be invited in for a reception. In other words, Tursunboy's house served as some sort of informal social welfare agency from which needy villagers could obtain support. When we asked villagers if they considered him a corrupt official, many ironically replied:

> Tell us who doesn't 'steal' these days? Who follows the law? Tursunboy is totally different from other state officials whose wealth is *harom* (unlawful in Sharia law). Of course, he steals from the state, but he is a 'conscientious thief' (*insofli o'g'ri*) and shares his wealth with everyone in the village; therefore, his earnings are *halol* (lawful in Sharia law).

Tursunboy's case provides a useful illustration of the existence of an alternative (to state law) morality and informal norms in Shabboda, where villagers regard illegal transactions as morally acceptable and an *halol* practice, given the state's inability to secure the basic needs of its citizens. From a legal standpoint, Uzbekistan's Anticorruption Law (No. O'RQ-419, adopted 3 January 2017) and the Criminal Code (No. 2014-XII, adopted 1 April 1995) would classify most of the transactions, practices, and interpretations described above as instances of corruption and illegality. However, in the eyes of locals, Tursunboy was a good state official according to local needs and standards.

These observations remind us of the 'living law' of the Bukowina. Eugen Ehrlich (1912) described a century ago in his book *Fundamental Principles of the Sociology of Law*. One important insight we gained was that state law is almost non-existent in everyday life in Shabboda. Instead, village life is regulated by informal norms which promote an alternative version of how people should behave. Thus, state law (and supranational law) lies in tension with the 'inner orders' ('living law') of other social associations in contemporary Uzbekistan. From a legal standpoint, the above practices and interpretations observed in the Shabboda context can be classified as instances of corruption and illegality according to Uzbekistan's legislation. Our informants understood that Tursunboy would not be able to accumulate so much wealth and cater to the needs of poor families if he strictly abided by state law and relied only on his official salary. Interestingly, villagers interpreted Tursunboy's actions from a religious perspective, as evidenced by their use of religious terms. The use of the *halol/harom* binary was commonplace in the village, whereas only a handful of the villagers we encountered discussed corruption in terms of a legal/illegal binary. Although the 'living law' described here can be interpreted as an instance of corruption according to both the nation-state law and international legal definitions of corruption, it is, however, acceptable within the rural communities in Ferghana as a legitimate practice—regardless of whether the actions involved are legal or illegal. Our observations enable us to argue that the behavioural instructions promoted by the 'living law' influence social behaviours and everyday life more effectively than the laws of the state.

This pattern is not unique to Uzbekistan. A similar situation was also observed in Mexico and Bolivia, where corruption was morally acceptable if state officials showed generosity towards and solidarity with the people (Lomnitz 1995, Lazar 2005). However, the above observations should not be viewed as an attempt to make the case for a 'culture of corruption' thesis (De Sardan 1999, Lazar 2005, Smart and Hsu 2007). Instead, we found that villagers took a clear stance and exhibited a different attitude when discussing cases involving high-level corruption. In actuality, from our conversations, we learned that villagers distinguished between low-level (petty) and high-level (systemic) corruption. This became visible in the way villagers distinguished between 'good corruption' and kleptocratic practices (*harombo'rlik*). They frequently referred to the corruption scandals in the upper echelons of government (e.g., Gulnora Karimova's case discussed in Chapter 2). Some of the villagers were even aware that Uzbekistan was ranked by TI as one of the most corrupt countries in the world. Referring to the fact that state officials themselves broke the law on a daily basis, most villagers stated that they felt no moral obligation to obey the laws or report corruption cases to the Anticorruption Agency or to the prosecutor's office. As such, people's willingness to challenge corruption was also affected by the extent to which they had confidence in the rule of law and the government's anticorruption measures (*cf.* Gong and Xiao 2017). The malfunctioning of state bureaucracy and the 'unrule of law' were thus locally perceived as the primary drivers of corrupt practices and behaviours.

Despite villagers' condemnation of corruption, we observed the existence of a 'dual, conflicting morality', through which they distinguished between low-level or petty corruption needed for 'getting things done' (*ish bitirmoq*) and high-level corruption and kleptocratic practices (*harombo'rlik*) which had nothing to do with 'survival'. Locals used various terms and categories when we asked them to describe the difference between petty corruption and high-level corruption. For example, they used the expression *hursand qilmoq* (making one happy) or *til topishmoq* (finding a common language) when they talked about how they bribed the utility fee collector to avoid high electricity bills. In addition, the term *harombo'r* or *porabo'r* (corrupt) was used to talk about their experiences with the public prosecutor's office or judges.

Our observations thus allow us to argue that corruption carries different meanings and logics within different levels and associations in society. There is also a difference between the masses of low-level officials and the smaller group of kleptocratic officials and elites. Without distinguishing between different types and levels of corruption, we run the risk of labelling the diversity of informal and nonlegal practices (*cf.* Gibson-Graham 2008) under the rubric of corruption, regardless of their different motives and functions. Thus, in line with Nuijten and Anders (2007) and Blundo (2007), we argue that classifications and typologies can provide useful points of departure and a much-needed orientation in the study of complex phenomena such as corruption, which is often prone to becoming mired in juicy stories and anecdotes.

Case studies

In this section, we attempt to shift the reader's attention from the 'thick description' (Geertz 1973)

to 'concrete examples'. To facilitate this shift, we present two ethnographic case studies focusing on informal, illegal transactions and practices that take place within the daily life of the *mahalla* and *urug'*, the two main social associations in Uzbekistan. The first case study is constructed around two *mahalla* members: Sardor, the deputy chief of a provincial police department (high-level state official), and Rahmon, a district-level traffic policeman (low-level official). The second case centres around Ahmedov's *urug'*. We must emphasise that these two case studies were possible thanks to our ability to establish trust and maintain regular contact with the informants over a long period of time (2009–2018). Because we were socially and physically immersed in the field site, we regularly visited the village's social spaces (*guzar*, *choykhona*, etc.) and life-cycle events. We also had direct, regular conversations with the main characters of our case studies—Sardor, Rahmon, and their family members—and with members of Ahmedov's *urug'* during our fieldwork trips. Before moving to the empirical case studies, we provide some additional clarifications regarding the *mahalla* and *urug'* in order to help the reader better distinguish between these two social contexts.

The term *mahalla* is commonly used in Shabboda (as well as in other parts of Uzbekistan) to refer to the neighbourhood community. As we mentioned previously, the Shabboda village consists of 28 *mahalla* (neighbourhood community). Most people in the village identify themselves through their *mahalla*. If a village resident is asked where they come from, the answer is, 'I am from *mahalla* X'. Thus, villagers use the term *mahalla* to refer to the neighbourhood community in which they live. Therefore, the *mahalla* includes all of the people living in the same neighbourhood regardless of their familial or kinship ties (Urinboyev 2023).

The term *urug'* arises when villagers talk about their larger kinship group or extended family members who are related by blood, through a shared name and ancestry. *Urug'* includes grandparents, uncles, aunts, cousins, nephews, and nieces from both the patrilineal and matrilineal families. Normally, *urug'* members do not live in the same household or *mahalla*, but they live close to each other, for example, in the same village or district. Thus, *urug'* is a collection of several *oila* (immediate families) who live in the same village or district.

Mahalla

Oqtepa, where this case took place, is one of the *mahalla* in the Shabboda village in rural Ferghana, with a population of more than 2000 people. Most of the residents in this *mahalla* are *dehqonlar* (farmers) who produce cucumbers and grapes. However, given the focus of our research, we were particularly interested in two *mahalla* members—Sardor and Rahmon, both state officials and the centre of everyday *mahalla* talk.

Sardor was a very high-level state official and worked as the deputy chief of a provincial police department, whereas Rahmon was a district-level traffic policeman. However, in everyday *mahalla* talk, Sardor, despite having such a high official status, did not have a good reputation. Many of the *mahalla* residents we encountered at *guzar* and weddings called him a communist, a term carrying a negative connotation and used in relation to law-abiding state officials who do not share their political influence and resources with their kin and *mahalla*. This social pressure rested on *mahalladoshlik* (a shared *mahalla* origin) obligations and mutual aid practices that constituted the backbone of social relations. *Mahalla* members frequently talked about how they had helped Sardor or his family members in the past when he did not yet possess such legal and political influence. Given this history, they argued that Sardor should support his *mahalla* members when they confronted problems with the law. For instance, they argued that in situations involving traffic law violations, 'just one phone call' from Sardor could relieve his neighbours from needing to bribe a traffic police officer. Given that the local government no longer provided funding for road asphalting, the *mahalla* roads were uneven and bumpy. The *mahalla* simply could not afford to asphalt its roads given the economic realities of the post-Soviet period. The *mahalla* members took a clear stance, insisting that Sardor, as a member of the *mahalla*, had a moral obligation to cater to their needs and, if he really wanted to help, he could solve the problem easily by ordering local government officials to asphalt the roads.

In reality, as a high-level state official, Sardor held substantial power and could easily divert resources to the *mahalla*, but he always rejected their requests and asked them to solve their problems through formal channels. Thus, because of his attempts to keep his public office separate from the private sphere, Sardor was regarded as a communist by many of the *mahalla* members we encountered at the *guzar* and during life-cycle events. They opined that Sardor was neither a good *mahalla* member nor a good state official due to his law-abiding behaviour and lack of willingness to use his power to benefit the *mahalla*. Pressure was also felt by Sardor's family members, who encountered sarcastic remarks on the *mahalla* streets, at the *guzar*, and during wedding ceremonies.

In contrast, low-level official Rahmon was a man of respect and enjoyed a rather high social status and good reputation in the *mahalla*. Unlike Sardor, Rahmon provided patronage to *mahalla* residents by, for instance, helping them avoid or navigate around state law. Rahmon was particularly praised for his ability to act as a bridge between high-level state officials and ordinary residents in terms of negotiating the sum of informal payments for a job or university admission issues, and bending state laws to meet the interests of *mahalla* residents. Rahmon's capacity to address the needs and concerns of his *mahalla* members not only placed him in a higher social position but also accounted for the enhanced prestige his family members and kinship group enjoyed during *mahalla* social events. Whilst observing the *mahalla's* wedding ceremonies, we noted that Rahmon and his family members were always offered seats at a 'best table' and served more quickly than others. Rahmon's high status and reputation were also visible in the daily talk at the *guzar*: residents often commented on his *odamgarchilik* (humanity and care), a trait many state officials lack in Uzbekistan. Thus, given his sensitivity to the needs and concerns of the *mahalla*, Rahmon was considered the 'pride of the *mahalla*'.

Legally, according to Uzbekistan's Anticorruption Law, Rahmon's actions could be classified as an abuse of public office and, therefore, were punishable as a criminal act under anticorruption legislation. But, according to the *mahalla's* 'living law', Rahmon's illegal acts had nothing to do with corruption, since his actions were not driven by egoism or greed. There was no formal reason why Rahmon should have helped *mahalla* members at the risk of breaking state law, and he was aware that his actions could cause him legal problems. A number of empirical studies (Lazar 2005, Urinboyev and Polese 2016, Urinboyev 2020) have demonstrated that social sanctions such as gossip, rumours, and ostracism may be related to outputs and productivity. As Rahmon's social prestige and reputation related to both the *mahalla* and the state, he understood that a loss of reputation, gossip, and social ostracism were too harsh to face (as illustrated in the previous section through various folk sayings). As such, corrupt acts were 'not merely selfish and private but profoundly social, shaped by larger sociocultural notions of power, privilege, and responsibility' (Hasty 2005, p. 271).

However, Sardor's decision not to follow *mahalla* norms reveals that Shabboda was not a bounded, homogenous social space in which loyalty to and respect for the *mahalla* explained all kinds of actions and transactions.

Whilst Sardor (and his family members) faced *mahalla* pressure, he made his position clear, drawing a sharp line between his public position and private life. As a result, he was designated a communist by *mahalla* members, but a *halol odam* (honest man) by his family and kinship group, who respected him for his law-abiding behaviour. Thus, the meaning and logic of corruption in micro-level arenas are fluid in that the interpretation of certain acts and behaviours as moral/immoral, appropriate/inappropriate, and legal/illegal is not static, but changes in accordance with the situation and context.

Urug'

In this case study, we focus on Ahmedov's *urug'* and their strategies to reassert their high social status in the village. Ahmedov's *urug'* consisted of five immediate families who lived in different *mahalla* within the Shabboda village. Whilst each of these five families lived in a separate household (*oila/xo'jalik*) and managed their finances independently (*alohida ro'zg'or*), they were all in a mutual dependence relationship. Like other kinship groups in the village, Ahmedov's *urug'* met regularly. During life-cycle events and holidays (Eid, Navruz, weddings, birthday celebrations, funerals, etc.), all *urug'* members gather and discuss what has happened since the last time they met. However, *urug'* members also gather during emergency situations, such as when someone from the *urug'* falls ill, needs a large sum of money, or gets into trouble possibly jeopardising the reputation of the entire *urug'*. In such circumstances, the *urug'* attempts to ensure that all its members are taken care of. The *urug's* capacity to provide for its members not only creates solidarity within the kinship group but also enhances the *urug's* prestige and reputation within the village. Thus, money is not the issue, and when the *urug'*'s *obro' etibor* (reputation) is at stake, all of its members unite and do their best to re-establish their status. As we demonstrate below, these *urug'*-based moral and affective repertoires carry important implications for re-contextualising the role and meaning of informal/illegal transactions.

From the late 1990s until 2009, Ahmedov's *urug'* was one of the most reputable and richest kinship groups in Shabboda. This stemmed from the fact that one of the members of the *urug'*, Nodirbek, worked in key positions in the regional government (*viloyat hokimiyati*) and was later promoted to the Ministry of Agriculture in Tashkent. But, this situation changed shortly after Nodirbek's removal from the government in 2009, something which negatively impacted the social status of the *urug'* in the village. Following these developments, Ahmedov's *urug'* lost their high social status and good reputation in the village. This change was also felt by Nodirbek, since he was no longer offered a 'best table' when invited to wedding feasts. Ahmedov's social status was further damaged when Bakhtiyor, one of the *urug'*'s rising stars, failed to be admitted to a prestigious law university in Tashkent. This event led to speculation that Ahmedov's *urug'* would never be able to recover and regain its social status.

These events forced the *urug'* members to mobilise their economic resources and invest them in Bakhtiyor's education, hoping that he would restore the *urug'*'s reputation in the future. During the *urug'* gathering, each of the families contributed US$3000, amassing a total of US$15,000. The idea behind this initiative was that this money would be given to 'people of influence' in Tashkent so that they would guarantee Bakhtiyor's admission to the university. Thanks to his many years of work in public administration, Nodirbek had many connections and networks (*tanish-bilish*) in Tashkent. Through these connections, Nodirbek was able to secure Bakhtiyor's admission to the law university. Ahmedov's *urug'* also used marriage to boost Bakhtiyor's career after graduation. Because Bakhtiyor was studying at such a prestigious law university, he had a good chance of marrying a girl from a powerful family. Following *urug'* members' zealous matchmaking efforts, Bakhtiyor married the daughter of a high-level state official from a neighbouring village. As a result of these strategic moves, a few years after his graduation, Bakhtiyor became a judge at one of the district courts, something that eventually reasserted Ahmedov's high social status and good reputation in the village. During our last visit to the fieldwork site, we learned that Bakhtiyor (and more generally, Ahmedov's *urug'*) once again enjoyed a high social status in the village due to Bakhtiyor's ability to divert the local government's funds to the village, an outcome resulting from Bakhtiyor's growing power and influence within the government.

This case study highlights two main issues. First, the illegal practices described in the case study (e.g., a bribe made to enrol Bakhtiyor at the law university and Bakhtiyor's ability to divert local government resources to his village) encompass a wide range of moral and affective repertoires that go beyond mere economic interests. This case also illustrates the importance of 'alternative currencies', such as respect, prestige, and reputation (Pardo 1996, Zanca 2003) in explaining the motives behind an individual's decision to engage in informal, illegal practices and transactions. It also shows the existence of a non-monetary economy deeply embedded in micro-level social structures. Hence, we need to move beyond the 'legal/illegal', 'licit/illicit' binaries and, specifically, the argument that petty corruption serves as a survival strategy for ordinary citizens and low-level state officials. As shown above, in micro-level arenas, petty corruption may also be driven by non-economic considerations and affective repertoires. Second, the case study provides useful insights into the nitty-gritty of everyday life and social relations in Uzbek society, in which various social groups compete for status, power, influence, and privileges. Given that the abovementioned kinship groups and their status-based interactions form part of the institutionalised practices embedded within everyday life and social relations, it is not appropriate to label them as instances of corruption or a 'cancer' that needs eradication. These kinship-based practices should be situated within a broader socio-legal context because they are not merely spontaneous actions on the part of participants; they also represent the institutionalised social practices or 'living law' which are part-and-parcel of everyday life. Therefore, the study of corruption should be sensitive to these micro-level social dynamics.

Living law, non-monetary economy, and corruption in a micro-level context

The case studies presented in this chapter demonstrate that informal transactions may also be driven by 'non-monetary currencies' allowing people to build personal, social, and professional relations. Hence, informal or illegal practices not only mirror kleptocracy, individual greed, economic interests or survival strategies, but also reflect social norms generated through kinship, social status, hierarchies, affection, reciprocity, and reputation. When these micro-level structures are perceived as corrupt and battled, there is a risk that the basic social fabric ('living law') of society weakens and becomes distorted, possibly eroding social solidarity and stability. By emphasising the existence of non-economic and non-monetary motivations to engage in informal transactions, we have also further attempted to place corruption beyond the kleptocracy, dysfunctional institutions, dishonest officials, or survival explanations. As such, we argue that economic-based attempts or normative approaches should be complemented with socio-legal approaches that consider the role of social norms and solidarity. Any anticorruption strategies should be built upon a deep knowledge of social norms and local context that determine the 'rights' and 'wrongs' of everyday social behaviours.

References

Blundo, G., 2007. Hidden Acts, Open Talks. How Anthropology Can "Observe" and Describe Corruption. *In*: M. Nuijten and G. Anders, eds. *Corruption and the Secret of Law: A Legal Anthropological Perspective*. Farnham: Ashgate, 27–52.

De Sardan, J.-P.O., 1999. A moral economy of corruption in Africa? *The Journal of Modern African Studies*, 37 (01), 25–52.

Ehrlich, E., 1912. Das lebende Recht der Völker der Bukowina. *In*: M. Rehbinder, ed. *Eugen Ehrlich, Recht und Leben*. Berlin: Duncker & Humblot, 43–60.

Geertz, C., 1973. *The Interpretation of Cultures*. New York, NY: Basic Books.

Gibson-Graham, J.K., 2008. Diverse economies: Performative practices for other worlds. *Progress in Human Geography*, 32 (5), 613–632.

Gong, T., and Xiao, H., 2017. Socially embedded anti-corruption governance: Evidence from Hong Kong. *Public Administration and Development*, 37 (3), 176–190.

Gupta, A., 1995. Blurred boundaries: The discourse of corruption, the culture of politics, and the imagined state. *American Ethnologist*, 22 (2), 375–402.

Hasty, J., 2005. The pleasures of corruption: Desire and discipline in Ghanaian political culture. *Cultural Anthropology*, 20 (2), 271–301.

Lazar, S., 2005. Citizens despite the state: Everyday corruption and local politics in El Alto, Bolivia. *In*: D. Haller and C. Shore, eds. *Corruption: Anthropological Perspectives*. London and Ann Arbor, MI: Pluto Press, 212–228.

Lomnitz, C., 1995. Ritual, rumor and corruption in the constitution of polity in modern Mexico. *Journal of Latin American Anthropology*, 1 (1), 20–47.

Nuijten, M., and Anders, G., 2007. *Corruption and the Secret of Law: A Legal Anthropological Perspective*. Farnham: Ashgate.

Pardo, I., 1996. *Managing Existence in Naples: Morality, Action, and Structure*. Cambridge: Cambridge University Press.

Rivkin-Fish, M., 2005. Bribes, gifts and unofficial payments: Rethinking corruption in post-Soviet Russian health care. In: D. Haller and C. Shore, eds. *Corruption: anthropological perspectives*. London and Ann Arbor, MI: Pluto Press, 47–64.

Smart, A., and Hsu, C.L., 2007. Corruption or social capital? Tact and the performance of guanxi in market socialist China. *In*: D. Haller and C. Shore, eds. *Corruption and the secret of law: A legal anthropological perspective*. Farnham: Ashgate, 167–190.

Urinboyev, R., 2020. *Migration and Hybrid Political Regimes: Navigating the Legal Landscape in Russia*. Oakland, CA: University of California Press.

Urinboyev, R., 2023. Islamic legal culture in Uzbekistan. *Legal Pluralism and Critical Social Analysis*, 55 (3), 402–429.

Urinboyev, R., and Polese, A., 2016. Informality currencies: A tale of Misha, his brigada and informal practices among Uzbek labour migrants in Russia. *Journal of Contemporary Central and Eastern Europe*, 24 (3), 191–206.

White, J.B., 1994. *Money Makes Us Relatives: Women's Labor in Urban Turkey*. Austin, TX: University of Texas Press.

Zanca, R., 2003. 'Take! Take! Take!' host-guest relations and all that food: Uzbek hospitality past and present. *Anthropology of East Europe Review*, 21 (1), 8–16.

Chapter 7

The interplay between law, society, and (anti)corruption in authoritarian regimes

Final reflections on law, society, and corruption in Uzbekistan

This book was conceived as a critical reflection on and memoir from our decade of ethnographic fieldwork in Uzbekistan. In this book, we explored the interplay between law, society, and corruption under the conditions of an authoritarian polity, ubiquitous corruption, and a weak rule of law. One recurring pattern we observed is that corruption remains persistent and widespread in the country despite the current political leadership's innumerable institutional and legislative initiatives. This is because post-Karimov anticorruption policies primarily aim to combat mid-level and petty corruption, whilst elite-level corruption and kleptocratic practices remain beyond the reach of the anticorruption agenda. We encountered numerous low-level state officials (traffic police officers, tax officials, and prosecutor's office employees) and social sector workers (in kindergartens, schools, and hospitals) seemingly nostalgic for the Karimov era. That nostalgia was explained by the tacit acceptance of petty corruption and informal practices by the Karimov regime, practices which provided many low-level officials and social sector employees with the opportunity to generate additional income. In some ways, this created an informal wealth distribution system enticing many low-paid state officials and social sector workers to work in the public sector despite their low salaries. As one of our informants explained:

> The rules of the game under the Karimov government were clear: the system was repressive and did not allow any critical voice. But there was some sort of informal contract under which both high-level and low-level officials were allowed to 'eat' (i.e., take bribes) and share the benefits, a system that kept both parties in a relationship of mutual dependence. However, the rules of the game have changed after Karimov: nowadays, a small number of people at the top are 'eating' without facing any legal consequences, whilst an army of low-level officials, with meagre incomes, are the main targets of anticorruption campaigns.

DOI: 10.4324/9780429952968-7

Notwithstanding the above tendencies, it should be noted that corruption has become a buzzword in post-Karimov Uzbekistan, as manifested in numerous legislative initiatives and institutional reconfigurations. In turn, these changes are also reflected in the latest 2023 Corruption Perceptions Index (CPI) released by Transparency International on 31 January 2024, showing that Uzbekistan has improved its position on the CPI since 2019.[1] Unlike late-President Islam Karimov's government, which suppressed any forms of critique and dissent, many people we encountered in urban and rural areas of the country openly talked about corruption and government inefficiencies. This was largely due to the post-Karimov opening and the rapid proliferation of social media, which fostered critical thinking and new ways of thinking within Uzbek society. Whilst observing and analysing Uzbekistan's current anticorruption environment, it is thus possible to observe two parallel and contradictory tendencies. On the one hand, the people we encountered welcomed the post-Karimov loosening that resulted in a certain degree of free speech and openness in the country. The emergence of a public debate condemning corruption and government inefficiencies on social media platforms and in daily life serve as clear examples of these positive changes. On the other hand, elite-level corruption and kleptocratic practices remain taboo topics in public discussions. Despite the government's official reform proclamations, little progress has been made in establishing equality for all before the law. High-level state officials and *hokims* (governors) continue to stand outside and above the law, an outcome largely resulting from the lack of independence in the Anticorruption Agency and the General Prosecutor's Office. Ordinary people are critical of high-level corruption but understand this is a red line that cannot be crossed. These post-Karimov societal expectations and sentiments were reflected in various anecdotes, biographical trajectories, statements, and rumours, which we collected during our informal conversations with various interlocutors in urban and rural areas of Uzbekistan. Here, we present some of the most provocative statements we recorded during our fieldwork, representing the views and positions of various social groups and actors in Uzbekistan:

> *According to the international corruption rankings, we are the second most corrupt country in the world. Which country is first? I don't know, but I am sure we paid a bribe not to be in first place.*
>
> *The cycle of bribery in Uzbek culture commences at the very beginning of life, symbolised by the tradition of offering suyunchi to a midwife during childbirth [as detailed in Chapter 5]. This practice persists throughout one's lifetime, culminating in the act of providing a bribe to a gravedigger in exchange for a more favourable burial site upon death.*

1 https://www.transparency.org/en/cpi/2022/index/uzb

> *It is impossible to eradicate the corruption in our society without taking radical measures. All corrupt officials should not only be arrested, but also shamed in front of the public. Why is it necessary to have mercy on such people? They are parasites sucking society's blood.*
>
> *If everyone is religious and pious, corruption will stop by itself. Therefore, the government is doing everything possible to reduce the influence of Islam on society and the public administration. Only Islam can help us combat corruption.*
>
> *There are two types of state officials in Uzbekistan: those who have been caught taking bribes and those who have not yet been caught taking bribes.*
>
> *The state sometimes catches corrupt state officials to show ordinary people that there is justice. If the state does not do it, the people will conclude that there is no justice and that state officials can do whatever they want. This is a demonstration intended to cheat people. Or they catch corrupt officials if someone needs their place. In such cases, they stage a corruption raid, creating a vacant position after arresting them. In other cases, employees of the State Security Service or Prosecutor's Office intentionally use anticorruption campaigns and catch corrupt officials to show that they are working, leading to a promotion in their career and rank. In short, anticorruption campaigns are used to cheat ordinary people.*
>
> *The establishment of an Anticorruption Agency is like giving a lamb to a wolf. This institution is not independent and fully subordinate to the President. Copy-pasting Western models does not solve the problem.*

These anecdotes and statements illustrate the existence of a plethora of normative, moral, cultural, and affective repertoires in Uzbekistan's legal landscape that coexist and/or vie for determining the basic parameters of people's social behaviours. They also reveal people's attitudes to and beliefs about the role and legitimacy of the state and its legal system and institutions. As we have shown in the preceding empirical chapters, Uzbekistan's political and legal authorities have little or no legitimacy in the eyes of ordinary people, particularly given their incapacity to valorise anticorruption laws and policies. Many people we encountered expressed concerns about the ever-growing gap between the government's reformist intentions and rhetoric and the everyday realities, resulting in the evaporation of people's belief in the genuineness of reforms. These developments, therefore, carried a pernicious effect on state–society relations, leading to citizens' widespread noncompliance with the state's laws and policies. As a result, in contemporary Uzbekistan, the state and its legal system operate in a condition of normative pluralism, competing or co-existing with informal legal orders (e.g., social norms, customs, etiquette, traditions, religion, personal morality, etc.). This leads us to suggest that the prevalence and persistence of corruption in authoritarian and weak rule of law contexts such as Uzbekistan should be examined not only by focusing on the question of why people obey or break state law but also by exploring why people are more inclined to follow non-state, informal forms of normative ordering.

Complexity of understanding (anti)corruption in authoritarian regimes

The vignette presented in the section above brings us back to the opening argument in the first chapter of this book, where we argued for developing a new conceptual framework for studying, understanding, and combating corruption in authoritarian polities. In undertaking this task, we constructed a hybrid compliance model building upon several theoretical perspectives in the field of socio-legal studies—namely, socio-legal perspectives on legal compliance, the concept of 'living law', the legal pluralism perspective, and the concept of legal consciousness. Armed with these socio-legal frameworks, we suggest that when exploring the question of why people obey or break the law (i.e., when people engage in corrupt and illegal practices), we should not only focus on state law and legal institutions as the main determinant of social behaviour. Instead, we need to reckon with plural, non-state, informal forms of normative ordering shaping people's attitudes towards the law and social behaviours as much as, or possibly more than, state law. In arguing thusly, we called for the necessity of moving beyond the established legal centralistic and economistic-based paradigms (i.e., the principal–agent model) and, thereby, focus on informal forms of normative ordering, everyday power relations, conflicts, contradictions, social sanctions, and norms constituting the basic social fabric ('living law') of a society. These points are especially valid in studying (anti)corruption in authoritarian regimes where political and legal authorities lack legitimacy and social acceptance.

Accordingly, this book represents our response and attempt to move beyond the established frameworks through the use of socio-legal theories, which allowed us to position legal compliance/legal behaviour in a normatively pluralistic context—reading, seeing, and understanding (anti)corruption through the experiences of law enforcement actors, civil society activists, mid- and low-level state officials, local government officials, community leaders, religious actors, and ordinary citizens. When examining these experiences from multilevel and socio-legal perspectives (i.e., focusing on macro-, meso-, and micro-level arenas), it becomes clear that a myriad of structural variables, power positions, and contextual and situational factors shape the 'corruption experiences' of state officials and ordinary citizens. This in-depth socio-legal inquiry into the multilevel orders of corruption reveals that the meanings, logics, and moralities of corruption can take many distinct forms on different levels of society. Furthermore, we find that we cannot merely rely on 'black and white' perspectives that possibly neglect intricacies, everyday dynamics, and the alternative orders informing the meaning of corruption and informal practices in non-Western settings.

Many of these processes have been discussed in detail in this book by analysing Uzbekistan's legal and institutional transformations since 1991, alongside the use of personal stories and experiences from state officials and ordinary citizens as empirical illustrations. In Chapter 2, we described how Uzbekistan transitioned from a tightly closed and repressive governance towards a softer form of authoritarianism, a governance pattern resembling a hybrid political regime. Islam Karimov, who ruled the country between 1991 and 2016, did not allow any form of public criticism of corruption and government inefficiencies and was reluctant to implement the advice and recommendations from international organisations. In his speeches, Karimov often stated that international organisations cannot teach Uzbekistan how to organise its system of governance and that the country can independently decide how to shape its own future (Karimov 1993, 1999). Unlike his predecessor, Shavkat Mirziyoyev opened up the previously closed and inaccessible country to the outside world and initiated a dialogue with many international organisations. As a result, Uzbekistan's new leadership adopted numerous laws, policies, state programmes, strategies, and initiatives, as we showed in Chapter 3. However, the analysis of Uzbekistan's post-Karimov governance trajectories demonstrates that the implementation of these laws and policies has been chaotic and selective. These shortcomings were clearly illustrated in Chapter 4, where we discussed how loopholes and ambiguities in the laws and arbitrary and selective enforcement of anticorruption laws led to the proliferation of high-level corruption and kleptocratic practices within the upper echelons of power. In Chapter 5, we focused on the meanings and logics of corruption in meso-level arenas, where we presented our field observations and case studies focusing on the 'corruption experiences' of mid- and low-level state officials. Based on the analysis of personal stories and experiences of state officials in meso-level arenas, we argued for the necessity of distinguishing between the predatory practices of kleptocratic elites and high-level state officials and the daily coping strategies of low-level state officials. In this chapter, we suggest that the 'one-size-fits-all' approach, which neglects the local needs, morality, and conditions, is too simplistic and that people engage in informal and extra-legal practices not just for personal enrichment, but also due to the conditions and circumstances resulting from their urge to secure their basic needs or to get things done. In this sense, corruption is not only driven by personal venality and greed but also by circumstances and situations, making it a 'last resort' (McMann 2015) under an opaque political and legal environment. In Chapter 6, we focused on the social life of corruption in micro-level arenas, examining the interconnections between informal and extra-legal practices ('corruption' from a legal standpoint) and society's basic social fabric, visualised in informal norms and non-monetary currencies (respect, prestige, reputation, and honour). In Uzbekistan, like many other non-Western societies (e.g., De Sardan 1999, Lazar 2005, Polese 2008, Blundo and De Sardan 2013), social norms play a more salient role than state law in moulding people's social behaviours in private domains, community life, and state/professional arenas. On the one hand, social norms and non-monetary currencies create social cohesion and play a functional role in Uzbek society. On the other hand, when these norms migrate to state institutions and are thus applied in the professional sphere, they may lead to the proliferation of nepotism, cronyism, and conflicts of interest in the public administration system. For example, the social norm 'do what elders say, respect and don't challenge them' carries pernicious effects when applied within the public administration system. What are the consequences of this? In state institutions, the head or manager of an organisation is characterised as an 'elder', and employees are obliged to carry out any tasks assigned by their line manager, even if they are against the law. In this case, we can see how the social norm may lead to adverse outcomes in professional activities. Thus, micro-level norms shape the nitty-gritty of everyday life and social relations. Whilst the political and legal authorities may look omnipotent due to the widespread presence of law enforcement structures in the country, everyday law and order-making is decentralised, and micro-level normative orders determine the final outcomes of centrally adopted laws and policies.

Implications for a global anticorruption agenda

Based on our decade of ethnographic fieldwork in Uzbekistan, in this book we put forward the following propositions, which we hope will contribute to scholarly and policy debates on (anti)corruption.

First, anticorruption reforms should simultaneously focus on different levels of governance, covering macro-, meso-, and micro-level processes, institutions, actors, and practices. It is insufficient to combat petty corruption. Instead, the focus should also be placed on high-level corruption and kleptocratic networks typically linked to the upper echelons of government.

Second, informal and illegal transactions and practices (or 'corruption' from a legal centralistic perspective) may be deemed legitimate practices in social contexts where the state fails to secure the basic needs of its citizens. In such contexts, informal and illegal practices and arrangements often make up for the incapacity of the state (cf. Torsello and Venard 2016). Therefore, before attacking informal and illegal practices embedded in livelihood strategies, there is a need to introduce alternative structures that provide viable means for securing livelihood needs.

Third, anticorruption laws and policies require a broader societal trust and legitimacy. Any change to political leadership and the accompanying anticorruption reform agenda must be followed by concrete actions. The state must demonstrate a credible commitment to the general public, in so far as anticorruption is not simply cheap talk, but a genuine and honest effort. This implies that anticorruption should not just focus on capturing and imprisoning low-level corrupt officials, but must also focus on combating high-level corruption, a step crucial to shifting popular perceptions regarding the image and legitimacy of the state (as prescribed by the normative perspective on legal compliance (Tyler 2006)). Everyday discussions, narratives, and discourses on corruption are key lenses via which the role and legitimacy of the state are imagined, reconstructed, and enacted (Gupta 1995). This leads us to argue that anticorruption efforts need to focus not only on introducing harsh penalties and/or economic incentives so that state officials are not tempted to 'use their office for private gain'. But also such efforts need to focus on altering the popular perceptions and corruption narratives through which the state and its role and legitimacy are imagined, shaped, and negotiated.

Fourth, anticorruption efforts should also focus on reducing the gap between legal norms and informal, unwritten rules and practices. This implies that it is insufficient to adopt anticorruption laws and harsh penalties, but there is also a need to increase the law's expressive power (McAdams 2015) and legitimacy in society (Tyler 2006). That is, the law's role lies in coordinating social behaviours through the provision of clear rules and sending a message to society about proper social behaviours. The state is rarely the only actor in society and faces enormous resistance from other (informal) social forces and associations in implementing its policies and laws. These associations interact and struggle with one another over material and non-material issues, attempting to impose their own norms and symbols on everyday social relations. To serve as a focal point for behaviour, state law should be aligned with people's morality and legitimate in the eyes of ordinary people.

Fifth, connected to the above, there is a need to design socially embedded anticorruption laws and policies, reckoning with both formal and informal norms shaping people's social behaviours. This implies that anticorruption reform is not simply related to introducing new laws, economic incentives, or harsh penalties, but is a broader social engineering project where efforts to study, diagnose, and combat corruption should focus, simultaneously, on the following three arenas of compliance: deterrence—that is, the use of penalties or sanctions to enforce compliance with rules and norms (Gibbs 1975, Levitt and Miles 2008, Paternoster 2010); legitimacy—that is, the belief in the existence of a fair and impartial order (authority) rendering people more prone to obey the law (Tyler 2006); and coordination and communication—that is, coordinating social behaviour through the provision of clear rules and sending a strong message to society regarding proper social behaviour (McAdams 2015). This task, in turn, entails focusing on moulding people's legal culture/consciousness (Ewick and Silbey 1998, Hertogh 2018) and aligning anticorruption laws and efforts with society's basic social fabric and non-monetary currencies, i.e. the living law of everyday life (Ehrlich 1912).

These five propositions bring us back to the opening question we posed in this book: do mainstream frameworks in the field of (anti)corruption (e.g., the 'principal–agent model' or the 'collective action approach) help us understand the multifarious meanings, logics, and moralities of informal and extra-legal transactions and practices in authoritarian regime contexts? Our short and clear-cut answer to this question is that the everyday experiences of corruption are multidimensional and multilevel, shaped by a complex chain of interactions amongst structural variables, power geometries, contextual and situational factors, and affective norms and repertoires. Thus, corruption should not be understood merely in terms of the legal culture, ways of thinking, and circumstances typical for Western societies. We hope that this book is read as an attempt to broaden the scope of (anti)corruption research, which is still largely confined to 'one-Western-size-fits-all' approaches. Whilst the fieldwork observations and experiences in this book originate in Uzbekistan, we argue that our insights from a decade of fieldwork in Uzbekistan are potentially useful when analysing (anti)corruption in other socio-legal contexts also characterised by an authoritarian polity, dysfunctional institutions, and a weak rule of law. That said, our ambition lies in inspiring further research on (anti)corruption in authoritarian regimes, which will hopefully generate new empirical data and theoretical perspectives.

References

Blundo, G., and De Sardan, J.-P.O., 2013. *Everyday Corruption and the State: Citizens and Public Officials in Africa*. London: Zed Books.

De Sardan, J.-P.O., 1999. A moral economy of corruption in Africa? *Journal of Modern African Studies*, 37 (1), 25–52.

Ehrlich, E., 1912. Das lebende Recht der Völker der Bukowina. *In*: M. Rehbinder, ed. *Eugen Ehrlich, Recht und Leben*. Berlin: Duncker & Humblot, 43–60.

Ewick, P., and Silbey, S.S., 1998. *The Common Place of Law: Stories from Everyday Life*. London: University of Chicago Press.

Gibbs, J.P., 1975. *Crime, Punishment, and Deterrence*. New York, NY: Elsevier.

Gupta, A., 1995. Blurred boundaries: The discourse of corruption, the culture of politics, and the imagined state. *American Ethnologist*, 22 (2), 375–402.

Hertogh, M., 2018. *Nobody's Law: Legal Consciousness and Legal Alienation in Everyday Life*. London: Palgrave Macmillan UK.

Karimov, I., 1993. *Building the Future: Uzbekistan - Its Own Model for Transition to a Market Economy*. Tashkent: Uzbekiston.

Karimov, I., 1999. *Biz kelajagimizni o'z qo'limiz bilan quramiz (We are constructing our future with our own hands)*. Tashkent: O'zbekiston.

Lazar, S., 2005. Citizens Despite the State: Everyday Corruption and Local Politics in El Alto, Bolivia. *In*: D. Haller and C. Shore, eds. *Corruption: Anthropological Perspectives*. London and Ann Arbor, MI: Pluto Press, 212–228.

Levitt, S., and Miles, T.J., 2008. Economic Analyses of Deterrence: Empirical. *In*: S. Durlauf and L. Blume, eds. *The New Palgrave Dictionary of Economics*. Cham: Palgrave MacMillan.

McAdams, R.H., 2015. *The Expressive Powers of Law*. Cambridge, MA: Harvard University Press.

McMann, K.M., 2015. *Corruption as a Last Resort: Adapting to the Market in Central Asia*. Ithaca, NY: Cornell University Press.

Paternoster, R., 2010. How much do we really know about criminal deterrence? *The Journal of Criminal Law and Criminology*, 100 (3), 765–824.

Polese, A., 2008. 'If I receive it, it is a gift; if I demand it, then it is a bribe': On the local meaning of economic transactions in Post-Soviet Ukraine. *Anthropology in Action*, 15 (3), 47–60.

Torsello, D., and Venard, B., 2016. The anthropology of corruption. *Journal of management inquiry*, 25 (1), 34–54.

Tyler, T.R., 2006. *Why People Obey the Law*. Princeton, NJ: Princeton University Press.

Index

3G licencing 45

Administrative Liability Code 57, 61–62
Africa 7–8, 10
agriculture: agricultural reforms 43–44; agricultural production 4, 41–42; minister for agriculture and water management 80, 114
Akfa enterprises 74
alternative orders 6, 122
anthropology 11–12, 14, 23; *see also* legal anthropology
anticorruption: agenda 49, 118, 123–125; assessment of 57, 64; in authoritarian regimes 6–7, 11, 15–24, 50, 61–63, 83–84, 92, 121–123, 125; development anticorruption of legislation 58–61, 63–66, 71; educational initiatives on 58, 66; forums 66; frameworks 6, 8–10, 13–16, 24, 65–67, 121, 124–125; global movement of 7–8, 13, 15–16, 25; (international) ratings 65, 69; interventions 15, 19–20, 105; and legislation 28, 56–61, 63–66, 71, 113; legislative boom 68, 71, 82; measures 27, 47, 56, 59–60, 65–66, 69, 71, 101–102, 110; Mirziyoyev reforms 50, 63–66, 71; monument 47; political economy of reforms 39; programmes 9, 28, 50, 55–56, 58–61, 65–66; public awareness on 60, 65–66; reform agenda 46, 48, 51, 63–68, 123–125; rhetoric of 2–3, 50–51, 120; specialised institutions 58, 61–64, 67, 71; training for civil servants 58, 66; yearly programmes 58; *see also* anti-corruption
Anticorruption Agency of Uzbekistan 58–59, 64–66, 68, 79, 110, 119–120; goals and objectives of 59–60
Anticorruption Commission 58, 58n6; *see also* Republican Interagency Commission on Combatting Corruption
Anticorruption Law of 2017 3, 50, 56, 59, 64, 78, 101, 109, 113; selective enforcement of 68, 83; *see also* 'On Combating Corruption'
Anti-Corruption Network for Eastern Europe and Central Asia (ACN) 56, 68
Anticorruption Weeks 66
artificial intelligence (AI) 58
Asia 7
authoritarian 4, 6, 15, 43, 83–84, 90, 116; contexts 9, 15–16, 19–21, 24, 92, 101–102, 120–122; global authoritarianism 15; modernisation 45–51, 60–61, 67; and political stability 40–41, 43, 46, 90; softer form of authoritarianism 27, 39, 48, 67; (tightly closed) regimes 1, 6–7, 9, 11, 16, 62, 67, 125
autocratic 15; *see also* autocratisation
autocratisation 15

bardak sistema (messy/disordered system) 2
'Beshkapa' (village of) 4–5
'black-and-white' perspective 6–7, 21, 27, 85, 121

black market foreign currency exchange 2, 89
bloggers 49–50
bombila (informal taxi drivers) 89–90
bottom–up: logic of ethnography 28; perspective 105
bribe(s) 3, 8, 14, 26, 62, 76, 92–93, 96, 108, 110, 112, 115, 118–120; and criminal liability 17, 61–62; and foreign officials 44–45, 61–62; *see also* bribery
budget 5, 41, 50, 60, 74, 99–100; state 5, 76, 79; *see also* public spending
businessmen 72, 99, 107; local and prosecutors 76–77

Cabinet of Ministers 56, 57, 67–68, 73, 78, 82; Resolution 'On Additional Measures to Ensure Compliance with the Rules of Conduct by Public Civil Servants' 57, 78
case studies 28, 87, 92–116; of Ahmedov 114–116; of Bakhtiyor 114–115; of Dilshod 93–95; of Nodirbek 114–115; of Rahmon 111–113; of Sardor 111–114; of Tursunboy 108–109; *see also* key informants
Central Asia 16, 39–41, 44, 56, 105; *see also* Central Asian states
centralised management (and government) 43, 87
central-level political institutions and business elites 3, 16, 25, 28, 71–72, 98
Chamber of Commerce & Industry of Uzbekistan 63
cheating 70, 120
childbirth 119–120
choykhona (teahouse) 105–106, 111
choyxona (teahouse) 4, 25, 105–106, 111; *see also choykhona*
Civil Code 57, 61, 81
civil servants 6, 61–62, 64, 66–68, 73–74, 78, 83; and (draft) decrees on 57, 67, 72, 75; and knowledge of legal changes 58, 82
civil society (organisations) 8, 9, 14, 27, 58–59, 65, 66, 121
clientelist practices 40
Code of Criminal Procedure 57, 61, 79
coercion 19, 20, 22, 44
collective action approach 7, 10, 24, 125; and framework on corruption 6
'On Combating Corruption' Law 3, 56, 58, 63, 68, 79
Committee for Roads 5
Committee on Judicial Legal Issues and Anticorruption of the Council of the *Oliy Majlis* 58–59
communist 112–114
community-based mutual aid practices 25, 107–108, 112
conceptual framework 10, 14, 29, 121
'On Conflicts of Interest' 57, 68, 75, 79
conflict of interest(s) 57, 68, 72, 74–75, 77–81; definition of 63, 78
constitution: amendments to 47, 56–57, 75; constitutional system 40, 98; of Uzbekistan 61, 101
coping strategies: daily 26, 92, 122; informal 29, 42, 43, 87, 97, 102, 104; among low-level officials 29, 67, 87, 97; in the Karimov-era 43; as survival 42, 87
corruption: as an adaptive strategy 98; anthropological studies of 11–12; and the business environment 75–77; as a cancer 8, 13, 115–116; charges of 45, 47, 49–50; and cheating 70; consequences of 14–15, 19, 49–50, 118, 123; and corrupt officials 50, 81, 120, 124; and crime 8, 14, 17, 59–60, 79, 98–100; culture of 14, 110; daily interactions 43, 87, 105–106; definition of 5–6, 9, 12–13, 15, 26, 63, 92, 101, 110; experiences 27–29, 67, 87, 92–93, 104, 108, 110, 121–122, 125; and formal institutions 6, 43; good *vs.* bad 108, 110; among high-level officials 73–77; indicators of 3, 25, 39, 43; international ratings and standards of 43, 47–48, 50, 57, 71; investigation of 24, 49–50, 60, 75–77, 79–81; legal production of 98–101; as legitimate practice 13, 76, 94–95, 110, 123–124; and local needs 6, 102, 109; and loopholes 58, 77–78, 84, 122; meanings and logics of 87, 92–95, 104, 111, 121–122, 125; monitoring of 3, 43, 56–58; new forms of 98–101; as a norm 102, 104, 109–110, 113, 116, 121–125; paradox of 41–43, 48, 85; penalty for 3, 9, 16, 41, 43, 50, 71, 124;

prevention (measures) 58–60, 63–66, 68, 71–72, 78; public perception of 48, 94, 124; raids 47, 50, 62; as a reflection of informal rules 4–6, 26, 70–71, 89–90; research on 4, 13–15, 20–21, 25, 43, 59–60, 72; risks and risk assessment 64–65; as ritual practices 25–26, 92; scandals 44–45, 47–48, 110; as standard operating procedure 10–11; among state and society levels 45, 47–50, 71–72, 79–80, 87, 89, 97, 112–115, 119, 122; survey on corruption experiences 3, 62–63; as survival strategy 13, 29, 41–42, 87–89, 95, 110, 115–116; systemic 1–2, 9–11, 16, 50, 110
Corruption Perceptions Index (CPI) 71, 119
Criminal Code 57, 61–63, 109
criminal liability 61–62, 79
critical reflection 13, 15, 118–119
cronyism 77–78, 123
culture 12–15, 39, 51, 60, 88; of corruption 14, 110; of informality 72, 81–84
currency: convertible 2; exchange 2, 89; non-monetary 13, 26, 104, 106, 115–116, 122–124
customs 20–22, 81, 120; *see also* religious norms

daily interactions 43, 105–106
data collection 1, 25–27, 72
'On the Declaration of the Incomes and Property of Civil Servants' 57, 67–68, 73, 75
decrees 56–57; draft 'On Conflicts of Interest' 57, 68, 75, 79; draft 'On the Declaration of the Income and Property of Civil Servants' 57, 67–68, 73, 75
'decriminalising' illegal practices 89
dehqonlar (farmers) 112
Democracy Index 43
democracy/-ies 11, 14, 39–40; democratisation 9, 39–40; scepticism of 40
Department on Combating Economic Crimes 59
deterrence-based strategy 16–18, 124
development strategy of Uzbekistan 51, 58
disordered system 2; *see also* bardak sistema
dissent 10, 19, 119; *see also* free speech
Doing Business Index 3
dolya (entrance fee/share) 44, 89

Eastern Europe 7, 39, 56
economistic-based approaches 8, 12, 16, 24, 87, 102, 121; or economic-based approaches/perspectives 14, 24, 92, 104–105, 116
economy 8, 11, 14, 21, 23–24, 29, 39–40, 43–44, 46, 48, 60, 63, 79, 95, 99–101, 105–108; central economic planning 41, 47; growth of 7, 42, 48, 51, 67; informal 2, 41, 89–90; liberalising of the 46–48, 61, 115–116; shadow 89; Uzbek 41–42, 44, 79, 112, 115–116, 124
e-governance initiative 2
Ehrlich, Eugen 22–24, 91, 109, 124
elite-level officials: corruption and kleptocracy 28–29, 43–45, 50–51, 68, 72–73, 75, 79–81, 89, 94–95, 97, 110–113, 115, 118–119, 122–124; *see also* high-level officials
empirical data 1, 3, 15, 25, 27, 28, 55, 72, 82, 85, 101, 125
entrepreneurs 4, 26, 57, 63, 73, 99; attempting to work legally 76–77; in big business 75–76; medium-level business 76
'equality of all before the law' 83–84
ethical business 14, 46
ethnography 1, 27–28; ethnographic case studies111–115; fieldwork 4, 24–27, 88–89, 105, 118, 123; material 28, 39, 67; toolkit 24–25
exchange rates 2, 89, 91
expenditures (public) 8
exports 4, 42
expressive perspective 16, 18–19
extortion 49
extra-legal (and informal practices) 3–6, 28, 44, 92–102, 104–105, 122, 125

female leaders 26
Ferghana region/valley 4, 24–26, 29, 83, 88, 90, 93, 95, 105, 110, 112; *see also* Ferghana
'focal points': for behaviour 92; multiple moralities 104

Foreign Corrupt Practices Act (FCPA) 45
foreign investor(s) 2, 8, 44, 46–48, 100
Fozilov, Bakhtiyor (oligarch) 49
free speech 14, 19, 46, 119; press freedom 49–50
Freedom House 1, 43

Ganiev, Shukhrat 83–84
gap (monthly get-togethers) 25–26
Gazeta.uz 48, 74, 79–80
Geertz, Clifford 25, 67, 111
General Prosecutor's Office (GPO) 5, 58–59, 63, 66, 72, 76, 98–100, 119–120
'getting things done' philosophy 89, 95, 97; how things get done 92, 102; *ish bitirgmoq* 110
gift exchange 26, 76, 102, 107
golden middle (*zolotaya serdina*) 2
gossip 12, 26, 104, 106–107, 113
governance 1–4, 27–28, 42–45, 57, 60–61, 67, 77–84, 87, 98–101, 122–123; trajectories 46–51
government: local-level 5, 27–28, 47, 55, 65, 82, 99–100, 107, 109, 112, 115, 121; regional 114; *see also hokimiyats*
gradualist approach: to transition 40–41
gross domestic product (GDP) 41, 51
gruz (burden) 93
*guzar (*village meeting place) 4, 25, 105–106, 111–113

halol (lawful) 109–110, 114; *halol odam* (honest man) 114; *halol/harom* binary 110
halq qabulhonalari (people's reception houses) 2, 46
harom (unlawful) 109, 110
harombo'rlik (predatory practices) 108, 110
Haydarov, Olimjon 49
health care 67, 95–98, 101, 107
'hidden' transactions 74, 89
hierarchies 26, 91–92, 107, 116
high-level officials 15, 28–29, 43–51, 72–73, 111–115, 118–119, 122–124
hokimiyat 5, 99, 114; *see also* Mirziyoyev, Shavkat, local governments
hokims (governors) 83, 99, 119
honest principal 8–10, 15
honour 26, 106, 122
hotspots (social) 4, 25–26, 89
human rights 40, 46, 100
hybrid compliance framework (or model) 16, 21–24, 29, 121
hybrid political regime 27, 48, 67, 122

*Ijtimoiy Fikr (*Public Opinion) 3, 62–63
Ikramov, Sanzhar 49–50
illegal practices 12–14, 83–84, 89, 100, 121, 123; and political and economic practices 18, 27, 39, 83–84, 89, 104, 115–116
incapacity of the state 101, 123
income-generating activities 105
inequality (economic and social) 8, 48, 51
informal alliances 98–101
informal coping strategies 29, 42, 43, 87, 97, 102, 104
informal economy 41, 89–91
informal income-earning opportunities 47, 76, 79, 89–90, 118
informal interviews 25, 28
informal legal orders 13, 20–23, 90, 101, 120
informal norms: alternative modality 23; and moral codes 13, 23, 26, 83, 104–105, 109, 122, 124; and nonlegal practices 22, 82; and social associations 2, 13, 21–24, 104–105; and village life 101–102, 106
informal payments 95–98
informal practices: acceptance of 2, 19, 95,118; culture of informality 72, 81–84; and extra-legal practices 5, 7, 94–95; and nonlegal practices 6, 121–122; and non-monetary currencies 104–106, 115, 116; political and economic practices 67, 72; as social norms 14–16, 25, 27, 67, 97; and transactions 1; *see also* illegal practices
informal rules 4, 6, 10–11, 26, 71, 89–90, 102
informal welfare infrastructure (or system) 42–43, 100–101, 107, 109
informant 2, 14, 25–28, 50, 72, 109, 111, 118; *see also* key informant(s)
infrastructure projects 5, 80–81
institution 2, 3–7, 9, 16, 19–20, 28, 116, 119–120, 125; central 3–5, 11, 14, 16, 25–26, 28, 42, 45–46, 51, 58,

62, 65–66, 71–73, 77–78, 108, 123; lower-level 3, 5, 59–60, 90, 108
institutional: context 6, 11, 39–40, 55, 71, 119; framework 9, 58, 61, 63
instrumental perspective 16–18, 71
interdisciplinary communication 13–15
Internal Affairs (Ministry of) 58n6, 59, 68, 72, 98, 100
International Anticorruption Day 66
International Anticorruption Excellence Award 47
international conference 3–4, 6
international corruption ranking 3, 119
international organisation(s) 4, 8, 11, 15, 21, 122
interviews: informal 25, 28; (key) informants 25, 28, 72; semi-structured 25
investment: foreign 46, 48, 100
Islam (in society) 120
Istanbul Anti-Corruption Action Plan 56, 63

judge(s) 12, 44, 66, 99, 110, 115
juristic law and statutes 22
justice 17–18, 120

Kamchik 90–91
Kandiyoti, D. 41–43
Karimov, Islam 1–4, 39–51, 54, 55, 60–64, 71, 82, 89–90, 93, 95, 98–99, 118–119, 122; post-Karimov era 2–3, 45–51, 55, 60, 63–66, 71, 82, 93, 98–99, 118–119, 122
Karimova, Gulnara: and corruption schemes 44–45, 97, 110
karnay (traditional Uzbek musical instrument) 88; *see also surnay*
kengash (local administrative body) 46
key informant(s) 28, 72; Abdulla 98 101; Akmal 5–6; Azim 4–5; Dilshod 92–95; interviews with 25, 28, 72, 84, 93, 95; Odil, Ozod, Salima, and Shuhrat 70; Umida 95–98
kinship 13, 29, 42, 78, 105, 111–116; obligations 12, 104
Kleptocrat 1, 13, 51, 104, 116; kleptocratic elite/high-level officials 6, 15, 19, 29, 43, 87, 94, 95, 97, 108, 111, 122; kleptocratic network 43, 44, 74, 123; kleptocratic practices 40, 43, 49–51, 68, 95, 97, 110, 118–119, 122; *see also* kleptocracy
Klitgaard, R. 8–9, 71
komanda (teams/groups) 77
kompromat (compromising material) 84
kryshovanye (protection): 'patronage/roofing' 72, 76, 99
Kyrgyzstan 11, 46; ethnic conflict 40

labour: forced 47; informal 82; law 62; relations 62; rights of 73; Uzbek labour migrants 42
Labour Code 62, 78
Lasslett, K. 44–45, 48–49, 95, 97–98
Latin America 7–8
law in action 7, 16, 22–24, 28, 55, 68, 72, 75, 82, 89–92, 97, 102, 104–105, 109–110, 113, 116, 121, 124; 'social contract' 42, 47, 90; *see also* 'living law'
law in books 55, 75, 82, 90; *see also* 'law on paper'
'law on paper' 82, 90
law(s): law-abiding behaviour 94, 112–114; arbitrary enforcement 6, 83, 122; bylaws 55–57, 61, 62, 64–65, 82–83, 98; law enforcement bodies and officials 4, 8, 9, 21, 25, 27, 29, 40, 43–44, 47, 55, 58, 62, 64, 67–68, 70, 79, 87, 90, 92–95, 98–101, 121, 123; and regulations 20, 25, 55–57, 61, 68, 73; and society 70–85
legal anthropology 11–12, 14–15, 23
legal architecture 57–58
legal centralistic perspective (and approaches) 8, 14–15, 24, 87, 92, 102, 104–105, 121, 123
legal compliance, perspectives on 7, 14, 16–22, 24, 71, 92–95, 121, 124
legal consciousness/culture 6–7, 15–16, 23–24, 59–60, 63, 94, 121, 124–125; and the business environment 39, 44–51
legal framework by decrees (*qonun osti hujjatlari*) 61–64, 82
legal norms 13, 17–18, 23–24, 59–60, 72, 75, 81–84, 109, 121, 124; and unwritten rules and practices 84, 91, 92, 101–102, 104–105
legal sanctions 17–19, 43, 68, 71, 124
legal statutes: Labour Code 62, 78; 'On Combating Corruption' 56, 58, 63, 68, 79; 'On Courts' 72; 'On Internal Affairs Bodies' 72; 'On the Prosecutor's Office' 72, 98–100

legal system 4, 22, 28, 39, 81–82, 84, 87; attitudes and beliefs regarding 19, 22, 24, 71, 120
legislation on anticorruption 28, 56–61, 63–66, 71, 113
legitimacy (of the law): of political and legal authorities 17–19, 22, 46, 49, 107, 120, 124; and social acceptance 17, 24, 40, 42, 50–51, 71, 120–121, 123–124
liberal–democratic context 15
liberalisation (political and economic) 47–51, 61, 67; ultra-liberalisation 89
life-cycle events 25, 28–29, 105–107, 111, 113, 114
livelihood needs 42, 51, 72; strategies and corruption 89, 108, 123
living law 7, 16, 22, 24, 28, 71, 72, 91, 102, 110, 124; 'how the law works' 28, 72, 75, 105; informal rules 89, 102; inner orders 109; and practices 23, 71, 89, 97; 'rules of the game' 70, 118; as a social perspective of norms 23, 92, 104, 110, 113, 116, 121; *see also* law in action
lobbying 76
local-level interactions 2, 21, 43, 70, 87, 102, 105–108, 125
logics of (or to) corruption 87, 92, 95, 101, 104–105, 111, 121–122, 125
loopholes 58, 77, 84, 122; *see also* legal loopholes
low-level officials 26, 29, 81, 87, 92–95, 97, 111, 118
loyalty 19, 44, 51, 83, 107n1, 113; *see also* sadoqat

macro-level and the law 14, 87; developments 28, 70–85; social arenas 70
mahalla (local community) 3, 5–6, 25–26, 29, 42, 88–89, 105–108, 111–114
mahalliychilik (localism) 77–78
'making-ends-meet' strategy 95, 97
Marxist–Leninist ideology 39
masjid (mosque) 105
mass media 43, 47, 59, 73
maternity hospital (district-level) 87, 92, 95–98
McAdams, R. H. 18, 124
memoir 118
meritocracy 51
meso-level: corruption practices 29, 92–93, 122; social arenas 87, 98–102, 104
micro-level: normative order 104–105, 107, 123; social arenas 5–6, 15–16, 27–29, 42, 85, 104–116, 121–122
migrant labourers 42, 107
ministries: Ministry of Agriculture 114; Ministry of Finance 61, 68; Ministry of Internal Affairs 58n6, 59, 68, 100; Ministry of Justice 58n6, 59, 61, 64, 68, 82; Ministry of the Interior 49–50, 61
Mirziyoyev, Shavkat: anticorruption measures 47, 50, 58, 63, 71; and dialog with international community 47; and local governments 46, 100; opening up of Uzbekistan 47, 122; as President 1–2, 46–51, 61; as Prime Minister 46; and reforms 2, 46–51, 82
modernise/-ation 2, 40, 45, 48–51, 55, 60, 67
Mominov, Abduqodir 49
moral code 11, 12, 26; and legal culture 13, 17, 21, 23, 94, 102, 105; multiple moralities 23, 97
moral obligations 12, 17, 23, 26, 104, 112
MTS 44
'multilevel orders of corruption' 85, 121–122
mutual aid practices 25, 107–108, 112
My Road (*Mening yo'lim*) 5

nahor oshi (morning pilaf feast) 88
National Anticorruption Council 58–59, 68
National Security Service 44, 47, 58n6, 59, 61, 68, 120; *see also* State Security Service
nation-state laws 13, 22–23, 101, 110
natural resources: export of 42, 51; extraction of 43
nepotism 72, 77–81, 123
nikoh toi (wedding ceremony) 88
noncompliance 17, 19, 83, 92–98, 120–121
non-democratic regimes 15, 19
non-governmental organisations (NGOs) 8, 58, 58n6, 59, 122; *see also* civil society organisations

non-monetary currencies 13, 26, 104, 106, 115, 116, 122–124; and alternative currencies 115
non-Western: settings 6, 16, 92, 122; societies 10, 14, 123
normative: legal acts 64, 73, 75, 78; micro-level orders 7, 22, 24, 123; moral, cultural and affective repertoires 120; ordering 7, 19–24, 92, 120–121
normative perspective 16–19; and legal compliance 71, 124
normative pluralism 20, 22, 120
norms 10–11, 17–18, 28, 59–60, 63, 70, 92, 94, 104, 121, 123–125; formal *vs.* informal 12–13, 20–24, 72, 75, 81–84, 124; informal 2, 21–24, 26, 102, 104–105, 109, 122–123; social 6, 10, 14–16, 29, 91, 105–107, 113, 116, 120

Obod Mahalla (Prosperous *Mahalla*) 5
Obod Qishloq (Prosperous Village) 5
observation 6–7, 28, 84, 90, 95, 101, 107, 125; among low-level state officials 25, 89–91, 109–111, 122
odamgarchilik (humanity and care) 113
officials: accountability of 80–81; as kleptocratic practices among 87, 111, 118; mid-level and low-level 94–95, 97; monthly salaries/incomes of 118
oila (immediate family) 29, 105, 112
oilalar (immediate families) 105
Oliy Majlis (Parliament of Uzbekistan) 25, 28, 40, 57–59, 64–68, 73
Olmazor City 76
'one-size-fits-all' perspectives/approaches 13, 15, 122
Open Budget programme 5
Open Society Foundations Eurasian Programme 50, 62
openness and transparency 60, 63, 66, 77, 119
oqsoqol (*mahalla* leader) 88
Oqtepa 112
Organisation for Economic Co-operation and Development (OECD) 56, 68
Ortiqhodjaev, Jahongir 48–49, 73–74, 76
Ostrom, Elinor 10
Ozodlik 49, 81n23

Parliament Senate and Legislative Chamber of 25, 28, 40, 57–59, 64–68, 73; *see also* O*liy Majlis*
participant observation *see* observation
patronage 43–44, 73, 76, 113
people of influence 25–26, 91, 107, 115
people's reception houses 2, 46; *see also halq qabulhonalari*
personal morality 17–20, 120
Persson, A. 9–10, 15
petty corruption 50, 61, 68; in daily life 115; *vs.* high-level corruption 68, 110, 118, 123
pillars of reforms 47
pluralistic legal contexts 21, 88–92, 94; normatively 121
police 43, 89–90, 107; district-level 98–101; provincial police department 111–112; traffic 28, 67, 89–95, 97, 108, 112, 118; *see also* law, law enforcement officials
political: environment 3, 9, 23, 28, 39–51, 67–68, 122; stability 40–41, 43, 46, 90; transition 1–3, 40, 48–51, 67
post-communist: contexts 21; period 42, 96; political, social and economic transformations 108; societies 39–40; *see also* post-independence; post-socialist; post-Soviet
post-independence 40–42, 96
post-Karimov era: governance trajectories and legal reforms during 28, 39, 42, 45–51, 55, 122; legislative boom/explosion 68, 71, 82; *see also* Karimov, Islam; Mirziyoyev, Shavkat
post-socialist 7
post-Soviet 2, 11, 39–43, 112
poverty 8, 41, 99–100, 108
predatory practices 19, 29, 87, 97–98, 108, 122
president (of Uzbekistan): 5, 44–45, 57–59, 64, 67, 75–76, 80, 83, 99, 120; decrees 3, 51, 56–57, 65, 73, 79–80, 98–100; Office of 46; online portal (virtual reception portal') 46; Presidential Administration 50, 68; speeches of 58
prestige 13, 104, 106–107, 113–115, 122
principal–agent model 6–10, 15, 17, 18, 24, 71, 92, 121, 125; limitations of 14

private property: protection of 65
prokuratura (prosecutors) 98–101
'On the Prosecutor's Office' 72, 98–100
prosecutor's office 28, 57, 76, 98–100, 110; district level 29, 87, 92, 98–100; *see also* General Prosecutor's Office
Public Opinion 3, 62–63; *see also* Ijtimoiy Fikr
public spending 8, 41, 60
pul qistirish (giving money) 107n1
punishments 17, 58, 71, 80, 83, 104; punitive measures 41, 43

Qalampir.uz 74
qishloq (village) *105*
qon (blood/kinship/nepotism) 78
qonun osti hujjatlari (legal framework by decree) 82
qualitative method(s) 25

Rakhmonkulov, Akram 74
Rassiychi (local entrepreneur) 4; *rassiychilar* (successful entrepreneur) 26
Referendum of April 2023 47
reforms 3, 9–10, 39, 43, 51, 56, 66–67, 71, 120, 123; partial market 40–42; reformist agenda 46, 67, 120
'regulatory guillotine' method 82
religious norms 22–23, 25, 28
remittances 42, 105, 107
repressive measures and systems 1, 27, 39, 46, 48, 60, 67, 90, 118, 122
Republican Interagency Commission on Combating Corruption 58; *see also* Republican Interdepartmental Commission on Combating Corruption
Republican Interdepartmental Commission on Combating Corruption 3
resource allocation 41, 44
respect, displays of 13, 26, 41, 104, 106, 107n1, 108–109, 113–115, 122–123
rights and freedoms of citizens 70, 98
road works and asphalting 5–6, 99, 112
rule of law 3, 39–40, 78, 98–100, 108, 110; good governance and 43, 46–47, 72; promotion of 9, 39, 63, 71; *vs.* unrule of law 110; weak 1, 6, 8–10, 16, 19, 118, 120–121, 125
Rule of Law Index 43
rules of the game 70, 118
rural areas 25, 41–42, 48, 90, 119
Russia 4, 11, 26, 39, 42, 107; *see also* Russian Federation
Russian Federation 107

sadoqat (loyalty) 77
salaries: meagre incomes of state employees 42, 73, 95–97, 118
Saliev, Ergash: and daughter, Nargiza Ergashevna Salieva 74
Sardoba dam collapse 49, 79–81, 83, 97
sector management strategy 100–101
security: and stability 40–41, 80
'selling tickets to drivers' 93–94
Senate and Legislative Chamber of Parliament 58–59, 63, 67–68, 73
separation of powers 47
SFI Management 75–76
Shabboda (village of) 29, 88, 105–116
shadow economy: taxi sector 89–92
shock therapy approach 40
social arenas 5, 7, 25, 28, 72; meso-level 27–28, 85, 87, 92–102, 121, 123; micro-level 5–6, 15–16, 27–29, 42, 85, 104–116, 121–123
social associations: and informal norms 22–23, 28–29, 105, 109, 111
social behaviour 13, 17, 20, 22–24, 83, 90, 101, 104, 106, 110, 120–121, 123–124; and instability 8, 13, 40, 82; and norms 6; and relations 1, 21–22, 26, 29, 42, 47, 49, 81, 90, 105, 112, 115, 123–124; and reputations and respect 12, 26, 104, 106, 112–116, 122; and social cohesion 123; and social control 17–18, 29, 43, 105; and social sanctions 12, 24, 29, 43, 92, 104, 106, 113, 121; and social status 12, 13, 26, 104, 107, 113–116; among women 106–107
social media: activist 70; platforms 73, 119
social order 6; maintenance of 22, 40
social practices 28, 116
social sector worker 118
'social state' 47, 101
social welfare: programmes and systems 40, 42; policies 40, 100; services 43, 107, 109
socio-legal: analysis 87; approach 66–67, 72, 116; context 16, 29, 87, 116,

125; ethnography 27; frameworks 121; multi-level perspectives 27, 104, 121; perspective on legal compliance 7, 16–20, 71, 121
sociology of law 22, 109
soum 2, 74, 76, 80, 91, 91n4, 93n5, 93–94, 96
Soviet Union: collapse of 2, 39, 41, 67; era 39, 41–42, 95–96; legacy of 40, 43; welfare system 40
'stability at any cost' 40, 43
State Programme on Combating Corruption 58
State Security Service 58n6, 59, 68, 120
State Tax: Committee 68, 74; Department 76; Inspectorate 76; Service 100
'strong–weak state' 43
state–society relations 1, 15, 42, 49, 79, 120
supervisory powers 98
supranational law 13, 22–23, 109
surnay (traditional Uzbek musical instrument) 88
surveillance 9, 19, 22, 43, 71
survival: means of 29, 41, 89, 95, 110; strategies 13, 42, 87, 115–116
suyunchi (informal payment; literally, 'joy') 96–97, 96n8, 119
Svensson, M. 2, 10–12, 27, 81–82, 91
svoi (ours/our own) 24, 26

Tajikistan: civil war 40, 46
Takilant 45, 45n1
tanish-bilish (cronyism/networks/contacts) 78, 115
taqsir (title of address for leaders) 109
Tashkent 48, 66, 76–77, 80, 100, 114–115; fieldwork in 1–4, 24–25, 28, 72, 73, 76, 89–90; State Tax Department 76
Tashkent City 24, 48, 73, 75–76
tax 6, 62; burden and high tax rates 41, 44; evasion 76; 'hidden policy' and tax benefits 74, 76, 79; office 25, 76, 98–101; tax officials 47, 76, 89, 98–99, 101, 118
Telia 44–45, 50
theoretical perspective(s) 121, 125
thick description 25, 67, 111
third wave of autocratisation 15
Topalang HPD Holding 80
top–down perspective 14; legal centralistic approaches 105
toyana (gift, tribute) 88
traffic police 28, 67, 89–95, 97, 108, 111–112, 118
traffic safety enforcement 25, 29, 87; and informal practices 92–95; traffic ticket quota 93–94; *see also* traffic police
transactions: informal and extra-legal 1, 6, 12–15, 23, 26, 29, 48, 84, 87, 89, 92, 94, 97–98, 101–102, 104–105, 108–109, 111, 113–116, 123, 125
transition: economic 40–41; political 67; post-Soviet 41–42; from repressive authoritarianism 27, 39, 48, 60, 122
transnational: anticorruption laws 16, 25; business 4
transparency 60–61, 63, 77
Transparency International (TI) 1, 3, 7–8, 11, 13, 15, 43, 50, 71, 92, 101, 110, 119
Tursunboy: case study 108–109

Ukraine 11
unemployment 41, 46, 48, 107
United Nations Convention against Corruption (UNCAC) 55–56, 61–62, 68–69, 92, 101; Implementation Review Mechanism (IRM) 56; Uzbekistan's accession to 55–56
United Nations Development Programme (UNDP): anticorruption e-platform 65
university admissions 113
unstable political situation 40
unwritten rules 70, 81–84; and behaviour 94–95; and legal gaps 84, 124
Uppdrag granskning: Swedish Telia scandal 44–45, 50
Urinboyev, R. 2, 10–12, 21–22, 27, 42, 81–82, 90, 94, 111, 113
urug' (extended family/kinship group) 29, 105, 111–112, 114–116; *urug'-aymoqchilik* (clanism/kinship) 78
Uzbekgidroenergo 80
'Uzbekistan affair' 44–45
Uzbekistan Railways 80

valyutchiki (currency changers) 89
VimpelCom 44–45
virtual reception portal 2, 46, 48

weak rule of law 1, 6, 8, 16, 118; contexts 6, 9–10, 19, 120, 125; *see also* rule of law
weddings 25, 26, 29, 88, 91, 106–107, 112, 114; and definition of corruption 12, 15, 92; perspectives of 13, 97
Western: regarding Western models 15, 39–40, 43, 94–95, 97, 120; networks and organisations 11; Western *vs.* non-Western practices 6, 10, 14, 16, 91–92, 122–123, 125
Western-backed reforms 39
Western-centrism 6, 13, 24
Western-style constitution and government 40, 43
whistleblowers: legal protection of 62, 64
World Bank 3, 7–8, 13, 15, 92, 101
World Economic Forum 8
World Justice Project 43

Made in the USA
Monee, IL
14 September 2026

62978584R00083